William John Knox Little

Sacerdotalism

If rightly understood, the teaching of the Church of England

William John Knox Little

Sacerdotalism

If rightly understood, the teaching of the Church of England

ISBN/EAN: 9783337262372

Printed in Europe, USA, Canada, Australia, Japan

Cover: Foto ©Lupo / pixelio.de

More available books at **www.hansebooks.com**

SACERDOTALISM

PUBLISHERS' NOTE

In consequence of this Volume having been originally issued in four Parts and expanded by the Author during revision, it will be found that in a few cases the numbering of the pages has been repeated.

SACERDOTALISM

IF RIGHTLY UNDERSTOOD, THE TEACHING OF THE CHURCH OF ENGLAND

BEING

FOUR LETTERS

Originally Addressed, by Permission, to

THE LATE VERY REV. WILLIAM J. BUTLER, D.D.
DEAN OF LINCOLN

BY

W. J. KNOX LITTLE, M.A.
CANON RESIDENTIARY OF WORCESTER AND VICAR OF HOAR CROSS

LONDON
LONGMANS, GREEN, & CO.
AND NEW YORK: 15 EAST 16th STREET
1894

All rights reserved

PREFACE

THE *occasion* of the following volume was, as will be seen by the reader, a passing controversy. To the utmost of my power, whatever might appear in any degree personal has been now suppressed. At the best of times, I cannot but feel that controversy is a doubtful blessing; and it is sorrowful and painful if—even when it is pressed upon one as a duty—any expression unnecessarily pungent or angry should find, anyhow, a more or less *permanent* place in words written in defence of the Truth.

The *cause* of the controversy, however, lies much deeper than the circumstances of a passing discussion seem at first sight to imply. And this it is which seems to me to justify such a volume as this.

The Anglican Communion has ever professed, and professes now, to be a true part of the Catholic Church. She believes herself to be *that* part of the Society founded by Jesus Christ, and having its birthday at Pentecost, which by the providence of God is appointed to minister in this land.

According to her view, which is supported by history, serious quarrels have occurred in the family of God, and among them that special quarrel which is known by the name of "the Reformation." At that time the Anglican Church insisted with determination, as she had often insisted before, that the great Patriarchs of the West—the Popes, as we are in the habit of calling them—had in several matters departed from Catholic tradition, and arrogated to themselves excessive powers. This departure from the Apostolic constitution of the Church she refused any longer to endorse. A quarrel was forced upon her in consequence. Doubtless there were faults on both sides; but the Anglican Church faithfully maintained that, while asserting her right to reform abuses, and to translate and rearrange her Office-books, she did not desire to separate from the rest of Western Christendom.

The separation, however, came; chiefly from political animosities, and the overweening assumptions of the then reigning Pontiff.

Since then, unhappily, the chasm has widened. On the one hand, the Latin remnant of the Catholic Church, which still held France and Spain and Italy, made increasing claims as to the powers of the Popedom, and placed an increasing strain on faith by insisting upon permissible *opinions* being treated as matters of *faith*, until matters culminated in our own days in the unhappy Vatican Decree. On the other hand, the sense of independence, desire for liberty, a deep feeling of the soul's relation to God, unbalanced by a sufficient sense of its relation to the Body of the Church—which is the Body of Christ—led many into positive schism, and dangerous repudiation of the Divine organization of the Church and of many revealed doctrines of the Faith. And so the quarrel with Rome laid the Anglican part of the Catholic Church open to the danger of succumbing to extreme and dangerous influences from the party of revolt.

By the mercy of God she stood firm. She remained faithful to her *Catholic* heritage, and merely rejected more modern accretions which clung to the Latin part of Christendom.

Naturally she had a deeper sympathy than the Roman Church could have with the party of revolt. She gained much by withstanding usurpations on the one hand; she was in danger of losing something by sympathy with a true effort—running wild—on the other.

The consequences have been what might be expected. Those within her whose sympathies were deepest for the revolt against Roman usurpation, have ever tended to go too far, and—while resisting all that is merely Roman—have been inclined to lose sight of what is, not Roman at all, but truly Catholic.

Against these—while sympathizing with what is true in their contention—she has steadily in all her authorized utterances set her face; whilst against Rome she has faithfully protested whenever Rome departed from Catholic tradition. The result has been that a party within her have striven, with varying success, to drive her from her Catholic moorings. They have never succeeded in inducing her to abandon the Faith and practice of Catholic Christendom by any overt act, but they *have* succeeded from time to time in obscuring her witness to the Truth, by introducing teachings and traditions into the minds of many of her children, which have lowered her practical efficiency, and which, if not silencing, have at least rendered, to some extent, inoperative, her proclamation of the Catholic Faith.

So far has this Puritan effort prevailed, that again and again it has succeeded in making her children look upon their Catholic heritage as something alien and belonging to Rome.

The binding formularies of the Church, however, have stood against all attacks. The sorrowful thing has been that often, within her frontiers, there have been, not only lay people, but actually some of her commissioned servants, her priests, and even her bishops, who have been more faithful to this invading Protestant tradition than to her distinct statements of Catholic truth. The consequences have been grave indeed. On the one hand, Roman controversialists have made absurd charges against her—charges which they find it impossible to sustain by fact and history. On the other, her less faithful sons have gone the length of accusing those who are rigidly faithful to her teachings, of *disloyalty* to the Church (to which *they* are, doubtless all-unconsciously, disloyal) and of leanings towards the Roman Communion.

Out of this has grown a serious struggle. Her less loyal children have, more or less, joined hands with those who *dissent* from her teachings in angry denunciation of those who are faithful to them.

Those who *dissent*—the Dissenters—are, in this matter, logical and consistent. Those who, not being professed Dissenters, deny her plain witness are at once illogical, inconsistent, and unfair. Their untenable position has rendered them at times bitter and angry with all who cling to the teachings of the Church. Their *practice* is a strange one, though they *themselves* are often, one may charitably believe, acting in good faith.

"The High Church party," as those have been called who have remained faithful to the Church's teachings, have been denounced from time to time as "Romanizers," or "Tractarians," or "Puseyites," or "Ritualists" by men who, binding themselves by her authoritative formularies, deny almost every truth which those formularies in the plainest language teach.

At the same time, it is fair to say that the old "Evangelicals" witnessed to a truth. Men like Simeon and Cecil were men of whom any Church may be justly proud. *Their* effort was to put *spiritual life* into what had become almost the *dry bones* of orthodoxy. The true successors of these first holy and devoted "Evangelicals" are, in a great measure, the "Ritualists" of to-day. The professing followers of these great men have, many of them, become the dry and hard opponents of the truths —more definitely stated—which these men really loved.

The result has been *mis-statement*. Angry passions, and strong prejudice, and *odium theologicum* have embittered a misunderstanding which ought never to have existed at all.

There have been, doubtless, faults on both sides, and men who ought to have made their meaning clear, have sometimes been content to state or act upon the truth in a hard or too uncompromising spirit. This has led the way to many mischiefs; and truths which are part of the heritage of the Church have been, in the dust of controversy, misunderstood, and those who *in their hearts* are sincere believers have allowed themselves, while condemning Roman accretions, to condemn, often through misunderstanding, real and blessed truths of the gospel of Christ.

It is not necessary to approve of or support *everything* that has been said or done by so-called "High Churchmen;" but none the less is it undesirable to condemn wholesale *real* truths accepted always by the Catholic Church, and therefore by the Church of

England, and which, when rightly understood, are in accordance with the mind of her Divine Founder.

The Catholic Church is the home of the *common sense* of eternity. There are *objective* truths which must never be forgotten—the fact of the visible Church, the truth of a spiritual *succession* of the ministry, the *necessary* office of bishops, the *real* functions of the priesthood, the *effectual* force of sacraments, the *practical value* of the penitential system, and so on,—these must never be forgotten; while, on the other hand, men must be helped to understand personal responsibility, and the need in each soul of a serious and perfect response to the offered mercies of God, and to the certain facts of the Faith.

In view of some unhistorical and absurd assertions of Rome, the Catholics of the English Church ought to be helped to understand the reality of her teaching and practice.

It is, surely, a very terrible thing that, in view of the witness of Catholic Christendom, in view of the plain statements of the Prayer-book, men have been encouraged, within the Anglican Communion, to glory in Latitudinarianism, and to treat Christianity *only* as a philosophy or ideal, rather than *a system of truth, and a ministration of grace*, as witnessed to by the Catholic Church. It is terrible because it is *untrue*, and because it is *unpractical*. That, and that only, is a *practical* religion which teaches men what to *be* and what to *do*. That, and that only, is a *true* religion which embodies the teachings of Christ, handed on by His Church. It is *true* to teach men the *Incarnation* and its results. The Eternal Word became Man. To extend the results of His wonderful condescension, He established the

Church, His Body, endued it with His power, and *officered* it, according to His will, by the sacred ministry. To submit to the truth, and to use grace,—*this* is, so far forth, to be a Christian. The Catholic Church, the Sacraments, the Apostolic Ministry, — these are the witness to, the extension and the practical application of, the Incarnation. "Pietism," with no sort of basis but that supplied by individual opinion, is dangerous, because it is passing, and because it may lead wrong.

Again, the Catholic Faith is *practical*. It is practical, if a soul is " baptized into " Christ; if that soul, *not* by its own act, but by God's act, does not " accept " Christ, but " is accepted by Him." It is practical to teach the young who have been baptized, when their intelligence is sufficiently developed to hold personal communion with God in prayer, and to learn from those in authority the truths of revelation. It is thoroughly unpractical—pursuing the absurd customs of Puritanism—to put into their hands the Bible, " without note or comment," to find out what religion they can from it for themselves. This superstitious use of the Scriptures prevails even now, apparently, in the minds of controversial Protestants. It is practical to bring children, when they have reached the years of discretion, to Confirmation, if, with the laying-on of hands of the bishop and prayer, they receive a gift of the Holy Ghost. It is more than unpractical to do so, if the whole thing is merely a more or less edifying ceremony, and the bishop has in fact no more, in succession from the Apostles, to convey than anybody else. It is practical, that if people fall into sin, and feel the need of making their confessions, they should be taught to do so, and should understand that when the Church tells them that the appointed minister can minister to them absolution, she is not playing with them, but *means* what she *says*. It is worse than unpractical to tell them that, though she talks about the priest and absolution, she really *means* that there is no such thing as either the one or the other! It is practical to teach them that they are to prepare with care for the Communion, and, when not communicating, should be devoutly present, when they can, at the Eucharistic Service to commemorate the Lord's death, and to show forth before God the merits of the Passion of Christ, if our Lord is *really* present there according to the promise. It is worse than unpractical to teach them, either that there is some sort of presence, but not a *real* presence—whatever this may mean—and that you ought to make your communions, but that, on the other hand, it does not really very much matter whether you do or not. Catholic Faith and Catholic Practice are practical guides in human life. Mercifully, many good Protestants, whether in the Church or outside of it, are Catholics without knowing it; but Protestantism *as a system* is at once unpractical and untrue.

Of course, as I have admitted, "Evangelicals" have, anyhow in the past, represented one aspect of the truth. We have all known dear and devout persons, whether in the English Church or among Dissenters, who have loved our Lord with a sweet and tender devotion, and who, if they have lost something by *not knowing* the Catholic Faith in its fulness, have been examples to us all, by *living* what they did know. But there has been a party in the English Church, very unlike the devout "Evangelicals," who seem bent on stirring up strife, and attacking those who believe in what the English Church states. No one can have any desire to drive out, or quarrel with, devout members of what is called "the Low Church party."

Persecution is not the way to advance the truth, as men both within and without the Church have learnt to their cost. In recent times certain associations of extreme Low Churchmen have tried the weapon of persecution against their brethren in so far as it has been possible in modern days. They have failed. Catholics in the Church of England have no desire to follow their example; we can have no desire to exclude Low Churchmen, so long as they see their way to hold their place within the pale of the Church. *How* they conscientiously can do so, in the face of our formularies, is to me, I confess, unintelligible. I can understand a Dissenter, where he is good, and devout, and earnest, and not merely political, and using any stick he can find, irrespective of truth and duty, with which to beat Churchmen—*and* I can respect him. He *dissents* from the teaching of the Church, and accordingly he becomes a *Dissenter.* I am sorry, but I understand. A "Low Churchman" I cannot understand. He is an unintelligible enigma to me. He appears to hate the very name of "Catholic," and he *says* he believes "in the Holy Catholic Church." He is indignant with you if you do not call yourself a "Protestant," while no such title ever once occurs in the formularies which he professes to recognize as binding upon him. He detests the word "priest," and raves against "absolution," and yet belongs to a Church which says in the most solemn moments to him, if he is her ordained minister —and if he is not, at least within his hearing—" Receive the Holy Ghost, for the office and work of a *priest* in the Church of God. Whose sins thou dost forgive they are forgiven, and whose sins thou dost retain they are retained." How "Low Churchmen" can *square* their beliefs and their positions with the statements of the Catholic Church in England, to which they adhere, I cannot myself in the least understand. Brought up among them in boyhood, I myself was struck long ago with the discrepancy between their habitual utterances and the plain teachings of the Prayer-book. I am convinced that their extraordinary statements have driven many of the young, who have been in the habit of looking at plain facts, into unbelief, unless when, by God's mercy, they have found that the teaching of the English Church is truly Catholic, and that she does not encourage this juggling with words, and playing fast and loose with her statements, but *means* what she *says*.

But although I cannot pretend to understand the position of these good people, I cannot doubt that they are, for the most part, honest in their intentions. It is difficult for me to imagine a man consecrated as a bishop, denying all *Divine* authority and all *necessity* of the Episcopate. It is difficult for me to understand a man ordained to the priesthood with the solemn words quoted above, repudiating the name and idea of "priest"—when every one knows what that name means, and what that idea is—and playing with the term "presbyter" by way of getting out of his difficulty. It is difficult for me to understand a man inviting people to come to him "or to some other," to make their confession when they need it, and then being angry with his brethren as God-forsaken "papists" if they appear to have *meant* what they actually said. It is difficult to understand the standpoint of such persons. But it is not my business to condemn them. The Church is large; there are many aspects of truth, and I have no doubt that their hearts are better than their heads.

What we have a right to do, and what at times it

is necessary to do—with whatever pain—is to remind them, that if we are not interfering with *them*, they ought not to interfere with *us*. Low Churchmen may, if they like, hold the most unintelligible position in Christendom, and settle with their own intellects and consciences how they can do it; but they have no business to come out—especially when unassailed—and assault the Catholic laity and the Catholic priesthood in the Church of England for holding truths and practising devout practices to which they have bound themselves, and in fact for teaching and believing the Catholic Faith.

That "party" in the Church which has been so singularly unfaithful to her formularies, is never tired of giving distressing hints that the Catholic laity and the Catholic priesthood have something mysterious and dark and terrible *behind* what they say. There is *nothing behind*, and they shall have no justification in saying so, certainly as far as I am concerned. We believe that the English Church is a true part of the Catholic Church; that she has a *true* Episcopate in succession from the Apostles, a *real* Priesthood, a *real* Sacrifice, a *real* Altar, a *real* Presence of her Divine Master in the Holy Mysteries, *real* gifts of grace, of absolution, and blessing given through her appointed ministry; a *real* mission to this people—not to fall in with every current of popular opinion, not to "play to the gallery" when any part of Revelation is not quite satisfactory to human weakness, but to witness with love and earnestness and unflinching courage to the unchanging truth, the "everlasting gospel," the Catholic Faith.

Our position I believe to be quite unassailable. When it is assailed, the assault always consists of rhetoric and denunciation.

As an example of this, I might refer to one criticism of my "Letter" which has reached me while writing this preface.

The critic is angry with me for *odium theologicum*. He talks of my "piteous protests" (I am unable to find them). He considers me "clever and adroit" (the usual resource of people who cannot argue and can only insinuate!). He talks of me as a "so-called priest." The writer professes to be a Churchman; at least, he writes in what, oddly enough, professes to be a Church paper. If he turns to his Prayer-book, I am afraid—especially if he turns to the Ordination Service—he will find that my erroneous views have stronger support than his opinions. He seems shocked at the notion of "confession of secret things ... meant for no one's ear but the so-called priest who asks for them." (Does he imagine that sinners go to confess *public* things, that can be talked about generally or put in the newspapers?) He prudently "passes over" all that I have said about a supposed "Act of Convocation," which (so it was erroneously asserted) was passed to forbid Confession and Absolution, but calls attention to the fact that I acknowledge that "a *caveat* was entered against the practice, threatening to deprive the clergy who resorted to it." This is a striking instance of the kind of "criticism" with which we are met by "Churchmen" who deny the teachings of the Prayer-book. The critic is wise to "pass over the Act of Convocation," as such an Act—which was brought against me in evidence by my assailant—never existed; but the said critic, it will be noticed, points out that I *acknowledge* the "caveat"! Did I, or any other believer in the Prayer-book, ever deny that "caveats" have been entered from time to time by unbelievers, against the truth ? The said "caveat" comes in a Puritanical document, which probably never came before Convocation at all, and which certainly never was passed by Convocation! This is the kind of "criticism" by which direct statement and argument are answered! To go on with the same critic—as a suitable example among many—I find that "all ministrations in which God's forgiving love may be urged" are meant when you speak of "Absolution." This he seems to think "gospel truth;" this I consider Jesuitry and juggling with words. He thinks I "beg the question" by believing that the First Prayer-book plainly taught Confession and Absolution. If it did not, I should like to know what it *did* teach; if it did not, I should like to be told what is the use of employing words when, according to the "use" of Protestant criticism, they may apparently mean anything under the sun. I find that I also "beg the question" by assuming that St. Paul's statement about the "washing of water" refers to Holy Baptism! Well, if it does not, I should like to know what it *does* refer to; I should like to know what other "sacrament of the gospel" employs the "washing of water and the word" except Holy Baptism. I learn from the same critic that the Exhortation in the Communion for the Sick is "awkward and embarrassed," *because* I had said—quoting Bishop Forbes—that the language of the Twenty-fifth Article about the five lesser sacraments, might be so described. I submit that any one reading that language intelligently *must* see—and I have shown reason why—that it *is* rightly so described; but to apply it to the Exhortation, which is *as definite as it can be*, is—I must be forgiven for saying—pure nonsense. I am informed, also, that "penance is not an ordinance of Christ, but of the Church of Rome." Although this is not true, I could understand its being said by a Dissenter; but that a "Churchman" professing to believe in the Prayer-book which contains the Commination Service, should venture on such a statement, is to me quite unintelligible! Then I gain this information, that "the blasphemous assumption by sinful man of the power to absolve a fellow-sinner from his sins, in the form, 'I absolve thee,' is nowhere found in the Word of God;" and "no language can adequately express the danger of such a perversion of the truth." Very well: my critic has a perfect right to his opinions, although I regret them, as they are contrary to the revealed faith given to us by our Lord; but what he has no right to do, is to attack me or others who believe and obey what the Prayer-book says, when he—professing, apparently, to be a Churchman—describes the teaching of the Prayer-book as "blasphemous assumption."

I have alluded to this criticism not because it is more irrational, or more beside the mark, than others of the same kind. Those who in the Church of England deny Catholic Faith and Practice are obliged to resort to this sort of denunciation and Jesuitry; *argument* they have not. Not an approach to an answer has reached me. Plenty of abuse, plenty of rhetoric, plenty of denunciation, plenty of painful twisting of words, but no *answer*.

As I have said, I have no desire to attack "Low Churchmen." There are good and devout men among them, who are "of the truth;" but if men *will* stir up strife, if men *will* attack those who believe that the Prayer-book means what it says, it is necessary to point out that, however they may justify their position—

which is difficult to understand—the Catholic laity and the Catholic priesthood in the Church of England are true to the Prayer-book *and* (indeed for the matter of that) true to the Bible.

On criticisms from Dissenting sources I need not touch, as the controversy is one *within* the frontiers of the English Church. I need only say that while by some critics of *some* Dissenting Bodies I have certainly been treated with the unkindly scorn and the evident ignorance of the subject that might naturally be expected; by others—and notably by one who writes in the organ of the Congregationalist Body—my arguments have been treated with intelligence and fairmindedness, if not, of course, with entire assent. This is what one would have expected from that Body of Dissenters in this country, who have most claim to real learning and understanding of the questions at issue.

I have every hope that, more and more, devout and thoughtful and instructed members of the Dissenting Bodies will see their way to the Catholic Faith, and to rejoining—with a strong grip of the truth—the Church, their Mother. Difficulties are many, but we may hope and pray. I am convinced that the more clear-minded and less prejudiced of them, the more they examine the question, will find that the Catholic Church in England —whilst wisely patient of many frailties and aberrations —is, in all her authoritative teachings, consistently and thoroughly Catholic, and is *the* home for those who desire to be faithful in word and life to "the truth as it is in Jesus."

Meanwhile, *this* controversy is, as I have said, one within our own frontiers, though one cannot but be thankful that those who *dissent* should be interested in it. God's Word never returns to Him void. Any steady contemplation of the truth, to "men of goodwill," *must* have good results. I cannot but hope, with one of my more kindly critics, that my book may be widely read among those who *dissent* from the Church's teaching; although, as I trust, with results, by God's mercy, very different from those which, not unnaturally, he seems to contemplate.

Well, then, it comes to this. No mere statement, no mere accurate statement of doctrine, will save a soul. No! But also no more will mere *pietism*, or sentiment, or superstitious repetition of shibboleths, which has no basis in fact. Every soul must by faith and love appropriate the gifts of grace, but the gifts of grace must be really given before the soul can appropriate them.

We must be *real*.

If there is no succession from the Apostles in our Episcopate, why does the Church call bishops "Fathers in God"? Why keep them at all? Why teach us to preach at ordinations as to the *necessity* of the Three Orders?

If there be no succession, *and* no Priesthood, why our Ordinal? Why is the bishop to say, "Receive the Holy Ghost for the office and work of a priest," when he *means*, "I can't give, so you can't receive; you are *not* a priest, for there is no Priesthood"?

If there is no Real Presence in the Holy Sacrament, why are children taught that the Body and Blood are "verily and indeed *taken* and *received*"? And why are we taught to pray to God that He will, by our reception of the Holy Sacrament, by our eating "the Flesh" and drinking "the Blood" of Christ, cleanse our bodies *by His Body*, and our souls *by His precious Blood*?

If there is no Regeneration in Baptism, why does the Church insist on the priest saying, "Seeing now, dearly beloved, that this child *is regenerate,*" etc. ?

If there be no power in the Priesthood to absolve, why is a man in the agony of a dying hour to be "moved to make a special confession of his sins;" and why is the priest to be told to absolve him, saying, " I absolve thee"?

If all these things are false, then men who enter the ministry have been cajoled into a false position, and made the victims of a lie. If they are false, sweep them away, cart them out, throw them overboard; *but,* whether *that* is done or not, do not allow those in authority *first* to require of men who, in the heyday of their youth, desire to devote themselves to God, to swear that, *ex animo,* they believe all this, and *then,* when they *act* upon what they believe, denounce them in unmeasured language, amid the plaudits of an unthinking crowd of worldlings, as traitors to the Church to which they have sworn allegiance.

Either Sacerdotalism is true, or the teaching of the Church of England is a hollow and a disgraceful sham.

Sacerdotalism, of course, *is* true. The Church of England is right. Those who deny the gospel truth of Sacerdotalism, and who *pose* as loyal members of the Church of England, *they,* I repeat, may settle the matter with their intellects and their consciences; but they have no right to describe as disloyal, men who in simplicity and straightforwardness have believed that the Church *means* what she *says.*

This is what I have been driven to insist upon in the following book. It is a *defence,* as I have said, against what I consider *an unprovoked attack.* However large the boundaries of the Church may be, men who make—as it seems to us—very free with the language of the Prayer-book, and with their obligations in the ministry, at any rate should leave us to do our work in peace. Doubtless the Church has always had her troubles; doubtless many minds approach truth in many different ways; doubtless the largest allowance is to be made that is possible for divergence of opinion; but it is necessary to show that Catholic Churchmen are the very reverse of disloyal to their Prayer-book. This surely is a point of honour, this surely is a duty. I have tried in the following pages to do this; but I repeat, that however certain of our position I am, and however clear it is as daylight that we are faithful to the teachings of the Church, as a matter-of-fact I detest controversy, and love "the things which make for peace."

As I close, I am startled and saddened by the intelligence that he to whom these letters were written has been called to his rest. In his last letter to me, only the other day, he had expressed his warm approval of my action in this matter, and his sense of the extreme need of believing Churchmen speaking out in defence of the Faith, and of the extreme danger to souls of the efforts of men of some ability and possessed of attractive gifts *in* the Church and entirely—even if unconsciously—disloyal to her teachings. He had also assured me of his conviction that, if opponents did not travel "beyond the record," they could not answer my arguments. In this he showed his usual acuteness and good sense. My argument all along has been: "This is the teaching of the Church of England; she may be right or she may be wrong, but *this* is what she teaches." In every attempt to answer me which I have yet seen, opponents travel "beyond the record." They never face the question. They cannot, as I believe. When not abusing me, they give *their ipse dixits* as to the meaning of Scripture! That, I need hardly say, is no argument. That method of *answer* may satisfy the constituents of some party paper; it cannot satisfy reasonable men. The question is *not* what any section of controversialists *think* that Holy Scripture means. We who "believe in the Holy Catholic Church," believe that the Church, and she alone, can teach us the *meaning* of Scripture on points of doctrine. To her interpretations of Holy Scripture every English Churchman is bound. That, however, is not the question. The question is—*What does the Church of England teach?* My dear friend who is gone saw clearly that Sacerdotalism, rightly understood, *is* the teaching of the Church of England. He saw clearly, as he wrote to me, that unless men travel "beyond the record"—unless, in fact, they evade the question—they can find no answer. So it has proved. They have not attempted to *meet* my contentions; they have gone off into other questions. They have given *their* views of scriptural interpretations, and what not, but they have abandoned "the record." It remains unanswered, because, I believe, unanswerable—as the late Dean of Lincoln felt—that to be true to the teaching of the Church of England you must be true to Sacerdotalism. That, of course, is a blessed fact, for it is only another way of saying that the Church of England has been true to the Catholic Faith, to the Gospel of Christ.

Meantime he is gone. We have to mourn another of those faithful servants of God, who has never flinched in his defence of the Faith, and in his consistent effort to *live* what he *taught*. A life of steady labour has closed in a peaceful death, and he has been laid, amid the tears of many, in an honoured grave. Sacerdotalist as he was from head to heel, while he abhorred unnecessary or ill-tempered controversy, he equally abhorred unfaithful "caution,"—which has been so deadly a bane to our Church,—for he had the warm-hearted love of a Christian, and the genial manliness of a genuine Englishman. We can ill afford to lose such in an age when the combination of Christian love and real backbone is not too common. "Taken away from the evil to come," he has left us an example of courage and constancy, and yet—able as he was in helping *here* the cause of the kingdom of God—perhaps he can do even more for it *there*. May he rest in peace! May his works follow him! Anyhow, for us it remains earnestly and lovingly to contend for the Faith as *he* contended, while, amidst our sorrows, we remember that *he* is gone where battle is over, and controversies, thank God, can no more be needed, where—it is sweet to remember—"beyond these voices there is peace."

W. J. KNOX LITTLE.

HOAR CROSS VICARAGE,
Septuagesima, 1894.

CONTENTS

PART I.
CONFESSION AND ABSOLUTION.

PART II.
FASTING COMMUNION AND EUCHARISTIC WORSHIP.

PART III.
THE REAL PRESENCE AND THE EUCHARISTIC SACRIFICE.

PART IV.
THE APOSTOLIC MINISTRY.

PART I.
CONFESSION AND ABSOLUTION.

My dear Dean,
  I am glad to be allowed to address this letter to you on many grounds. First of all, from personal affection, and from admiration for the great and solid work that you have done for so many years in the Church of England, I am glad to protect my protest under the shelter of your name. Then further, the recollection that you are the vicar who trained some of the very best priests in the Church of England—among them our dear friends Dr. Liddon and Mr. Mackonochie —now gone to their rest—and my very beloved friend Mr. Noel, and others who are with us still,—this supplies me with a reason for being thankful to have the opportunity of acknowledging obligations under which you have placed us all. Then, again, I like also to remember, now that you have gone from us, that I once had the honour of working with you as a fellow-canon in Worcester. Yet beyond all these, there are further and deeper reasons why I am glad to be allowed to address this letter to you; and these reasons may be stated thus—
  No one has more fairly, more courageously, and, in the best sense of that much-abused word, with greater *moderation*, than yourself asserted the truth, in its right interpretation of that part of our Divine Lord's arrange-

ments for the government of His Church, which is called "Sacerdotalism."

You have not only spoken faithfully on the subject; you have consistently lived as one who realizes the blessed truth of real sacerdotalism should live. I am sure that, with me, you have felt that it is a great sorrow that some who ought to be faithful ministers of the Church of England should misrepresent her clear teaching on this solemn subject, and thereby (not intentionally, of course) should do a great injury to souls. Just as "clericalism" has been used with much effect by atheists and unbelievers in republican France to arouse violent passions against the Truth, so among ourselves it has been saddening to find that, even among priests of our part of the Catholic Church, the word "sacerdotalism"—used in an invidious sense—has been employed in order to stir up passion and prejudice, and to misrepresent the teachings of the Church of England.

I, my dear friend, as you know, am a sacerdotalist from head to heel. It is difficult for me to understand how a Christian can be anything else. But whatever be the difficulties in this matter for really devout persons who are not in communion with the Church of England, it is still more difficult to understand—it is really almost unintelligible—how any *Priest* of the English Church, who has *ex animo* accepted her formularies, fails to be—in the true sense of the word—a "sacerdotalist."

When, then, I find a priest of some eminence and learning writing with what I may almost call violence against sacerdotalism, I naturally ask in what sense he uses that word. It cannot, surely, be in the sense in which you and I should use it. To my question, however, I find no quite satisfactory answer in certain papers which have appeared lately in a leading magazine. For the striking thing is this: that while we find plenty of declamation, there is no precise *definition* of what "sacerdotalism" means. Under these circumstances, I am obliged to hunt about with diligence to discover what is included under that term by such controversialists. In doing so, I find so much as this: that any one who teaches Confession and Absolution, "non-communicating attendance"—as they call Eucharistic worship—the practice of keeping the fast before receiving Communion, the doctrine of the Real Presence, and the doctrine of the Sacrifice of the Altar, and generally the doctrine of the Christian Priesthood,—that anyone, I say, who upholds these, is apparently a "sacerdotalist," and —and *this* is the point—*therefore* disloyal to the Church of England. For myself, my dear friend, I uphold *all* these doctrines and practices, but I object to them being misrepresented. I am sure that if they are freed from the fogs and accretions with which angry opponents surround them, they are comprehended not only in the teaching of the Church of England, but also in the gospel of Christ. My business is, then—in default of a clearer definition—so far as I can understand their meaning, to disabuse the minds of our opponents of misunderstandings on these points, and to show that if I am a loyal son of the Church of England, and, indeed, if I am a faithful gospel minister within her ranks, I *must* be a "sacerdotalist."

You, I know, will do me the justice to believe that I do not love controversy. You will also agree with me, I am sure, that while controversy is, if possible, to be avoided, there may be occasions when it is thrust upon one; occasions when to ignore it entirely is to be unfaithful to matters of *principle*, and when one is called upon—lest one should appear to be regardless of the sanctity of Truth, or lest one should be guilty of wilfully allowing others to misunderstand one's meaning —to speak out in the plainest way.

You will notice, then, that, among the points I have enumerated above, there are *three* devout *practices* and *three doctrines*, the upholding of which seems at any rate—so far as I can discover from the recent writings of the controversialist referred to—to constitute "sacerdotalism." I shall take the practices first, and afterwards deal with the doctrines and the general question.

Of these *practices*—not unconnected, of course, with doctrine—the first and most serious is what our opponents call Auricular Confession. It is asserted with regard to it that it is dangerous; that it is contrary to the teaching of the Church of England; and that it is opposed to Scripture. All these propositions can, I think, be shown to be false.

The practically important one, however, as regards the present controversy is the second, viz. that it is *contrary to the teaching of the Church of England*, for whether the Church of England be right or wrong, we all of us who are her priests are bound to be loyal to her teaching so long as we exercise our ministry within her fold. To this point, then, chiefly I address myself; but before I do so I must call your attention, my dear friend, to the present state of facts.

This letter has, as I have implied, its origin in a recent controversy.

In the July number of a well-known magazine in the year 1892, a person of eminence in the Church, both from his position and from his ability, delivered his mind, apparently *à propos de rien*, on the enormities of "sacerdotalism."

He represented himself as constrained by a sense of duty to oppose "the current of popular opinion," which seemed, apparently, to him to be running in the direction of this terrible danger. This was startling. Judging by the controversies of the last thirty years, and by the difficulties which any of us who have taken our stand upon the exact teaching of the Church of England have had to encounter, it had never appeared to most people, I imagine, that the severer views of the discipline of the Church were what would be described as "popular." It was all the more wonderful because he *also*—in fact, side by side with this sense of overwhelming duty to oppose the "popular" tendency to "sacerdotalism"—seemed to feel that it was the temper and conduct of the clergy in this matter which were the real reasons why a wise and despairing laity were driven into "indifference to religious questions"! The two views were scarcely consistent with one another, but that seemed of small consequence. "Sunday rest" was failing, we were told. "Sunday worship" was "losing hold." A "serious disruption" might come, or "the intellect of England" might be "dissociated from the faith," all in consequence of the very natural and proper disgust felt by Englishmen towards "sacerdotalism"! And all the time this "sacerdotalism" was a "current of popular opinion," which, with deep self-denial, and sacrificing his dislike of controversy, he felt bound in duty, lest he should appear guilty of "pusillanimity," to oppose. Then, while throwing himself into the breach, he determined to do it with "calmness and courtesy," and warned those who might criticize or answer his paper, that they must take him as a model in this. The great question to be settled was the truth about "sacerdotalism," which, on the one hand, as I have said, he seemed to think was a dangerous "current of popular opinion," which he stood almost alone in endeavouring to stem; while, on the other, it appeared to be the aberration of a number of clergy only, giving way to "autonomy and licence."

The main drift of the article seemed to be this: Neither the Bible nor the Church of England allow us to believe in a real "Priesthood;" therefore there is no truth in the doctrine of the Real Presence in the Eucharist—to assert which as a truth is to teach Transubstantiation; in Christianity there is no "Altar;" the practice of Fasting Communion is new and dangerous; non-communicating attendance is wrong; Confession and Absolution are things alien to the teaching of Scripture and of the English Church; and, in fact, all who hold and teach these doctrines and practices are disloyal to Scripture and to their Church. All these things—so the article in question seemed to assert—are "false and alien accretions."

As far as I know, no one did attempt to "criticize or answer" this article. It was read, and, I suppose, like many other magazine articles, it was forgotten.

A year passed. In the same magazine, in the July number of the current year, the same eminent person returned to the charge. The more recent article was more pungent. The charge of disloyalty was now fastened on to some individuals by name, and to two considerable societies, numbering in their ranks many hundreds of clergymen and laymen—the *English Church Union* and the *Confraternity of the Blessed Sacrament*. To sustain this charge, among other statements, he published, in a footnote, an entirely inaccurate "quotation" from the "Manual" of the latter society. To this his attention was called. The consequence was that he made a tardy and half-hearted apology for partial inaccuracy, when, as a matter of fact, *not a word* in the "quotation" was accurate. At the same time, apologizing with one hand, so to speak, he withdrew his apology with the other, by saying in effect that it was practically accurate, and by quoting, to prove this assertion, unauthoritative utterances of individuals who were said to belong to these societies.

It seemed to me that he was unfair, that he was in the highest degree inaccurate; that his tone and manner were scarcely consistent with the usual amenities of serious controversy; and that his teaching was contrary to that of the English Church, as witnessed by the Prayer-book and by the testimony of her greatest divines. Being a member for many years of the incriminated societies, I thought I had the right of any man who is attacked to defend himself. I did so, not from personal motives—for I care as little for personal attacks as my opponent can do—but I felt that a large body of men, better far than myself—some of them among the brightest ornaments of the English Church—had been wantonly and unfairly assailed. Well, this eminent person answered in a recent number of the same magazine. His answer seemed to imply that *I* had attacked *him!* He warned me off, in fact, into my proper place! I was accused of a cheap method of controversy by taking "snips" from his statements without the context, though he perfectly knew that "the context" was too extensive to quote in an article, and that it only made—if quoted—the "snips" more pungent and extravagant. When I used a handy phrase to express his method of dealing with souls, I was told, with scorn, that I thought myself "witty;" when I quoted a great Father of the Church and a great modern Divine as disproving his assertions, I was informed that they were mistaken or wrong. I was told —as a crushing blow—that *I* never entered *his* mind, that he had no thought of *me*, and had not assailed *me;* and, finally, that it was to be hoped that some one "better equipped" than I, would answer him. In fact, the article sought to turn the whole thing into a personal squabble with one who had assailed *him*, but who was beneath his notice, and unworthy of his powder and shot!

Notwithstanding all this, as a matter of fact, he was the aggressor. It is unworthy to pretend that he is an injured innocent assaulted by me! True, he never named *me*, and would doubtless never condescend to think of *me!* No, he only *assailed by name* two great societies, of both of which I am a member, and in whose actions and teachings I therefore share a responsibility. I consider that he has *gone out of his way to stir up strife*, when no one was meddling with him or any of his beliefs and disbelievings; that he has been inaccurate and unfair; that he has misrepresented the teachings of Scripture and of his Church; and that his recent lecture to me on charity is singularly out of place in one who could allow himself to come as a thunderbolt out of the clear heaven to assault his brethren, and should do it in the way in which he has done it.

This is the personal aspect of the question. *That* I now, as far as possible, dismiss from my mind. It is of no consequence to any one what he may be good enough to think of me. It is not, I think, to edification to carry on a personal squabble, connected with the most sacred subjects, in the pages of a monthly magazine. What *is* of consequence is—*Are these charges and assertions true or false?* I think them false. I think they are misleading. I think, whatever force they may have on men's minds, is derived from the constant appeal, in them, to popular prejudice and popular passion, and not to reason. I think they rest on statements untrue to Scripture and to the Church's teachings, and that if—*per impossibile*—they were true, the Church of England would not have a leg to stand upon.

I dismiss now all mere personalities. Lest he should suppose for a moment that his mass of crude and ridiculous assertions could not be answered, I shall deal with them *seriatim* by-and-by. I am no longer concerned with any controversialist or with any personal rudenesses and impertinences, but I am concerned with certain astonishing statements, and certain attacks, not only on good men, but also on the teachings of our own Church.

AURICULAR CONFESSION.

There are, then, several doctrines and practices included in the general charge of "sacerdotalism." To teach these, it appears, is to be a "sacerdotalist." These are untrue to Scripture and the Church, and therefore "sacerdotalism" is disloyalty. These may be taken *seriatim*. I begin with one.

Now, first as to "Auricular Confession." It has often been noticed, and I here notice it again, that when a point is to be made against this devout practice, its adversaries invariably describe it as "Auricular." That word is supposed to add to the horror of the situation! I need scarcely observe that all confession, as all conversation, must be "auricular," as it is only with the ear that we can hear.[1] The proofs against this practice

---

[1] It is impossible not to be struck by the weakness of opposing arguments when I find that a critic, who is greatly displeased with me, finds

being consistent with the teaching of Scripture and of the Church of England are hard to find. There are pages of declamation and violences of assertion, but proofs are few. All I can find, amidst the mass of declamation, are these: (1) That the commission in St. John xx. 21–23 and St. Matt. xviii. 20 is a gift to the Christian society, not to the Christian ministry. (2) That the use of Confession and Absolution may be abused; and that some stray sayings of Hooker, Jeremy Taylor, and of Bishop Wilberforce and Archbishop Tait are condemnatory of it. (3) That the receiving of confessions is forbidden by an "Act of the Convocation" of 1562.

As to the (1) and (2) of these proofs, I shall deal with them presently. To (3) I draw attention at once. I do so because it serves as a fit example of the accuracy of one who assails this part of the teaching of the Church. Now, I hope you will realize the assertion. It ought to be fully understood. It amounts to this. Priests who hear confessions or "practise" confession— that is the remarkable phrase used—are disobeying an "Act of Convocation" of 1562. I do not ask whether there *could* be an *Act of Convocation* to override the Prayer-book, which of course teaches Confession and Absolution as doctrines of the gospel, in the clearest terms; but, without going into that, it is worth while here and now to examine this *proof* that the English Church repudiates the "sacerdotalist" practice in question. The "Acts of the Convocation" of 1562 are referred to as containing a prohibition, under the gravest

nothing more cogent to urge than that "you might *write* your confession," therefore my remarks about its "Auricular" character do not apply! It would be absurd to take serious notice of such a criticism. When the opponents of the teaching of the Church betake themselves to such shifts as this, their case is weak indeed.

clerical penalties, of "practising" (*i.e.* receiving) auricular confession.

Now, (1) supposing there *had* been such an "Act of Convocation," it would have struck at a provision in the Prayer-book which the Queen's Highness had put forth three years before! I think you will agree with me that we know how luridly "the Occidental Star" would have glared at such presumption, had Convocation been guilty of it!

But it is worth while—as a specimen of the accuracy of rhetorical declaimers against the teaching of the Church—calmly to examine *the facts.*

My opponent has committed himself to this—that this prohibition of receiving confessions is among the "Acts of Convocation." His words are, "See Acts of the Convocation of 1562, I think, which, after directing the Ministry of God's Word, add, What Priest or Minister soever, under colour hereof, shall practise Auricular Confession, *shall be deposed from the ministry.*"[1] Well, here is a serious statement, and, in the dearth of evidence which marks this part of the attack, one naturally examines so strong a testimony with respect, as it is the only really weighty argument brought forward at all.

The writer in question seems to have been too hurried to be sure of the date. He *thinks* it is 1562. So far he is right. 1562 *is* the year to which this matter is to be referred. His quotation, however, does not seem to be quite accurate. He might have made his case seem even stronger by quoting it accurately. The matter stands thus: "Every person of age and discretion sufficient to communicate" is to "offer himself once a year . . . to be examined by his Parson, Vicar, or Curate, . . . upon pain to be excommunicate *ipso facto.* And before

[1] *Contemporary Review*, September, 1893, p. 360, note.

they be absolved, to pay"—either 6*s*. 8*d*. or 3*s*. 4*d*. according to their means. To carry out this examination of the laity as to whether they had learnt the Creed, the Lord's Prayer, and the Ten Commandments properly by heart, " every Parson and Vicar, by himself, or some sufficient Curate, shall give his attendance to hear his parishioners every Wednesday, Friday, and Holy Day, during the foresaid time, upon pain of deprivation, and loss of his benefice; and every Curate, upon pain, to forfeit 40*s*. At which time the said Parsons and Vicars shall take occasion to give some private, godly admonitions to their parishioners, if they know any faults or offences in them."

Then comes the crucial sentence, as follows : " What Priest or Minister soever, under colour hereof, shall practise Auricular Confession, *shall be deprived of all his livings, and deposed from the ministry.*"

Now, you will notice that this " Act of Convocation," as my opponent calls it, which is supposed to deal a deadly blow to " Sacerdotalism " in the Church of England, by forbidding priests to hear confessions, if it were an " Act " at all, would establish the most intolerable clerical tyranny over the laity that it is possible to imagine. I think a writer, so filled with horror of the danger to the laity, in making their confessions *if they choose*, and so very sensitive as to the dangers of "priestly domination," and infringement of the liberties of the laity, is hardly right in quoting so much of an " Act" as serves the purpose of an attack upon the doctrine of Confession, while keeping in the background the fact that such an " Act " would establish a most inquisitorial and intolerable tyranny. This is worth noting; but this by the way; for I say this on the assumption that there ever was such an " Act of Convocation." I do not believe that there ever was anything of the kind. If so, where is the evidence of it? If anywhere, in Cardwell, "Synod.," ii. 495. Now, there we learn that the passage concerned with this question was one sentence in a long paper, *not* of "Acts of Convocation" at all, but of *matters prepared for Convocation.* Go back from Cardwell to Strype, whom Cardwell quotes—you will correct me if I am wrong— I say whom Cardwell quotes, but quotes imperfectly. What do you find? You find that from Strype ("Annals," i. 473) we learn that Parker had set persons "on work to prepare matter for the Synod." Hence there are long draft *memoranda* of desirable proposals containing things *which were passed by*—which were, that is, *not passed at all—e.g.* that "the use of vestments, copes, and surplices," and "of organs," be "taken away or removed;" that "sponsors do not as heretofore answer in the infant's name;" that "no person do serve two cures at once;" that "the Articles of our Faith [*i.e.* the Apostles' Creed], the Commandments, the Lord's Prayer," be read every Sunday and Holy Day after the Gospel, together with some of those stringent provisions for the discipline of the laity referred to above; and among these is inserted this proposal about hearing of confessions, which comes in as a *caveat* after a passage enforcing the careful examination of the laity and the rather inquisitorial "godly admonition in private." Well, this "notable paper"[1] was prepared for the Synod, and we hear through Strype of two sets of *proposals or resolutions* which were presented to the Lower House on the part of the puritanizing members, one of which was only lost by a majority of one. *Neither of these,* however, contains the proposal to

[1] Strype, "Annals," i. 473, also quoted by Cardwell, "Synod.," i. 495.

prohibit the " practice " of Confession. Now, it is to be remembered that *neither of these* is an " Act " even of the Lower House, still less an " Act of Convocation." There was yet *another set of resolutions* actually adopted by the Lower House, but *not accepted* by the Upper House, *but not a word in it, so far as we know, of this extraordinary proposal.* It also is no " Act of Convocation." How much less can a *proposal* be called an "Act of Convocation" which, so far as appears, was *not even moved* in the Lower House! So much for the (3) *proof* of the wrong-doing of those who are in favour of the use of Confession and Absolution! So much also for the accuracy of my opponent's confident statements! It seems to me to be well at once to clear this out of the way. It would be hard indeed to imagine Convocation, even in its worst moments, doing such a thing. Had it done so, however, it might have been more or less a difficulty to those who uphold the Catholic teaching of the English Church. We have seen, however, that no such " Act " was passed.

This is the only statement in these articles which had the least appearance of being solid evidence on this matter; and you see how much it is worth![1]

The important duty in relation to the question before us is to examine *the positive teaching* of the English Church. The question whether a doctrine or practice has the sanction of Scripture, is of course of the highest

[1] An adverse critic observes that anyhow there *was a caveat* as to Confession and Absolution, *therefore* that the doctrine of the Church of England is opposed to this practice; *i.e.* there is a warning against the practice *in a document rejected by the Church of England, therefore* the Church of England denies the practice! In other words, you utterly *refuse* to deny something, which proves that you deny it! Such is Protestant logic!

importance, and every Churchman believes that the teachings of the Church *are* in conformity with Scripture. There are those who dissent from such teachings, and consider that they are in greater or less degree at variance with Scripture; but when the question is one of honesty and loyalty, the first thing to be determined is, "Does the Church teach and sanction this or not?" Whether or not men may think the Church's teaching not warranted by Scripture, at least they will agree that if any particular doctrine is according to the Church's teaching, those who uphold that doctrine are the men who, however mistaken they may be supposed to be, are the loyal sons of the Church.

I. Now, I assert that (without going into the scriptural question at present) Auricular Confession and Priestly Absolution are in accordance with the teaching of the Church of England. In order to substantiate this assertion, it is necessary to examine her authoritative documents, and there are some passages in the Prayer-book which have a special bearing on the point before us. The first of these is the Exhortation in the Communion Service. The passage in the Second Prayer-book [1] runs as follows: "Because it is requisite that no man should come to the Holy Communion but with a full trust in God's mercy, and with a quiet conscience; therefore if there be any of you, which by the means aforesaid cannot quiet his own conscience, but requireth further comfort or counsel, then let him come to me, or some other discreet and learned minister of God's Word, and *open his grief,* that he may receive such ghostly counsel, advice, and comfort as his conscience

---

[1] 1552. This is almost the same as in the present book, only that ours is somewhat stronger, as emphasizing "the benefit of Absolution" as being the chief thing to be sought.

may be relieved, and that by the *ministry of God's Word* he may receive comfort and the *benefit of Absolution*, to the quieting of his conscience, and the avoiding of all scruple and doubtfulness."

Now, it has been argued that certain expressions were here substituted for stronger expressions in the First Prayer-book for the express purpose of putting aside the doctrine and practice in question. This can be shown to be a complete mistake. It may be true, indeed, and it is very probable, that the alterations, like some others, were intended to conciliate the foreign reformers. But our Reformation divines, whether they were wise or unwise in going all the length they could for this purpose, never went so far as to depart from primitive practice and the teachings of the Fathers. That the change in the wording of the Exhortation implied no change of doctrine, and was not meant to introduce some novel Protestant theory, may be easily seen from the following considerations.

1. The *Benefit of Absolution*, about which various arguments—which really can only be described as shuffling arguments—have been used to empty it of any real meaning, was nothing more nor less than a phrase of earlier date than "Absolution;" and instead of weakening the teaching on the point, it strengthens it, by bringing before the mind the fact that the gift of Absolution is a real "Benefit."[1]

2. It has been asserted that the words, "by the ministry of God's Word," are meant to teach that Absolution is nothing at all except an exposition or lecture on some of the promises of Holy Scripture meant

---

[1] See Dr. Pusey's "Letter to Mr. Upton Richards:" "The Church of England leaves her children free to whom," etc., pp. 41, 42. Also Cardwell, "Doc. Ann.," i. p. 130. Also Carter (who quotes both), "Doctrine of Confession," p. 107.

as a help to individuals. To any plain man it would appear at once that if the Prayer-book uses language in this mysterious manner, in direct contradiction to its ordinary meaning, the less one has to do with the Prayer-book the better, as it would only confuse and perplex in the highest degree. When the Second Prayer-book was framed, everybody knew perfectly well the meaning of the term " Absolution." It was an ordinance, it was a ministerial act, and it had had that definite meaning for ages. You will remember the story that is told of an ecclesiastic who, on being asked—as his Puritan proclivities were well known—" What would you do if a man came to you to hear his confession?" answered, "I would make him sit down, and I should read to him the Comfortable Words." This illustrates the painful efforts made to distort the meaning of the Prayer-book. Had the framers of the Exhortation not meant *absolution* to be given, or had they wished to deny the doctrine, of course they would not have used the *expression*. When they speak of the " ministry of God's Word," they mean men to regard the " Word " as a part or instrument of the ministerial act in conveying the Grace of Absolution, certainly not as a substitute for it.[1] "Hooker," says Canon Carter justly, "understood the phrase in our Office in this sense." Hooker's words are, "They" (*i.e.* they who seek relief of the priest according to his invitation) " are to rest with minds encouraged and persuaded concerning the forgiveness of all their sins as out of Christ's own Word and power by the ministry of the keys."[2] Besides that " the expression under consideration is also consistent with a

---

[1] See on these points also Carter's "Doctrine of Confession," ch. vi., where they are more fully dealt with.
[2] "Eccles. Polity," book vi. c. 4, s. 114.

sacramental view of the ministry, and is used under this idea both in Scripture and by the Fathers. St. Paul, *e.g.*, speaks of Christ in Holy Baptism 'cleansing' the Church 'with the washing of water *by the Word;*'[1] St. Peter, again, of our 'being born again, not of corruptible seed, but of incorruptible, *by the Word of God.*' In both cases the grace of the sacrament is referred, not to the act of the minister, but to the word used in his ministry. . . . Again, St. Augustine, commenting on our Lord's saying, 'Now are ye clean *by the Word* I have spoken unto you,' adds, 'Why saith He not, "Ye are clean through the Baptism wherewith ye have been baptized"? saving that in water *also the Word* cleanseth. Take away *the Word*, and what is the water but water? *The Word* is added to the element, and it becomes a Sacrament, which itself also is a sort of visible Word.'"

3. But further, all through the Prayer-book the hearing of confessions and the ministering of absolution is treated as *an authoritative act* entirely confined to the priesthood. Deacons are allowed to expound the Scriptures. What would be the sense in a man who wanted absolution going to a priest, if all that it amounted to was that he should have the opportunity of hearing the Comfortable Words read to him? It is difficult to believe that anybody can seriously believe in or defend such a grotesque perversion of language. This exhortation, it has been truly said, comprehensively

[1] It is interesting to notice—in spite of Hooker, whom they usually quote—that an adverse critic says that I assume that St. Paul alludes to baptism by "the washing of water"! I should like to ask—If not, then what *does* he allude to? I know of nothing in the Christian Church in which "the washing of water" comes in except Holy Baptism. Men are driven hard to contravene the Faith if they fall back upon criticism of this kind.

expresses the several parts of the ministry. (*a*) The appointed minister is the priest. " Let him come to me;" for it is only a priest who can read this exhortation, as it is only a priest who can celebrate. (*b*) The instrument of the ministry is God's Word. (*c*) The blessing received is counsel and comfort, and the benefit of absolution. (*d*) The results are " the quieting of his conscience, and avoiding all scruple and doubtfulness."[1]

4. But a most important consideration, again and again urged, and again and again ignored by those who oppose Catholic teaching, is this—that when the Second Prayer-book was authorized, it was distinctly stated, in the " Act for the Uniformity of Services " (1552), that the First Prayer-book was " agreeable to the Word of God and the Primitive Church," and that " doubts in the use and exercise thereof " had arisen " rather from the curiosity of the ministers and mistakers than of any other worthy cause." Whatever change of language, then, there may have been in later books, we have a public and authoritative statement that *no change of doctrine was intended.* The most dexterous juggler with words cannot escape from the plain assertions of the First Prayer-book. Even if he tries to twist the expressions of the later book into meaning something else instead of Confession and Absolution, he cannot, with any sort of respect for the meaning of language, pretend that the First Book did not in the plainest way teach this doctrine and practice; and since *no change of doctrine,* we are distinctly told, *was intended,* if he has any doubt about the meaning of the language of the later book, he has only to refer to the First Book to clear away his doubt.

The teaching of the Exhortation in the Communion

---

[1] *Vide* Carter, *ut supra.*

Service, then, goes so far as this—*not* that Auricular Confession is *necessary* in all cases, but that it is *permitted*, in certain cases *advised*, and even *urged*, that it is a *benefit* and a *blessing*.

II. (1) The second important passage is, of course, in the Office for the Visitation of the Sick. The witness of this to the mind of the Church of England as to the truth and blessing of Auricular Confession is final, and cannot be evaded. It comes to us with all the authority of the settlement of 1661. The changes made then rendered the whole question more definite and distinct, by going back more closely to the pre-Reformation directions. In the earlier Prayer-book confession was left to the discretion of the sick person; in our present Prayer-book the priest is directed to take the initiative, and to use his influence so as to *move* the sick person to make a confession, if he thought it desirable. Not only so, the present Prayer-book also specifies that it is to be a special confession of his sins. Former Prayer-books offered, indeed, an opportunity to the sick person; in our present Prayer-book the priest is to *urge* it. How, then, can anybody, I would ask, with the slightest respect for the morality of language, pretend for a moment that the Church of England does not teach Auricular Confession?

(2) It is also to be remembered that the stronger terms of our present rubric were probably introduced to counteract that growing tendency to laxity, and the dangerous evasion of confession, which was becoming then, as unfortunately it has been since, a very grave danger to souls. The clergy, so it has been wisely said, had become rather slow and backward—a little bit lazy, I suppose, and perhaps half-hearted and cowardly—which is a serious danger to priests—as, unfortunately, they have sometimes shown themselves in later times,

we cannot doubt to the serious detriment of souls—in doing what was their duty, though a painful duty. Probably some of them found refuge in the terms of the rubric. Rubric-worship then, as rubric-worship now, in those who do not really mean what they say in the Creed—" I believe in the Holy Catholic Church "—was doubtless dangerous. The Savoy Fathers were determined that there should be no mistake. They met such persons on their own ground. They were not to escape from their duties by pleading a vague rubric. It was the *duty* of the priest henceforth, at any rate, to take the initiative, and to *exhort* and *urge* the sick man to confession.[1]

I repeat, again, whatever be the limits, whatever be the arrangements to be made in detail, any man who puts his hand to the statement that he accepts the Prayer-book *ex animo*, and then, in face of this rubric, declares that Auricular Confession is contrary to the teaching of the Church of England, is a curiosity, and might fairly advance a claim to be put in a museum!

(3) There has been, I know, an attempt made—which, were the subject not so serious, would be positively comical—to evade the force of this command by declaring that this is an absolution only from Church censures. When men say such things, my dear friend, we feel sorrow for them. They are suffering under the pressure of a disagreeable truth, to which they have bound

[1] The only attempt made to meet the force of this is that it was "a Romish form," and "never permitted till 1215, and the great Cardinal *Hugo*, William of Paris, and William of Auxerre, protested against it" as "false in doctrine and modern in form." I differ. It is "an Anglican form." It does not matter in the smallest degree in what year it was first permitted, nor is it of consequence what "great Cardinal" liked or disliked it. *The* point is—the Church of England has liked it and adopted it, and to its use all of us clergy are bound as Anglican priests.

themselves, and the force of which it is not easy to evade. I do not mean that they are consciously dishonest, but they have drifted into the habit of interpreting the teachings of the Church in accordance with formulæ invented by "this present evil world," and they have emptied the teachings of her who is the bride of the Lamb of their real meaning by traditional heresies and superstitions of Puritanism. It can scarcely be doubted, surely, by any serious person, that language so solemn, and so exact, and used at such a time as in the last moments of the probationary life of a soul in this world, could not possibly, I submit, relate to " Church censures." It is really difficult to repress a smile when one finds Protestant teachers so very jealous about respect to the directions of the Church, which usually they decry, that they urge the theory that they are to disturb the last moments of a dying man in order to remove " Church censures." We do not find them in the ordinary hours of life so sensitively alive to the regulations of the Church. Verily "the whirligig of time hath its revenges"!

But beyond all this, we know that this is taken from the old Latin Office, which *did* mention ecclesiastical censures as a separate thing, but also had, " I absolve thee from *thy sins.*" In our Prayer-book the sentence about ecclesiastical censures *was deliberately omitted*, while that about the absolution from sins was as *deliberately retained.* In the face of this, is it possible for any one to say that the directions in the Visitation of the Sick have to do with the censures of the Church only ?

But further, the priest has to ask the sick man about his " sins ;" he has to move him to confess his " sins." If Church censures only are the subject of absolution, then this is what the Church is supposed to do: in the most awful moment of human trial she is supposed to juggle with language, and to put one meaning on the word "sins" in her rubric of direction to the priest, and another meaning upon it in the words of absolution! A strange mother, to deceive and perplex her child at the moment of his severest trial!

But besides that, there are two considerations which really settle the question for any serious person. (1) The sins which are spoken of can, from the nature of the case, be only known to the priest by the confession of the sick person. Now, sins which come under "Church censure" are *notorious* sins, and (2) the removing of "Church censures" is no part of the office of a priest. There is not a word about any special commission from the bishop here—which would be necessary in dealing with ecclesiastical censures—but the ordinary exercise of the authority of a priest. It is also well to remember Mr. Cooke's remark, quoted by Canon Carter.[1] It is made *à propos* of the fact that when the Prayer-book was reviewed the Nonconformists objected to the form of Absolution. Then Mr. Cooke says, and justly, "How easy it would have been for the bishops to have answered, that nothing but a release from Church censures was meant, if such had been considered to be the object of the absolution!" But the bishops answered in a very different way. They affirmed the exact contrary. They said that "the form[2] of Absolution is more agreeable to the Scriptures than that which they desire, it being said in St. John xx.,

---

[1] "Doctrine of Confession," ch. vii.
[2] Cardwell's "History of Conferences on the Book of Common Prayer," p. 361; quoted also by Carter, "Doctrine of Confession," *ut supra*.

'whose sins ye remit, they are remitted'—not, 'whose sins ye pronounce remitted'—*and the condition needs not to be expressed, being always necessarily understood.*"

(4) The last statement of the bishops here, I think you will agree with me, is worth dwelling upon for a moment. One of the foolish fallacies constantly in vogue with the opponents of Catholic teaching is that absolution is not operative unless penitence is sincere, and that as the priest is not omniscient he cannot be sure of this. This kind of argument would cut at the root of all faithful action under the laws of Divine government. But just as our common sense would correct any such absurdity in the ordinary practices of life, so the common sense of the bishops made short work of this transparent evasion. There is always, of course, a *personal responsibility* ultimately and in the long run, but in every affair of life— not merely in these very serious matters—when we act for and with others, there are also always conditions understood of the fulfilment of which we can never be *absolutely* certain. We live in a world of probation and trial, and probability is necessarily the guide of life.

But this by the way.

(5) It is a further very remarkable thing that, through all the revisions of the Prayer-book, the form of the Absolution in the Visitation of the Sick has never been changed. Foreign Protestants and sectaries of all kinds pressed fiercely upon the Fathers of the English Church, especially in Edward VI.'s reign. Notwithstanding this, they did not succeed in persuading the Church of England to change the strongest form of Absolution that ever has been used in the Church. The truth evidently is that the "principles of the Reformation" involved the clear Catholic doctrine of Auricular Confession and Priestly Absolution, and that any man who denies these

is—perhaps unconsciously, but still really—unfaithful to the "principles of the Reformation."

I think, my dear friend, we are bound to keep it clearly before our minds, and the minds of others, that we learn from the plainest evidence, if we do not allow ourselves to be Jesuitical, or to juggle with language, that a prominent "principle of the Reformation" is the truth and duty and blessing of Auricular Confession and Priestly Absolution.

III. But those who desire to deny the Catholic character of the Church's teaching upon this important point fall back upon the Articles and even the Homilies. The first thing to be said on that point is that anything which is doubtful in either must be interpreted according to the teaching of the Prayer-book. *Lex orandi, lex credendi.* It is usual to quote the Twenty-fifth Article, however, as denying the Sacrament of Penance.

This assertion we must now examine. It must be acknowledged at once that "the language of the Article is awkward and embarrassed."[1] It speaks of the five lesser sacraments as having "grown," partly of "the corrupt following of the Apostles," partly are "states of life allowed in the Scriptures." At first sight, this looks as if it were intended to divide them into two classes, and opponents of Catholic teaching affirm (1) that the five lesser sacraments are not sacraments at all, because the Article says they are not "sacraments of the Gospel," and (2) that instead of being sacraments, they were some of them *merely* permissible states of life, and some of them corruptions of Apostolic teaching.[2]

---

[1] Bishop Forbes on the Articles, *in loc.*
[2] I notice that an adverse critic thinks I acknowledge that the Article is against my contention by adopting Bishop Forbes' phrase that the

This is altogether a mistaken view; for (1) the word "sacrament" has been used in a wide sense and a narrow sense. In the wider sense these five are sacraments, according to St. Augustine's description, "a visible sign of an invisible grace;" and this the Article does not deny. What it does deny is that they are sacraments *in the stricter sense*. What the Article technically calls "sacraments of the Gospel," that is, sacraments *with an outward sign ordained expressly by Christ Himself*, are recorded as being so ordained in the Gospel. In this latter sense, only Holy Baptism and Holy Communion are "sacraments." The Article means to place before us the special dignity and necessity of the two great sacraments, but does not deny a sacramental character to the five other rites. It could not be so, for those who framed the Article cannot have meant to contradict the Homilies of which they spoke with approval. Indeed, the passage on Common Prayer and Sacraments, in the Second Book of the Homilies, illustrates the meaning of the Article. The Homily there confines the term "sacrament," "in its fullest, strictest sense," to the two great sacraments; "recognizes," it has been truly said, "at the same time an intermediate class of sacraments, or sacramental ordinances, of which Absolution and Orders are mentioned as instances." Marriage, again, is directly called a "sacrament" in one of the Homilies. And Absolution is declared to have "the promise of forgiveness of sin." And Orders are said to

language of the Article is "awkward and embarrassed." How so? Can any one contend that it is anything else? It *appears* at first sight to divide the five sacramental ordinances in question into *two* classes: (1) "corrupt following of the Apostles;" (2) "states of life allowed in Scripture." Can any member of the English Church, I repeat, pretend that Confirmation falls under *either* of these heads? He cannot. Well, if so, the language *is* "awkward and embarrassed."

convey the grace of the priesthood. Taking the Article and Homilies together in the light of the teaching of the Prayer-book, it is quite clear that the Church of England means to draw a distinction between the two great sacraments and the others. Holy Baptism and the Holy Eucharist are pre-eminent. "What Circumcision and the Passover were to the Fathers, *they* are to the Israel of God. They alone are generally necessary to salvation," and they alone have outward signs instituted by Christ Himself, as recorded in the Gospels. Other sacramental rites, however, there are, and it has been shown that the Article cannot be supposed to deny that they are ordinances of God, and that they convey spiritual grace. It has been truly said, "It cannot be denied that seven ordinances have enclosed the whole Christian life in blessed bonds, not all necessary for all —nay, in the highest form of Christian life there is no room for Matrimony; and in the first fervour of Christian love, *they* were the exception who needed to be restored by the Sacrament of Penance—but these convey, *according to men's needs*, the grace of which they are channels. They have ever been regarded to have a mystical significance of their own, and severally from the beginning, have existed as practices in the Church."[1]

(2) As to the notion that the Article really intended to declare these to be either permissible states of life *or* corruptions of Apostolic teaching, this again is clearly a mistake; for this reason, among others, that Confirmation, for instance, is certainly not a "state of life," and as certainly it did not arise from a "*corrupt* following of the Apostles," seeing that it is accepted and insisted upon by the English Church in the most emphatic manner. Obscure and awkward as the language

[1] Carter, "Doctrine of Confession," *in loc.*

of the Article certainly is, it cannot mean this; and with regard to the question immediately before us, it cannot mean that the Sacrament of Penance arose from a "*corrupt* following of the Apostles," for in the Commination Service the component parts of the Sacrament of Penance, according to their accustomed and ancient definitions, are drawn out so that we learn that they are *contrition, confession,* and *worthy fruits of penance.* If the curious expression in the Article about the " corrupt following of the Apostles " refers to this sacrament at all, then it can only have meant to repudiate " not penance, whether public or private, simply considered, but some incidental doctrines, which had become intimately associated with the term, and formed part of the practical system then prevailing."[1] Very probably, too, that expression may have been intended to condemn, not the Sacrament of Unction, for which there is an appointed Service in the First Prayer-book, but the *abuse* of making it *extreme* Unction only. But that by the way.

IV. I need not now dwell at any great length upon the bearing on this subject of the words in the Service for the Ordination of Priests, because they must be considered more carefully by-and-by on the whole question of sacerdotalism. But we may notice this now : The Ordinal was prepared in 1549 by Cranmer and others who were working with him. In 1548 he put forth what is called Cranmer's Catechism. That Catechism may therefore be taken as explanatory of what the Ordinal was intended to mean. In 1562 was published the Homily for Whitsun Day, and it has been truly said that "these documents together form an authoritative

---

[1] Carter, "Doctrine of Confession," ch. vii. *ut supra.* See also Forbes on the Articles *in loc.*

catena of doctrine stretching throughout the most critical period of the Reformation."[1]

The following is the language of the Homily: "Christ ordained the authority of the Keys to excommunicate notorious sinners, and to absolve them which are truly penitent." The language of the Catechism is as follows: "Now, God doth not speak to us with a voice sounding out of Heaven, but He hath given the Keys of the Kingdom of Heaven, and the authority to forgive sin by the Ministers of the Church. Wherefore let him that is a sinner go to one of them; let him acknowledge and confess his sin, and pray him that, according to God's commandment, he will give him Absolution, and comfort him with the Word of Grace, and Forgiveness of his sins. And when the Minister doth so, then I ought steadfastly to believe that my sins are truly forgiven me in Heaven, and such a faith is able to stand strong in all skirmishes and assaults of our mortal enemy, the Devil; forasmuch as it is builded on a sure rock, that is to say, the certain Word and Work of God. *For he that is absolved knoweth for a surety that his sins be forgiven him by the Minister, and he knoweth assuredly also that the Minister hath authority from God Himself to do so.* And, thirdly, he knoweth that God hath made this promise to His Ministers, and said to them, 'To whom ye forgive sins on earth, to him also they shall be forgiven in Heaven.' *Wherefore despise not Absolution, for it is the commandment and Ordinance of God, and the Holy Spirit of God is present and causeth these things to take effect in us and to work our salvation.*"[2]

---

[1] Carter, ibid., ch. viii.; also Cooke's "Power of the Priesthood," p. 62, also quoted by him.

[2] Cf. "Catechism, Cranmer's Works," vol. iv. p. 283. The italics are

I repeat that the question before us for the moment is not as to *the truth* of the doctrine under discussion; but the question is whether the Church of England does or does not teach and sanction Confession and Absolution, or Auricular Confession or the Sacrament of Penance, by whichever name it be called. And I would appeal to any fair-minded man—whatever his opinions be as to *the truth* of the doctrine—whether it is possible, in the face of the teaching of the Prayer-book, of the Articles, of the Homilies, of the Ordinal, to deny that the Church of England does so teach? And whether it is not abundantly clear in regard to this matter, by a comparison of the words of Cranmer's Catechism of 1548, quoted above, with the words in the Ordinal—" Whose sins thou dost forgive, they are forgiven," etc.—drawn up by Cranmer and others in 1549, that *the intention of the English Church is to assert* the truth of Confession and Absolution, of the Sacrament of Penance, and of this special exercise of the power of the keys?

There can be no doubt, then, unless men twist language into non-natural senses, that if the teaching of Auricular Confession and Priestly Absolution implies " sacerdotalism," then " sacerdotalism " is the teaching of the English Church.

Men who dissent entirely from that teaching, and—acting in a consistent manner by reason of that dissent—remain " Dissenters," see this clearly. It is just twenty years ago since, in commenting upon a discussion which had just then taken place in Convocation, the *Nonconformist*, a Dissenting newspaper, wrote as follows:—

" When men can shut their eyes to what is clearly

mine. Cranmer is not usually considered by Protestants a " Sacerdotalist " in the evil sense of that word. Who can be stronger on Confession and Absolution?

implied by the reservation of the right to read the daily Absolution; when they are obstinately blind to the plain grammatical meaning of the Rubric and Absolution in the Visitation of the Sick; when they, in general, pervert to non-natural meanings the essential significance of the whole sacramental system they profess;—it is impossible but that paralysis should seize their understandings. Violating of necessity, however unconsciously, the unmistakable spirit of the Prayer-book, they have no right to say to transgressors in the opposite direction, 'Stand off; for I am holier than thou.' Say what they may, the principle of Auricular Confession and of Priestly Absolution stares us in the face, indelibly branded on the legal constitution of the Anglican Church." [1]

I am afraid, had I written such words, that it is not difficult to imagine the depth and extent of the scorn of opponents; but, in truth, it must be evident, to any who look at the matter calmly, how clear and persistent the English Church is as to that part of the gospel which is called by these opponents "sacerdotalism."

There are two points in this connection which it is well, perhaps, to dwell upon more fully, because of the extreme shiftiness of the arguments of such opponents.

(1) As to *Absolution*—oddly enough, they endeavour, in this connection, to make out a sort of general power of doing people good, or helping them, or teaching them. It is necessary to insist that such use or misuse of language would have been in the highest degree immoral. Our Reformers knew perfectly well, as everybody else knew, what meaning was attached in the minds of all men at the time to the word "absolution." Notwithstanding this, it has been actually argued that by the

[1] *Nonconformist,* July, 1873.

power of absolution is meant a power to preach that there is remission of sins offered to repentant sinners through the blood of Christ! Clearly, if this had been meant, it would have been the duty of the Church to say, "God hath given power and authority to His ministers to preach." If you mean "preaching," you have no business to say "absolution." This would seem obvious to most people; but it is necessary to insist upon it, as such an extraordinary statement is repeated again and again. Anyhow, whether it be right or not to call one thing by the name of another, the Church of England does not do so. For you will notice, my dear friend, that in the ordination of deacons the bishop delivers to every one of them the New Testament, and in doing so says, "Take thou authority to read the Gospel in the Church of God, and *to preach the same*, if thou be thereto licensed by the bishop himself." It is never said to the deacon, "Whose sins thou dost forgive, they are forgiven;" and no suggestion is made that he should be licensed *to pronounce absolution*.

It is well known that the Nonconformists desired the word "priest" to be removed, and the word "minister" to be used instead of it always in the Prayer-book. There are some who regret that the word was left in the Prayer-book. They think that it means nothing more than a deacon or minister, or even layman, and that its retention has led to this unfortunate "sacerdotalism" which they so greatly deplore. This is a mistake. The retention of the word "priest" did not lead to sacerdotalism, but "sacerdotalism"—being the doctrine of the Church of England—led to the retention of the word "priest." *This we know as a matter of fact.* The bishops at the Savoy Conference answered the Nonconformists as follows: "It is not reasonable that the word 'minister' should be only used in the Liturgy. For since some parts of the Liturgy may be performed by a deacon, others by none under the order of a priest, viz. *absolution and consecration*, it is fit that some such word as 'priest' should be used for those offices, and not 'minister,' which signifies at large every one that ministers in that holy office, of what order soever he be."[1]

But what is more, in the rubric before the Absolution in the Office for Daily Morning and Evening Prayer, the word "minister" was erased and "priest" substituted. The Church of England then, as it permits the deacon to preach and *the priest only* to absolve, makes her mind quite clear as to this point, that *preaching* is one function and *absolution* quite another. And, in view of this evidence, I submit, it may be legitimate for some men—being Catholic priests—to lament that they are not Protestant ministers, and that their Church did not depart from "sacerdotalism" and the Catholic teaching about absolution; but it is not open to them to say that she *did* depart from it when there is clear evidence that she did *not*, or to find fault with those who, being like themselves Catholic priests, are not desirous of acting as Protestant ministers. That by the way. But it is abundantly evident that *absolution is an ordinance* to be administered in the Church by a priest, and *only by a priest;* that its "benefits," which come from God through the power of the Passion of Christ, may be received by any penitent soul making

---

[1] Cardwell, "Hist. of Conferences," ch. vii. prop. ii. p. 42. What becomes of the retort to my argument that "the Reformers might have called ministers by other names than priest," *and they deliberately would not?* The retort is, "On the contrary, they deliberately did"! It has been declared that in my statement I speak "*in the teeth of all evidence.*" Let any one read Cardwell's account as above of the bishops' answer, and then say which of us speaks "*in the teeth of all evidence.*"

D

their confession to the priest, and that this Divine gift and sacred ordinance has its own meaning and object, and is not to be confused with any other whatever.

(2) As to *Confession*—there has further been an effort made, of an evasive kind, to promote the notion that if absolution means anything at all beyond preaching of forgiveness, it only means some sort of general declaration, and that special confession is not necessary before particular absolution. How any one can imagine such a thing in the face of those teachings of the Prayer-book which we have already examined, viz. the Exhortation in the Communion Service, and, above all, the rubric in the Visitation of the Sick, it is difficult to imagine, if one did not know the shifts to which men sometimes betake themselves in order to cover an impossible position. But there are some direct proofs, besides those in the Prayer-book, that confession, as a prerequisite to receiving the Grace of Absolution, has been believed and insisted upon by the Anglican hierarchy. Among such proofs I need only mention one. You will remember the story of Sir John Friend and Sir William Parkins, who were sentenced to death for conspiring against King William III. Certain clergy, it appears, "openly and scandalously gave them absolution, though they made no special confession of their sins." The archbishops, and as many bishops as it was possible to get together in London, issued a declaration accordingly.[1] In the declaration this occurs—

"Lastly. For those clergymen that took upon them to absolve these criminals at the place of execution, by laying, all three together, their hands upon their heads, and publicly pronouncing a form of absolution;

---

[1] Wilkins' "Concilia," vol. iv. p. 627. This is also quoted by Cooke, "Power of the Priesthood," p. 57.

as their manner of doing this was extremely insolent, and without precedent either in our Church or any way that we know of, so the thing itself was altogether irregular.

"The rubric in our Office of the Visitation of the Sick, from which they took the words they then used, and upon which, if upon anything in our Liturgy, they must ground this their proceeding, gave them no authority nor no pretence for the absolving these persons; nay, as they managed the affair, they acted in this absolution far otherwise than is there directed.

"That rubric is concerning sick persons, and it is there required, first, that the 'sick person shall be moved to make a special confession of his sins, if he feel his conscience troubled with any weighty matter, and then, after such confession, the priest shall absolve him, if he humbly and heartily desire it.' But here they absolved, and *that publicly*, persons condemned by law for execrable crimes, *without so much as once moving them at that time to make a special confession of their sins*—at least of those sins for which they were condemned. And, on the other side, here were persons absolved that did not humbly desire absolution, as feeling any such weighty matter to trouble their conscience.

"If these ministers knew not the state of these men's souls before they gave them absolution, as it is manifest two of them did not, . . . *how could they, without manifest transgression of the Church's order, as well as the profane abuse of the power Christ has left with His ministers, absolve them from their sins?*

"If they were acquainted with these men's sentiments

declared in their papers, then they must look upon them either as hardened impenitents, or martyrs.

"We are so charitable to believe that they would not absolve them under the former notion [*i.e.* as being impenitent]; *for that had been, in effect, sealing them to damnation.*"

This document is dated April 10, 1696, and it is signed by the two archbishops and twelve bishops. I may remind you that Tenison at the time was Archbishop of Canterbury.

But what I desire to call your attention to, my dear Dean, is this — that these archbishops and bishops teach: (1) That there must be a special confession of sin before particular absolution. (2) That Christ hath left power to His ministers to absolve penitents *from their sins* (not merely from Church censures). (3) That to receive absolution unworthily is as serious a matter as to receive the Eucharist unworthily. Indeed, the archbishops' and bishops' language here is unmistakably strong; for whilst the Exhortation in the Communion Service speaks of receiving Communion unworthily being a way to '*increase damnation*,'' the archbishops and bishops here speak of receiving absolution unworthily *immediately before death*, when there is presumably no time for further repentance, as being a means to *seal us to damnation*. Confession, then, of sins is clearly a prerequisite in the mind of the Church for the receiving of absolution, and absolution is a means of conveying pardon to the penitent according to the institution of Christ. This is clear enough, of course, to any one who does not wilfully shut his eyes to the Church of England formularies already considered; but here there is the very strongest corroborative evidence from the declaration of these archbishops and bishops, not by any means inclined to be prejudiced in favour of extreme "sacerdotalism." [1]

If I turn, my dear friend, to the great divines of the English Church, I am so overwhelmed by a mass of evidence on the subject that I would weary you, and all my readers, if I attempted to quote half of it. Allow me to remind you of some examples.

Here is what Bishop Montague [2] says: "Private confession to a priest is of very ancient practice in the Church; of excellent use and practice, being discreetly handled. We refuse it to none, if men require it, if need be to have it. We urge and persuade it in extremes. We require it in case of perplexity, for the quieting of men disturbed, and their consciences."

There is no doubt that our great divines draw the true line between confession as *compulsory* and confession as *voluntary*. So Marshall writes—

"This [private confession] they find recommended in very ancient records, and descending to them with the advantage of truly primitive examples; therefore they are loth entirely to lose sight of it; especially since they observe both *our own and most of the reformed Churches* to have been well-wishers to it; though they have left it, indeed, upon every man's conscience to resort, as he shall see occasion, to his spiritual guide either for comfort or counsel." [3]

Hooker, as you know, was quite distinct against *compulsion* in confession. He is a favourite authority, by the way, with some who oppose us when they can

---

[1] This is drawn out more strongly and clearly by Cooke, "Power of the Priesthood," p. 89.
[2] A.D. 1578–1641. "A Gag for the New Gospel."
[3] "Penitential Discipline," p. 41, quoted by Bennett.

find in him a stray sentence which seems to tell against the Faith. I do not think they would be inclined to be so enthusiastic as to *some* of his teachings, as I shall have occasion to notice on another point. But even Hooker writes as follows:—

"Were the Fathers, then, without use of private confession as long as public was in use? *I affirm no such thing.* The first and ancientest that mentioneth this confession is Origen, by whom it may be seen that men, being loth to present rashly themselves and their faults unto the view of the whole Church, thought it best to unfold their minds to some one special man of the clergy, which might either help them himself, or refer them to a higher court if need were."

Hooker also quotes Origen as follows: "Be therefore circumspect in making choice of the party to whom thou meanest to confess thy sins; know thy physician before thou use him."[1]

He also quotes St. Augustine as follows: "Let every man while there is time judge himself, and change his life of his own accord; and when this is resolved, let him, from the disposers of the Holy Sacraments, learn in what manner he is to pacify God's displeasure."[2]

Then Hooker concludes as follows: "But because of all men there is, or should be, none more fit for troubled and distressed minds to repair unto than God's ministers, he [*i.e.* St. Augustine] proceedeth further: 'Make the priest, as a father, partaker of thy affliction and grief; *be bold to impart unto him the things that are most secret,* he will have care both of thy safety and of thy credit.'"

You will agree with me also, my dear friend, and perhaps even opponents will agree with me in this, that

---

[1] "Eccles. Polity," bk. vi. (Keble's edit., vol. iii. p. 30).
[2] Ibid., pp. 31, 32.

a man's *deeds* are more eloquent than his *words*. You remember what Walton tells us of Hooker in his " Life." "About one day before his death, Dr. Saravia, who knew the very secrets of his soul [*for they were supposed to be confessors to each other*] came to him, and after a conference of *the benefit, the necessity*, and *safety* of the Church's Absolution, it was resolved the doctor should give him both that and the Sacrament the day following." [1]

There is something very touching in the story of Hooker and Saravia hearing each other's confessions, and giving one another absolution. There is something very saddening in thinking how many souls at the time must have stood in the same sort of need of the Church's ministrations who often, from laxity or carelessness in the priesthood, failed to receive them. We cannot be thankful enough to Almighty God for the revival of life in these later times in our beloved Church, whereby both clergy and laity are led to realize the blessing of this loving ordinance of Christ. We are, alas! all of us, too ready to think lightly of sin, and too open to the temptation to avoid the penitential discipline of particular Confession, and to slight the "benefit of Absolution;" but how shocking and how sad it is when—in the face of the plain teaching of our Church—sometimes a priest (and, occasionally I fear, it has been so, a bishop) positively dissuades men from the use of so blessed an ordinance of grace, and thereby really hinders souls!

But I go on. We are told of Bishop Bull, that "a few days before his death, in the presence of several persons, he made a solemn confession and declaration of the conduct of his whole life," and he received abso-

[1] "The Life of Mr. Richard Hooker," fol. edit. 1666, p. 25.

lution.[1] The same is told of Bishop Sanderson, and of other great English divines. You remember also that Bishop Latimer said, "To speak of right and true confession, I would to God it were kept in England, for it is a good thing."[2]

Bishop Andrewes, you remember, thanked God that his sins had been remitted through the power of the keys; and it was his habit, especially in Lent, to walk daily at certain hours in one of the aisles of the church, that if any came unto him for spiritual advice and comfort, he might impart it to them.

Dr. Crakanthorp[3] said, "We have abrogated neither Private Confession nor Private Absolution."

Bishop Morton[4] said, "It is not questioned between us whether it be convenient for a man burthened with sin to lay open his conscience in private to the minister of God, and to seek *at his hands . . . the comfort of God's pardon.*"

Bishop Cosin says that Sacramental Confession and Absolution are for the better preparation for the Blessed Sacrament.[5]

I might also, of course, quote to you the well-known words of Bishop Wilson on Absolution, Death-bed Repentance, and Auricular Confession, and, indeed, any

[1] Nelson's "Life of Bull," Oxford, 1846, pp. 393, 394. Here we are told that he preferred the form of Absolution in the Communion Office, but that he did not thereby condemn the use of the other form, nor had he "any doubt concerning the benefits of Sacerdotal Absolution."

[2] Bishop Sanderson (A.D. 1587-1662), speaking of a case of mortal sin, says, "She [must] also make an outward free confession of her said sins to him *to whom God hath delegated a ministerial power to remit sins, that she may receive comfort and absolution from his mouth; I mean the Priest*" (vide "Nine Cases of Conscience," sec. 13, published under the authority of Bishop Hall).

[3] A.D. 1567-1624. "Defensio Eccl. Anglicanæ," p. 565.

[4] A.D. 1564-1659. "Catholick Appeal," p. 270.

[5] A.D. 1594-1672. "Works," vol. ii. p. 121.

number of sayings from his works *all* teaching this truth fully; but I need not weary you with accumulating evidences of the mind of the great English divines on this subject, for the mass of evidence both from the Prayer-book and from our divines is so great that it would be impossible to exhaust it within any reasonable space. However, there is one piece of evidence to which I must call your attention.

If a practice is not authorized or permitted by a Church, then that Church would certainly not make laws to regulate that practice. If, on the other hand, a Church *does* make such laws, then it would be impossible to say that she puts aside the practice which she regulates. No reasonable being can deny this. Now, if every other proof were wanting of the fact that the Church of England teaches the doctrine of Confession and Absolution, and further that she contemplates the use of Private Auricular Confession by her members, *her own regulation on the subject would be sufficient and unanswerable.* In the 113th of the Constitutions and Canons Ecclesiastical, which were passed in the Synod of 1604, and which are still in force, "provision is made," as it has been truly said, " to secure the secrecy of confession by threatening one of the heaviest ecclesiastical penalties against any priest who shall reveal a sin committed to his trust in confession."[1] The Canon in question absolutely forbids the revealing by the minister, "if any man confess his secret and hidden sins to" him, of anything that has been told him, and this "under pain of irregularity." And *pain of irregularity,* as the Canonists tell us, "not only doth deprive a man of all his *spiritual promotions* for the

[1] Cooke, "Power of the Priesthood," pp. 106, 107.

present time, but makes him utterly incapable of any for the time to come; and therefore it is the greatest penalty, except *degradation from the priesthood*, which possibly a clergyman can be subject to." It is certainly true, then, "that a law to regulate the priest's conduct concerning Confession is the very strongest possible evidence that the practice of Confession is contemplated by the English Church."

But further, I may adduce the following evidence, which is entirely to the point in question, and I cannot do better than adopt the words of an able writer on the subject:—

"In the year 1634," he says, "the English Canons were introduced into Ireland, with certain alterations. It must be remembered that the Irish Church at that period decidedly leaned to Puritanism, and that the Irish Canons were drawn up by Bishop Bramhall and approved of by the Primate Ussher—two of the greatest opponents Rome ever had. And therefore it is not a little remarkable, and, at the same time, *a proof that private confession is not necessarily peculiar to the Roman Church*,[1] to find the practice of private confession recommended in such decided terms: 'Canon XIX. Warning to be given beforehand for the Communion: "Whereas every lay person is bound to receive the Holy Communion thrice every year, and many, notwithstanding, do not receive the sacrament once a year, we do require every minister to give warning to his parishioners publicly in the church at Morning Prayer, the Sunday before every time of his administering the Holy Sacrament, for the better preparation of themselves; which said warning be enjoined the said parishioners to accept and obey, under the penalty and danger of the

[1] The italics are mine.—W. J. K. L.

law. And the minister of every parish, and in cathedral and collegiate churches some principal minister of the Church, shall, the afternoon before the said administration, give warning by the tolling of the bell, or otherwise, that if any have any scruple of conscience, or desire the special ministry of reconciliation, he may afford it to those that need it. And to this end that people are often to be exhorted to enter into a special examination of the state of their own souls, and that finding themselves extremely dull, or much troubled in mind, they do resort unto God's ministers, to receive from them as well advice and counsel for the quieting of their dead hearts, and the subduing of those corruptions whereunto they have been subject, *as the benefit of absolution likewise, for the quieting of their consciences by the power of the keys which Christ hath committed His ministers for that purpose.*'"[1]

Let me further quote—

"In the Articles of Inquiry made by Bishops at their Visitations, we find constant reference to Confession. In 1619 Bishop Overall inquires, 'Whether doth your minister, before the several times of the administration of the Lord's Supper, admonish and exhort his parishioners if they have their consciences troubled and disquieted, to resort unto him or some other learned minister, and open his grief, that he may receive such ghostly counsel and comfort as his conscience may be relieved, and by the minister he may receive the benefit of absolution, to the quiet of his conscience and avoiding of scruple?' In 1636 the Bishop of Peterborough inquires, 'Doth your minister ... commonly premonish his parishioners if they be

---

[1] Cooke, "Power of the Priesthood." The italics are mine.—W. J. K. L.

troubled in conscience to confess and open their griefs to him, that they may receive the benefit of absolution?' The same inquiry is made in 1636 by the Bishop of Norwich. In 1638 Bishop Montague inquires, 'Doth the minister comfort the sick person, as concerning his soul's health, his state to Godward? *Doth he, upon hearing of his confession, which he shall persuade him to make, absolve him from his sins?* And hath he at any time discovered any part of his confession?' And in the Convocation of the year 1640, it was ordered that at all Episcopal and Archidiaconal Visitations this inquiry should be made of the churchwardens, 'Have you ever heard that your said priest or minister hath revealed and made known at any time, to any person whatsoever, any crime or offence committed to his trust and secrecy either in extremity of sickness *or in any other case whatsoever* (excepting they be such crimes as by the laws of this land), etc.? Declare the name of the offender, when and by whom you heard the same.' In 1686, in the Visitation Articles of the diocese of Ely, we find, 'Doth the minister visit the sick? Doth he *upon their confession*, repentance, and faith (being thereunto desired) *absolve them?*'"

In the face of all this, my dear friend, we look in vain in the pages of opponents, and especially in the recent pages of the controversialist to whom I particularly allude, for anything approaching evidence in the contrary direction. There is plenty of declamation, and the darkest suggestions of terrible evils which are not to be named, and which—so it is implied—can only come from the use of confession and absolution. Sometimes the ground is shifted, and it is said to be *unscriptural;* but that, let me remind you, is not the point. When a large body of clergy and laity are assaulted as being *unfaithful to the teaching of the English Church*, the question is not, "Is the teaching of that Church scriptural?" but, "*What* is the teaching of that Church?" Supposing, *per impossibile*, that the teaching of the English Church is wrong, and contrary to Scripture in this matter, then it may be the duty of those whose eyes are opened to see this, to secede from her, as consistent Dissenters have done; but those who, amidst her supposed errors, consider her (however mistaken they may be) to be in the right, and who teach and uphold her doctrine and practice, are, at any rate, her loyal sons. Scriptural or unscriptural—for *we must insist on keeping to the point* when such wild accusations are made against us—the Church of England teaches the doctrine and practice of confession and absolution, and if this be "sacerdotalism," then every fair-minded man must acknowledge (as I have shown that thoughtful Dissenters do) that whoever may be unfaithful to the teachings of our Church, it is not the "sacerdotalists."

But the real strength of any violent opponent to the Catholic teaching of our Church in this matter is not in argument or evidence—for they have not a grain of it to bring forward—but in exaggerating or misstating some things which have some truth in them, and then appealing to popular passion—what I have called "playing to the gallery." I will notice one or two of these.

(1) Men are scared away from this blessed means of approaching our Lord Jesus Christ by being told that "a man cannot forgive sins," or that we are "putting a man between the soul and God." It would be just as reasonable to say that in listening to a sermon "a man cannot convert a soul," and by attending to the teachings

of the pulpit we are "putting a man between the soul and God." Nay, it would be just as reasonable to say that in recognizing our parents as channels of natural life to us we are asserting that "a man can give us life," and we are "putting two people between ourselves and God." As a matter of fact, our Lord Himself reminds us that in the *absolute* sense of the word we are to "call no man *father* upon earth." Life natural, like life spiritual, can only come from God. This objection really arises from that foolish and proud *individualism* which is so natural to fallen man. We cannot bear to think that we must depend upon one another for many things, and that we cannot stand alone. God is the Source of all good things, but He uses many agents and channels. All callings in life may be said to be ministerial. If I go to the magistrate, he is in one sphere of life a minister of God's justice to me. If I go to the physician, he is in another sphere of life the minister of God's power of dealing with my material frame. If I look to my natural father, he is to me God's minister for the mystery of natural life, and of protection and guidance in my early years. If I go to my spiritual father and make my confession, he, in another sphere— in the supernatural sphere—is the minister of God's grace for forgiveness and cleansing. I am afraid that very often the objection *really* means that men *have not faith* in the promises of Christ in this regard, and do not *believe* in the power of supernatural grace.

(2) Then, again, it is sometimes contended that the doctrine and practice are to be repudiated as implying a sort of *magical* power in the individual priest. To any one who thinks carefully, and believes in the *Incarnation* and all its consequences, it is evident that the Church—the Body of Christ—ever united with her

Divine Head, holds in herself the forces of His life. The power of absolution coming from the Father is given to the Son—" power on earth to forgive sins "—because of His " everlasting Priesthood," and this He communicates to His Body the Church. When the ordained priest absolves the penitent, he acts as the divinely appointed and equipped minister to *apply* to the individual soul the grace won for His Church by our Blessed Redeemer, and residing in that Body because ever united to the Head. There is nothing *magical* about the action of the priesthood, but there is something indeed *supernatural*. To men who think of the Church of Christ as a merely human society this may appear unintelligible, but to those who believe in her as a *divine* society, united to an Unseen and Divine Head, it is equally unintelligible to imagine her ministry anything but *supernatural* and *divine*.

(3) But, then, *the* stress of "argument"—if one can dignify the wildest declamation by such a name—rests upon the supposed *misuse* of confession. Good people are scared by the awful hints and dark suggestions of the most terrible consequences which may follow from the use of this means of grace. Now, to any who can put aside mere prejudice and passion, and look at matters calmly and thoughtfully, it may be worth while to draw attention to the following points:—

In fallen humanity there is, alas! probably nothing that has not sometimes been *misused*. The noblest Arts, meant to raise us to the thoughts of the highest things, have been placed at the disposal of corrupting influences. Holy Marriage, meant to place under Divine sanction the tenderest of human affections, has been corrupted into a means, sometimes for mere financial advantage, sometimes for kindling and keeping alive the most evil tempers, sometimes for the gratification of degraded passion. Holy Orders have been misused for money-getting and "promotion" and worldly advantage. The Bible has been misused, and is even now grossly misused, to bolster up, by an eclectic picking and choosing of texts, every conceivable heresy in opposition to the Catholic Faith. Probably, indeed, no relic of a saint in the dark ages, or no mere *fetish* among heathens, has been turned to such superstitious uses as the Bible has by the various forms of Puritanism. The pulpit has been misused, and instead of being employed as the chair of truth, has before now been made use of to gratify the promptings of overweening personal conceit and ambition. It is not wonderful, then, if the ministry of reconciliation has been misused. *Usum non tollit abusus.*[1] It is a very shallow philosophy which would invite us to avoid the use of a very blessed Divine ordinance because sinners have sometimes misused it.

À *propos* of this very controversy, an eminent and thoughtful and highly cultured minister of a body of Christians which dissents from the Church of England, just as I am penning this letter writes to me these words—

"The confessional must have its uses, or it would never have survived all these years, and been revived in our own day by good and earnest men. I can understand how it might be helpful to others, even though I do not suppose that I could ever practise it myself, if only in providing, as it does, systematically and

---

[1] There has been a curious answer given to this obvious truth! "That is quite true of sacred things which Scripture sanctions and enjoins; but," etc.; *i.e.* those who answer thus beg the whole question! I answer, "Very well, Scripture *and your own Church do* sanction and enjoin this."

without offence, for that direct heart-searching questioning which would seem almost an impertinence in mere conversation, however private and confidential." He goes on then to speak of the charge of grave abuses against it, and then adds, "It is, of course, just the abuses that outsiders are most likely to hear of."

This is a noble utterance of a thoughtful and eminent and deeply religious and fair-minded Dissenting minister, and it "hits" precisely, as I think, my dear friend, "the nail upon the head" in two particulars—viz. first, (a) there may be plenty of evidences of abuses in the past, but abuses are just the things which opponents bring to the front and make much of. The devil delights in the abuses of sacred things. On the other hand, there is *enormous evidence* of the unspeakable blessing to souls from the use of the confessional; but while "Holywell Street" may drag together all the abominations it can find out, or invent, to discredit an ordinance of our Divine Master, devout persons cannot, from the nature of the case, publish to the world the innumerable and touching and splendid stories of the triumphs of grace in souls through the ministry of reconciliation. You and I can afford to smile at the unworthy declamation of those who "play to the gallery," and talk about only "namby-pamby" people going to confession, and "this dreadful confessional separating husbands and wives," and so on! We can afford to smile at this melancholy nonsense, because we know how many noble souls have been made more noble, how many manly boys and men have been made more manly, how many family catastrophes have been averted, how many weary souls have been comforted how many sinful souls have been brought to peace, by this blessed mode of approach to our Divine Redeemer.

But there are good and honest-minded people who unfortunately are deceived by all this declamation and "screaming," and it is necessary to remind them that it has nothing to do with "Popery," but is the plain teaching of their own English Church, and that because it may, like other things, have been *misused* by some, that is no reason why they, if they need it, should not *use* it properly.

(*b*) Then, again, my Dissenting friend reminds us of another important fact. It seems to me there are three ways in which God's ministers may deal with souls. "Deal with souls," of course they must, unless they are hopelessly and scandalously to neglect their very *raison d'être*. They may either content themselves by preaching to or teaching large bodies of their people collected together. If that is all they do, it is evidently, so it seems to me—though good so far as it goes—*quite insufficient*. The Church is not a mere society for lecturing on Divine Truth. If God's ministers only did that, they would be of no more use than would be a public lecturer on the science of medicine to a sick man needing a physician for his specific disease. I am very much afraid that this kind of unmeasured popular assault upon the Church's teaching which we have lately witnessed, may encourage careless or lazy priests to content themselves with fulfilling only this part— and far from the most important part—of their calling.

Then there is another method, viz. what I may call the "conversational."[1] This also is good so far as it goes. It is good that advice should be sought by Christian people from their ministers, and it is right

---

[1] This, some opponents think, is the only way the Church of England *does* allow for helping troubled souls! They are wrong in this, as I have shown.

that advice should be given and sympathy shown, and so on. But when you come to questions of personal *sin*, you come to very sacred ground. The interior life of souls is a very sacred thing. It can only be dealt with, I think, properly under Divine sanctions, and in the power of a Divine ordinance. That is just the reason why the ordinance of Confession is so necessary. I re-echo the words of my Dissenting friend quoted above, by saying that confession is valuable, " providing, as it does, systematically and without offence, for that direct heart-searching questioning which would seem almost an impertinence in mere conversation, however private and confidential."

They, it seems to me, are rash and audacious who attempt to deal with souls, as a minister of God is bound to do, merely by the "conversational;" not *they* who deal with them by the sacred ordinance of the "confessional." Of course, at all times the intercourse of human souls with one another is a very serious thing, and anything so serious may be misused, and has been misused, and is constantly misused, as we know in this sinful world, in every walk of life. In religion, the dangers of the "conversational" are also real, and if one cared, like the opponents of the Catholic teaching of the Church, to dwell upon the dark side of things, and to gloat over the troubles of the Church on earth, one might dwell upon the spiritual disasters which have resulted from the " conversational." But this kind of thing you and I, dear friend, would rather leave to others. The great preservative against an insufficient or unworthy, or careless, or worldly, or sinful use of the call to God's ministers to deal with souls is the confessional. I suppose that is why the devil hates it, and why the "world" scoffs at it with such violence. It is a special outcome of the love of Jesus. It protects God's minister in the awful duty laid upon him to deal with the sins of his fellow-sinners entrusted to his care, for it reminds him that above all he is only a *minister*, and the human representative for the moment of the Most Awful Presence. Everything, as I have said, has been misused by fallen man, but I can imagine nothing that so protects a man from standing upon lower levels than being placed in the serious position of a priest hearing a confession. He would be a devil indeed who could misuse such a position. Every other relationship of life, and other ministerial relations in religion, are more easily misused; and I suppose it is just because *this* ministerial function is so Divine and so blessed, and so calculated to lift the minister who exercises it into the highest thoughts, into the noblest feelings of fatherhood, into the closest sense of union with his Divine Master, that when, alas! it has been misused men have dwelt upon it in such a furious temper, while they seem to show such quiet indifference to all the accumulated misuses of human relationships which go on every day. The anger—the just anger—against any misuse of the confessional is a constant witness to its Divine origin, and to the protection that it above all things gives to the necessary intercourse between souls involved in the relationship of pastor and people.

(4) There is another kind of practical objection which I think weighs upon men's minds in spite of argument, and is made much of by opponents of Catholic teaching, viz. the fear lest it should make persons too introspective—lest people should be led to what was called "the numbering of sins." As a matter of fact, there is probably nothing which so *delivers* souls from introspection as confession wisely used. The English Church abolished

at the Reformation *enforced* confession, and rightly. "Where the Spirit of the Lord is, there is liberty." The result is that I do not suppose in any part of Christendom there are more thorough, good, honest, helpful, and manly confessions made than by Englishmen in the English Church. The Church does not require a detailed foolish introspective "numbering of sins." The soul "does what it can." It knows what is pressing upon its conscience, when the conscience is honestly and carefully examined, "by the rule of God's commandments," as the Prayer-book directs it; and what sins it may have committed but does not remember, it knows well enough —and every wise priest would tell it—are received as confessed through the illimitable merits of its Redeemer. It is no small thing for the young, especially our young men, fighting a severe battle of life amidst the dangerous temptations of the world, in the heyday of their opening manhood, to have some definite opportunity of escape from sins that press upon them, and may darken and destroy. They cannot go and *converse* with some minister, however pious, about the grave secrets of their souls. They feel a loss of self-respect in doing so. But they *can* use a Divine ordinance wherein the minister, under the most severe and solemn sanctions, is simply ministering to them the grace of Christ, and acting as a father in such fashion that their seeking at his hands guidance and the ministration of grace is in a totally different sphere from any intercourse they may hold with him at other times. The use of the confessional as sanctioned by the Church of England is the freeing of the laity.

I have said, my dear friend, that the question before us in this controversy, and in relation to this point of Confession and Absolution, is not whether it is scriptural or unscriptural, but whether it is or not the teaching of the Church of England. I have shown that it is the teaching of the Church of England, from the Prayer-book and her other formularies, from the testimony of her great divines, from the enactment of one of her canons, from the witness of a canon of a Church in communion with her, and from the testimony of fair-minded Dissenters who do not accept the doctrine—as witness my quotation (p. 48). I affirm that whilst Dissenters have a perfect right to take their stand against such teaching—although I may regret their missing part of the truth in doing so—no English Priest who has pledged himself to the formularies of the English Church has a right to do so, much less has he a right to hold up to popular indignation those laity and clergy who accept and act upon the teaching of the Church. It is quite impossible, I believe as regards this doctrine and practice, for any one to escape from the conclusion that Confession and Absolution is the teaching of the Church of England, except by unworthy casuistry, and a Jesuitical way of affixing non-natural senses to plain words, and juggling with language in a way that is not right.

There are only two remaining ways of escape from submission to the Church's teaching in this matter which, as far as I have observed, are attempted.

(1) It is pretended that Holy Scripture does not give directions for the practice, nor sanction the doctrine. As I have said, this is not really germane to the matter before us, for—scriptural or unscriptural—I have shown that the Church of England teaches it, and while we remain in her ministry we are bound by her teaching. Still it may be well for a moment to glance at this objection about Scripture, because, I think, it is entirely without foundation. To relieve a "burdened conscience,"

as it has been said, "by the open acknowledgment of its guilt, is an instinct of natural piety." In the Mosaic Law this is taken for granted, for regulations are made which imply confession of sin. You will remember in this connection Hooker's explanation of Confession under the Mosaic Law: "The Law imposed upon them [the Israelites] that special confession which they in their books called confession of that particular fault, for which we, namely, seek pardon at God's hands. The words of the Law concerning confession in this kind are as followeth;" and then he goes on to quote Numb. v. 6 and Lev. v. 5, and after dwelling upon the *special* sacrifices for *special* sins, he adds, "Finally, there was no man amongst them at any time, either condemned to suffer death, or corrected, or chastised with stripes, nor even sick and near his end, but they called upon him to *repent and confess his sins*."[1] The case of Achan you will at once think of, and Joshua's words: "My son, give glory to the Lord God of Israel; confess unto Him, and *unto me*." The Law foreshadowed and was a type of the Gospel. Human nature is human nature under both, and it was not intended that it should be worse off under the Gospel than under the Law. Special personal cleansings, special ministrations accompanied by confession of sin, are necessarily, then, to be looked for under the Gospel as means for applying to us personally the power of grace.

In the preparatory period immediately before the coming of the kingdom of God, the same is implied. When John the Baptist came preaching his great mission, people came to him not confessing their sinfulness, but confessing their *sins*. And it has been truly said that the commission to the Christian priesthood,

[1] "Eccles. Polity," bk. vi. ch. iv. 4 (Keble's edit. vol. iii. p. 19).

"Whose soever sins ye remit," etc., implicitly involved the practice of Confession. For confession had been required under the earlier dispensation "as a necessary condition for such remission of sin as could then be bestowed." The necessity of reconciliation under the new dispensation was more perfect, and for it the continuance of confession would, of course, be understood to be implied, unless it was expressly excluded. A "type," of course, "interprets its antitype." But, besides that, it would, of course, have been impossible for the commission to the priesthood to be properly exercised in direct application to individual souls unless the priest were sufficiently aware of their secret state to enable him to form a judgment as to their fitness. This he could only know by their own confession. And thus, as it has been said, "Bishop Cosin, commenting on the First Exhortation in the Communion Office, observes that 'confession of sins must necessarily be made to them to whom the dispensation of the mysteries of God is committed,' and quotes St. Basil adducing New Testament authority for the statement, 'For so they which in former times repented among the saints are said to have done. It is written in the Gospel that they confessed their sins unto St. John Baptist (St. Matt. iii. 6). In the Acts they all confessed their sins unto the Apostles of whom they were baptized (Acts xix. 18).' Cosin adds St. Augustine's application of a passage of St. Paul: 'He that willingly judgeth himself, lest against his will he be judged of the Lord, let him come to the priests, by whom the keys are ministered unto him in the Church, and receive of them that have the oversight of the sacraments, the manner of his satisfaction.'"[1]

---

[1] Carter, "Doctrine of Confession," p. 12.

It is curious and interesting that some have tried to evade the force of the fact that confessions were made to St. John the Baptist, by saying that he was not a priest. Well, he was certainly of a priestly family, and succession in the Old Dispensation went in the line of natural, and not of supernatural, generation; but, besides that, he was directly called and sent as a prophet, *before* the exact regulations of the New Dispensation, to gather disciples for a new life.

But on the principle of Confession in Holy Scripture, one of the most important statements is, of course, that made by St. James (v. 13-16). The force of this passage has been evaded by declaring that it refers to confession of faults between Christian people. Doubtless it *does* apply to such cases, but it by no means follows that, having that wide interpretation, it has not also a reference to a special intention to confession to a priest. Jeremy Taylor, for instance, considers that it refers to both.[1] But, however much the passage may point to the general duty of acknowledging our faults to one another, no one in his senses can deny that it takes for granted, *and is written under the sense that everybody knows*, that there is a special exercise of an appointed ministry; otherwise the direction to send for the priests of the Church (or "elders," if any one likes that translation better) would be useless. Confession and prayer are spoken of; then the penitent is spoken of as in consequence being "healed," or his "sins being forgiven him." And then I may quote to you the sayings of such men as Dean Comber and Bishop Wilson on this passage.

Dean Comber says, "Absolution seems to be positively enjoined by St. James to be given to the sick penitent by the priest that comes to pray over him

---

[1] "Holy Dying."

(you will notice how exactly the Church of England, in her Visitation Office, takes this view); for the Apostle adds, 'and if he have committed sins, remission or absolution shall be given him;' which is the right translation of the impersonal verb used in the original, and the practice of the primitive Church (the best of Commentaries) confirms this exposition, they being always wont to grant absolution to all sorts of penitents lying in danger of death."[1] And Dean Comber adds further, that the expression about "the righteous man" really means the minister of God; and he adds, "Here 'confess one to another' is the people to the 'elders of the Church,' for to them only Christ committed the power of binding and loosing, and 'when a man is overtaken in a fault, he that is spiritual must restore him;' and this was so received a doctrine in the primitive times, that the confession of sins to a priest, in the case of a troubled conscience, was esteemed an Apostolical institution."[2]

Bishop Wilson says, and supports his interpretation of the passage on Hammond's authority, "If we have committed sins against God, these are to be confessed to the elders of the Church, and ἀφεθήσεται αὐτῷ, he shall be absolved, or absolution shall be given him, *i.e.* upon his confession." Other teachers of the English Church refer *à propos* to the system of Confession of the Sick in the primitive Church.

Holy Scripture, then, teaches the *principle* of Confession as being of Divine revelation, and according to the will of God. It does not determine all manner of *details* about it. Persons who require that every detail of the usage of a sacred ordinance of this kind should

---

[1] "Guide to the Infirm," Stretton, who quotes it, and quoted by Carter, *ut supra*.
[2] "On the Offices," pp. 309, 310, quoted by Carter, *ut supra*.

be drawn out in Holy Scripture, really misunderstand the office of the Scriptures and the office of the Church. The New Testament is not a Directory for the details of Divine service, or of ministerial action. Our blessed Lord did not write a book; He founded a society. He promised to be with His society to the end. He taught His disciples, before He left them, the "things concerning the kingdom of God."[1] Even then they did not understand them all, but He promised that whilst in His lifetime there were "many things" which they could not bear, afterwards the Spirit of Truth would guide and teach them.[2] You might as well expect Holy Scripture to tell you how to say Matins and Evensong, or whether you are to wear the black gown or the surplice in the pulpit, as expect it to give minute directions about the confessional. What Holy Scripture *does* record is the *blessing*, and in many cases the *necessity*, of confession, not only to God, but to God in the presence of and using the ministrations of others; *and* the commission for absolving in the Name of God, so that appointed ministers may convey the grace of cleansing and forgiveness to the penitent soul.[3]

The Church has applied these teachings and principles. And our part of the Catholic Church, in applying them, has taught us the truth and blessedness of individual and private confession and absolution if we require it.

I think, then, my dear friend, that every loyal son of the Church of England will feel that her teaching upon such solemn doctrines and practices as, say, Holy Baptism and (as the Fathers called it, the "Second Plank") Confession and Absolution is the right inter-

---

[1] Acts i. 3. [2] St. John xvi. 12.
[3] St. John xx. 21, 22, 23 (as interpreted, as we have seen, by our Church and our great divines).

pretation of Holy Scripture, which he willingly learns and to which he loyally submits.[1]

As I have said, in this special controversy *the* point is not what Holy Scripture teaches, but what the Church of England teaches. However, of course we know perfectly well that the teaching of the Church is her interpretation of the Scriptures guided by the Holy Ghost. We feel that, if you attack the doctrine and practice of Confession and Absolution, you give no adequate meaning to the teachings of Holy Scripture from first to last as to the dealing with human sin.

Then, secondly, men try to evade the force of this overwhelming evidence by saying that occasions for confession and absolution are to be very exceptional. In great crises, they say, or just before death. Now, the Church of England is the land of liberty. Her principle has been evidently to throw much more responsibility upon the individual conscience, and much less upon the priest. When and how often private confession should be made is a matter for each conscience to decide, acting upon wise advice. There is one thing quite certain, and it cannot be escaped from, that our Church insists that her priests shall never, if they can help it, permit a soul to pass out of its present state of probation into the near vision of the Holy God without—if it have any weighty matter, any serious sin (and how many have not?) upon it—making its confession

[1] An eminent controversialist apparently does not believe this. He wishes I would tell him what I mean (*Contemporary Review*, September, 1893, p. 355). I answer by a handy example. Why is he bound to believe, as I am, in baptismal regeneration? The answer is, *because that* is the interpretation put by the Church upon the teachings of Scripture on Baptism. Other interpretations are put on these sayings by various Dissenting teachers. We are bound to accept, in these *doctrinal* matters, the interpretation and teachings of the Church. The Church *does* interpret Scripture for us in these things.

and receiving absolution from the priest. This cannot be gainsaid. To this every one of us is bound, and he who, being a priest of the English Church, neglects to perform this duty, or so leads men in life, by his denunciation of this holy ordinance, that their eyes are closed to their need of it, at least in dying, incurs a heavy responsibility indeed.

And can it be supposed by any reasonable man that that which the Church enjoins so strictly for the dying hour is never to be used till then? Surely not. Surely souls, if they are awake and feel their need, will, according to that need, use every means of grace they can.

I must now, my dear friend, pause as to this one point. I have, of course, not nearly exhausted the evidence, but I have said enough to answer these absurd calumnies. The Church of England teaches the *freedom* of confession. She does not teach that private confession and absolution are *necessary* in all cases[1] for salvation; but that where the communion of the soul with God is disturbed, this ordinance should be *used* before receiving Holy Communion; that it *may* be used whenever Christian people feel that they need it; and that it OUGHT to be used, at least in a very large number of cases, in preparation for death. Its blessed effects when rightly used are known to you and me. It helps to deepen repentance; it helps to make souls more watchful; it strengthens resolutions; it deepens reality; it guards purity; it confirms manfulness; it revives hope; it stimulates flagging strength. It can be used with the large liberty of the English Church.

[1] An adverse critic actually says that it is all very well for me to say it is *not necessary*, but that I must know well enough that, where encouraged, it will be used. I wish I did know this. I hope devoutly, for the saving of souls, it *will* be used more and more.

No one is driven to it. Each one can choose his own time and his own confessor. Blessed, most blessed, for many now struggling with sin in loneliness and desolation, if they realized and used this ordinance of grace. It is an outcome of common sense. It is taught and sanctioned by Scripture. It is proclaimed in unmistakable terms by the Church our Mother. It is a result of the love and sorrow of our Blessed Lord and Master. If this is "sacerdotalism," then the teaching of common sense, of the Bible, of the Church of England, is "sacerdotalism." You, my dear friend, and I, and every member of the Church, lay or clerical, are "sacerdotalists;" and it is our duty to strive and pray that *such* "sacerdotalism" should be more and more understood and loved and lived. For it is nothing else but "the truth as it is in Jesus;" it is nothing else but the "Blessed Gospel of the Everlasting God."

Yours affectionately,
W. J. KNOX LITTLE.

P.S.—The frequent quotations from Bishop Wilberforce and the one from Archbishop Tait I have not dealt with for this reason: They are unfair. Even if they were the mature views of those prelates, they could not override the teaching of the Prayer-book and a long line of great divines. I myself, however, have had testimony of an exactly opposite view from Bishop Wilberforce, and possess letters from Archbishop Tait greatly modifying the remark quoted. These hasty utterances of good men plunged in the midst of a controversy, taken away from their context, it is not—in my opinion—fair to use. Whatever these two prelates may have said or felt, I have shown, I contend, on evidence which cannot be set aside, that the doctrine and practice of Confession and Absolution form part of the authoritative teaching of the Church of England.

THE COLLEGE, WORCESTER,
Michaelmas, 1893.

ADDITIONAL POSTSCRIPT.

It is difficult always to get men to keep steadily before their minds what is the question at issue. I have reiterated, again and again, that *the* question is, "What does the Church of England teach?" In spite of this, I find some of my critics already going off, not merely into rhetorical abuse—which, of course, one expects from "the baser sort"—but into *their* views of the meaning of Holy Scripture! This, my dear friend, we have nothing to do with. When you and I say, "I believe in the Holy Catholic Church," we mean what we say, and *therefore* we mean that the *meaning* of Holy Scripture as to certain important doctrines—such as the Holy Trinity, the Virgin Birth, the Incarnation, the Real Presence in the Blessed Sacrament, Confession and Absolution—have been settled for us by the Church as the true *interpreter* of Scripture on these points. We believe, of course, that the Church of England, being *our* part of the Catholic Church, teaches the Catholic Faith on all these particulars and others as clearly as any other part of the Catholic Church. To see what Catholic doctrine is, and what the *meaning* of Scripture is on any of these important matters, we examine what the Church of England has handed on to us.

Now, in the extraordinary indifference to, and misunderstanding of, and carelessness about, the Penitential System, and the dealings of God with sin, which prevail among many at present, men who actually call themselves Churchmen have denied and denounced Confession and Absolution! This is astonishing; and I have shown in the earlier part of this letter that if they do so deny and denounce, they are contradicting the teaching of the Church of England. That is *the* point, and men may if they like—as Dissenters do, though of course I am sorry for their erroneous views—find fault with Catholic teaching, and therefore with the teaching of the English Church; but, whether they like it or whether they leave it, they have no business to say that it is *not* the teaching of the English Church, much less have they any right to denounce English priests for teaching precisely what the Church requires them to teach.

The Church of England, then, I repeat, teaches clearly and emphatically the blessed gospel truth of Confession and Priestly Absolution. There is a remarkable passage on the subject from a public man of some eminence, whose name is well known, and which I wish to quote to you.

When Lady Georgiana Fullerton wrote her novel, "Ellen Middleton," you may perhaps remember that she makes her heroine, in great trouble, find comfort and help by making her confession to an Anglican priest. Lord Brougham—who, as you remember, was an eminent statesman, but very far from a religious man—dashed off a letter to the authoress, telling her, in the conventional jargon to which we are so well accustomed, that this was "rank Popery." Lady Georgiana sent the letter to Charles Greville. You know the sort of person Charles Greville was—not at all theological, and, I suppose, by no means very religious; but a most intelligent man. I want to call your attention to his answer to his correspondent.

"London, Monday.

" I have been out of town since I saw you, and there was no ' E. M.' ['Ellen Middleton'] at Stoke, so I have not had time yet to compare Brougham's criticisms with the text—indeed, I can't read half of them till I do; but meanwhile, I write a few lines to say I think you may well do battle with him on what he says about *Absolution*.

"' What authority has a priest to absolve from sin ? ' he says; ' absolutely none. It is rank Popery to say so. The Liturgy does not venture on it, except in the Visitation of the Sick.' You are much more competent than I am to argue this question, and it is quite superfluous to suggest anything to you; but this criticism of his seems to me a mere tissue of errors and gross impertinences. He may reject the doctrine of the Church of England, and adopt any other creed he pleases, but most assuredly the doctrine of Absolution is the doctrine of our Church, and, according to it, *a priest has authority to absolve from sin*. If it is rank *anything*, it is rank *Church of Englandism* to say so. Nor is it true that it is *only* to be found in the *Visitation* Service. Not but what it would be quite sufficient to establish it as the doctrine of the Church, if it were found in any one of her authorized services, uncontradicted either by her Articles or anything in any other part of the Rubrics. But there can be no question on the subject, because the *Form of Ordering Priests* contains, in terms the most clear and unmistakable, this authority and power conferred upon priests."

F

Then the writer quotes the words of the Ordinal, "Receive," etc. His common sense and natural intelligence, unbiased by that kind of party prejudice which makes men empty words of their plain meaning, leads him to see clearly that the words of Ordination imply priestly power, and true sacerdotalism.

After this he alludes to some rather wild statement of Lord Brougham's about the Liturgy teaching "paganism," on which he says—

"You may leave him to settle that with the Liturgy. It is enough for you that whatever the Liturgy does teach must be taken to be the doctrine of the Church of England. I don't well know what he means by paganism. As to his sneers at the doctrine of Priestly Absolution, . . . who supposes that any 'mere man has the power of saving other men's souls'? Nobody can pardon or save souls, but the Almighty. But the priest is consecrated to His service, and receives with certain ceremonies a Divine commission, and God 'hath given *him* power and commandment *to declare and pronounce to his people being penitent* the absolution and remission of their sins.' This appears to me to be the office of the priest, his duty and his power. And this is the doctrine of the Church of England." [1]

You see, my dear friend, how the matter strikes an intelligent man by no means biased in favour of the Catholic Faith. We may well say with him—for there is no denying it—that if this doctrine "is rank anything, it is rank *Church of Englandism.*"

[1] "Life of Lady Georgiana Fullerton," translated from the French of Mrs. Augustus Craven, by H. J. Coleridge, pp. 139–141.

PART II

ERRATA TO PART II.

Page 74, line 1, *for* "demonstratively" *read* "demonstrably."

Page 98, line 10, *after the word* "practice," *instead of the next five lines, read as follows*: "He and Sozomen allude to the practice. Sozomen says, 'But amongst the Egyptians, in many cities and villages, *contrary to the custom received by all*, coming together on Saturday at evening, having already breakfasted (or supped, ἡριστηκότες ἤδη), they partake of the Mysteries (μυστηρίων μετέχουσι).'—Sozomeni, 'Hist. Eccles.,' lib. vii. c. xix. c. fol. ed., Paris, 1678. And Socrates says, 'The Egyptians near Alexandria, and those who inhabit the Thebaid, hold their assemblies on the Saturday, *but contrary to the custom of Christians*, they partake of the Mysteries. For after having feasted and filled themselves with all manner of food, they towards evening make the oblation and partake of the Mysteries.'—Socrates, 'Hist. Eccles.,' bk. v. chap. 22 D. fol. ed., Paris, 1678."

,, line 15, *instead of* "He" *read* "Socrates then."

,, line 17, *after the word* "then" *insert* "as well as that of Sozomen."

Page 133, line 8, *after the word* "are" *insert* "scarcely." *After the word* "justified" *insert* "in leaving; they are certainly justified in being devoutly present."

---

believe both practices to be devout and right; to be, for any Churchman, in the Anglican part of the Catholic Church, at least permissible, generally desirable, and often coming under the head of positive duty; that, therefore, if by these is meant "sacerdotalism," then "sacerdotalism" is the teaching of the Church of England.

I. We may, perhaps, first examine the question of Fasting Communion.

There are difficulties in the way of meeting assailants on this point, because of their habit of shifting their ground. In one passage in a recent controversy the attack seems to be on those clergymen who are said to teach that not to keep the fast before Communion is "a deadly sin."

Of this I say at once, as I have said before, that "if there *are* clergymen who teach this (although I myself do not know of any such), one may well believe . . . that they use very extreme language."

The question is not whether the Church of England *insists* that her children should keep their fast before Communion under pain of deadly sin—*that* she cannot be said to do; but the question is, Is such a custom opposed to her mind and teaching? Is it unscriptural? Is it uncatholic? Is it a bad custom? Is the practising it and teaching it and encouraging it a wrong "sacerdotalism," showing disloyalty to the English Church?

My opponents, I suppose, would answer all these questions in the affirmative. I, on the contrary, maintain that they must all be answered in the negative, and I proceed to show cause why.

(1) And first, my dear Dean, I turn to the *scriptural* aspect of the question. I do not think this is *the* point in the present controversy, as I have already said. The point is loyalty to the Church of England, whether scripturally she be right or wrong. *That*, it is important to keep before our minds; for the only chance which adversaries to Catholic teaching have, is shifting about, and using Jesuitical arguments, avoiding the point, and appealing, sometimes with abundant declamation, to Scripture.

However, though, I repeat, that is not *the* point in question at the moment, it is well to consider the scriptural ground of such a custom; for this, of course, has ever been before the mind of the Church.

Now, broadly speaking, how about *Fasting*, as a solemn duty, on solemn occasions, in Scripture? Well, those who are severe on Fasting Communion must acknowledge—if they will be honest—that all *their* tone of teaching on this subject is strangely out of joint with the Bible, which they so loudly profess to follow. St. Paul[1] speaks language about discipline of the body, about striking it severe and heavy blows, which, had it come from a Catholic priest in the Church of England, would have formed a foundation for lively and rhetorical denunciation, as you and I can well imagine, in certain quarters! He lays tremendous stress upon physical self-discipline. (Were it not St. Paul, one can imagine the robust denunciation of "detestable materialism!") St. Paul, who had been tried "above measure" by a Divine discipline of suffering, still, by a voluntary discipline of a severe character, brought his body into subjection lest he should in any way fail. The fears which the great Apostle entertained cannot, of course, have been imaginary. The whole thing has—for those who believe in the teaching of his Epistles as being Divine—God's seal upon it. He, even he, needed discipline of the body.

There surely is a grave danger of self-deceit if men in modern times imagine that *they*—to be true to Scripture—need no discipline of the body. To speak or think of bodily discipline and fasting as a "carnal ordinance," as some have done, is clearly to be in opposition to the teaching of the Spirit of God. Without the performance in some degree of such duties, we may be well assured that the spiritual life can have no

[1] 1 Cor. ix. 27, ὑπωπιάζω.

real soundness at all. If such a one as St. Paul needed such exercises as bodily discipline and fasting, certainly *we* do. Here I may quote well-known words which you probably remember: "It must be feared that it is one of the subtlest devices of the enemy, to persuade us that we may become spiritual through means merely spiritual; that we can cherish better the things of the Spirit by neglecting those of the flesh; that we can have the victory over the flesh without fighting against it; that, being in the body, we can transfer the conflict wholly to the soul; that we can cultivate spiritual feelings, desires, longings, love, without discipline of the body, which would obstruct them and weigh them down. This self-deceit is not a snare of these times only. It has been practised, on system, before as now. Only then by heretics, who, thinking the spirit alone worthy of God, the body, which He also created, all evil, thought it no evil to do all evil with it. It is so not unfrequently now with those who make spiritual feelings the test of holiness. It will ever be, that *they who think themselves more spiritual than the Church*, or seek these easier, shorter roads, will find their spirituality to be sickly and carnal, puffed up by some false spirit, rather than borne aloft by the indwelling Spirit of God."[1]

Now, fasting and self-discipline are lowly and unexciting courses, but they are *the* ways put before us by Holy Scripture. The *end*, indeed, is communion with God, spiritual affections, and the love and vision of the Most Holy; but fasting is a *means*, and an important means, insisted upon in Holy Scripture. Is it possible for men to close their eyes to this? Those who believe in the Divine authority of the Old Testa-

[1] Pusey, "Parochial Sermons," vol. i. p. 185.

ment, believe that "fasting and weeping and mourning" were appointed ways of approach to God;[1] that the penitence of Ahab and the repentance of Nineveh were accepted *through fasting;* that David, held up to us in this matter as an example, *fasted* for his sins; that the Day of Atonement was appointed as an unbroken fast; that the approach of such holy men as Moses and Elijah to God was prepared and secured *by fasting;* that Samuel, Esther, Jehoshaphat, Ezra, Nehemiah, and Daniel are all given as examples of the power and need of *fasting* as a preparation for entering on any serious and solemn duty, and a means of disciplining the soul for greater nearness to God.

You will readily remember, my dear Dean, that, even if men put aside the testimony of the Old Testament, they cannot escape from that of the New. Suffering, deliberate self-discipline *and fasting,* were *not* taken away, they were specially blessed by our Blessed Lord. He Himself fasted, and with great severity, in preparation for His most solemn undertakings. By His sacred Passion He gave a new virtue to this form of discipline, and made it "a token of His disciples, and a channel of grace." As He submitted to it in preparation for His own ministry, so He left it as a mark of His own people, of "the children of the bridechamber." Certainly, any fair-minded man, on studying the New Testament, would surely conclude that fasting is one chief mark and duty of a Christian. Is it so put forward by the representatives of that school which denounces "Ritualism"—*i.e.* Catholic teaching in the Church of England?

More, our Lord taught us *how* to fast.[2] And yet fasting has been called "unspiritual," and fasting before

[1] Joel ii. 12-14.   [2] St. Luke v. 35.

Communion " detestable materialism " ![1] Is it right for men to call a practice "unspiritual," which our Lord has taught us to do to God as our Father?

Then, again, the Apostolic teaching on the subject is, of course, quite at one with that of our Lord. It was *when fasting* that the Apostles were "separated" by the Holy Ghost for the work of their ministry;[2] *by fastings* as well as other things it was that St. Paul approved himself as a minister of God.[3] It would weary you to enumerate well-known instances. This is certain, that Patriarchs, Prophets, Apostles, Saints, Martyrs, and our Lord Himself, *taught and practised fasting as a religious duty, and as acceptable to God,* and as a proper means of preparation for and entering into the more solemn and serious things and occasions of religion.

Well, then, is there anything—even to those who take the lowest views on the subject—is there anything, I ask, to any serious Christian, more solemn, more moving, than the Communion of the Lord's Body and Blood? Apart from any further question, is it not astonishing, as a matter of elementary piety, that any should be found—if they believe in the teaching of the New Testament at all—to discountenance, not to say to denounce, the evidently pious custom of keeping the fast before Communion?

I am afraid, with all the professions which are made about "scriptural authority," men evidently do not believe, and do not care to be guided by, the New Testament. For, to consider it further, on this question of fasting it is perfectly astonishing the amount of Jesuitical casuistry which is used to escape from the

---

[1] Quoted by Dr. Farrar, *Contemporary Review*, July, 1892, p. 57.
[2] Acts xiii. 2.   [3] 2 Cor. vi. 4, 6, 7.

plain teaching of Holy Scripture. Something of this sort has been very truly said by a great teacher on such a subject.[1] People assert that *the* thing is to fast from sin. True; spiritual fasting and mortification are the chief things. Bodily fasting has this end in view. Do those who are so wholly spiritual that they despise bodily fasting, show themselves complete in sanctity in these things? Do they who neglect the means attain the end? It is contended that you should fast in speech, fast with the eyes, fast with the ears, fast with the limbs, fast as to money, as to dress, as to the esteem of others; only that to keep the physical fast is "legal" and "carnal," and obeying "the letter" and not "the spirit." True, these things are to be done—true, the *means* are not the *end;* but is it a fact that those who despise the teaching of Scripture and the example of the saints on bodily fasts are high examples of this spiritual completeness? Evil-speaking, gossip, harsh and angry words, reproaches, falsehoods, statements meant to feed vanity and exalt self—is the absence of these specially characteristic of all who despise the teaching of Scripture on fasting? Is there among them no looking for pomps and vanities, no gazing on what arouses evil thoughts, no coveting things seen? Is there no listening with satisfaction to words that do hurt, to evil tales, and unkind rumours, and corrupting language, and sayings which feed personal pride? Is there no luxury, and softness, and sloth, and indolence in this age? Are all ways of life simple and self-restraining? Is there no love of money, no pomp of apparel, no struggling to be first? Surely, my dear friend, we know that all this profession of a lofty "spiritual" way of using the gospel; all this supercilious contempt for the

---

[1] See Pusey, sermon on "Fasting," "Parochial Sermons," vol. i.

practical duties of self-denial laid down by Christ and His Apostles, is a hollow sham. Catholic teaching is practical common sense. Fasting is a religious duty, taught clearly by Holy Scripture, taught by precept and example by our Lord and His Apostles. It is not everything. It is a means to an end; but it *is* a means, and a divinely appointed means. It cannot be put aside with impunity. They who try to shirk such a duty are closing their eyes to the teachings of Holy Scripture and the precepts and example of Christ.

I repeat, then—looking at these—we should *expect* such a devout custom as Fasting Communion; for fasting has ever been one ordained way for preparing for the great things of religion, and nothing in religion can be greater or more serious than Communion in the Body and Blood of the Lord. *Primâ facie*, then, we should *expect*, I say, from the teachings of Scripture, and the example of Christ and His Apostles and all the saints, that Christians would be encouraged to keep their fast before so solemn a matter as the making of their Communion. We should be surprised if such was not the case, for it would be contrary to the whole drift of the teaching of the gospel; much more should we be astounded to discover that to do such a thing, or encourage men to do it, is positively wrong, and indeed " teaching for doctrines the commandments of men "!

Scripture, I maintain, *primâ facie*, is in our favour. We shall need overwhelming evidence indeed to lead us to believe that in this matter alone Scripture is quite inconsistent with itself!

Have we such evidence?

I suppose our duty is to examine, after the *general teaching* of Scripture on which we have already dwelt, (2) specific statements of Scripture which are said to forbid the custom, and what is meant by an English Churchman if he holds that "the Church" interprets these; (3) the evidence to be found in the history of the Church from the beginning; and (4) the teaching of the Church of England.

(2) As to certain specific statements of Scripture which are said to forbid the teaching of Fasting Communion. What are they? The palmary argument of opponents is that our Lord instituted the Blessed Sacrament "after supper." It is difficult to believe that fairly instructed persons who use this argument are in earnest, and sincerely believe what they say. It would be just as sensible to argue that you are a "sacerdotalist" for observing the Lord's day, instead of observing the Jewish Saturday. It is certain that our Lord when on earth *did* observe Saturday, and did *not* observe Sunday; but no one, as far as I know, has ever been called a "sacerdotalist" for departing from His undoubted habit of "resting the seventh day."

Well, there can be no doubt that the "supper" of which the Lord partook with His disciples was as exceptional in character as were those who joined in partaking of it. It was, in fact, a very serious religious ceremony. It was the winding up of the Old Dispensation by Him Who "fulfilled all righteousness." To compare taking part in it with our taking part in an ordinary meal, in breakfast or dinner, is worse than absurd. The Old Dispensation was, so to speak, wound up in the partaking of the Paschal Supper, the New Dispensation begun in the institution of the Holy Eucharist. Our Lord's case was a special and very exceptional one. It seems to me, therefore, that it is altogether wide of the mark to plead the circumstances of the institution as against Fasting Communion; from the nature of the case, the Paschal rite was developed by the Divine Lord Himself—not in the presence of any lay persons, or of a general congregation, but only in the presence of His Apostles—into the fuller reality of the Blessed Sacrament. It is only when people lose sight of the amazing difference between themselves and that first assembly at the institution that they can argue so lightly from the observance of the Paschal Supper to an everyday common meal. St. Cyprian implies the same—that in his judgment the case of the first Eucharist was to be considered exceptional.[1] It is really not to the point, then, when men object to keeping the fast on the plea of a closer imitation of our Lord and His Apostles. It would be just as sensible to insist on wearing sandals instead of shoes by way of imitating Christ. The ordinance of the Eucharist being "after supper" was not —no one can pretend it was—an essential point in the institution to be carried on for ever, and the fact that it took place "after supper" was, as we have seen, the result of exceptional circumstances.

The fact is that questions of this kind were to be settled by the Church. It is here that the real *crux* of such questions comes in. I had said that "the Church is the pillar and ground of the truth," and that the Church is to us the interpreter of Holy Scripture. I should have imagined that this proposition would have been endorsed by every Christian, whatever interpretation he might put upon the word "Church." Dr. Farrar, however, falls upon me with great severity for these assertions. This is interesting, for he, as I think, so evades my answers to him, and drops some things out of view, that a definite charge of this kind cannot

[1] Ep. lxiii. Dr. Farrar apparently thinks very badly of St. Cyprian. Still the testimony of the Blessed Saint has its value.

fail to arrest attention. He considers my "scriptural quotations extraordinary in their irrelevance;" in particular the above text is not, he thinks, "relevant." Accordingly, he explains that some commentators think the phrase applies not to "the Church," but to Timothy. He gives various reasons why he thinks so—all more or less interesting, still all such as are pretty well known to students of the Epistles, as they are the commonplaces of Greek Testament criticism, but all, I submit, beside the mark. It is not right, in a discussion like this, to ride off upon a side issue. I differ from Dr. Farrar's conclusions. I know what has been said about 1 Tim. iii. 15, and I think that the view of many commentators (the view, by the way, of the translators of the Revised Version), that it *does* apply to "the Church," is the true one. But—however that may be—all this Greek Testament criticism is beside the mark. Whether or not the translation in 1 Tim. iii 15 be correct, whether or not St. Paul ever said so, does any serious Christian deny—whatever his definition of "Church" may be—that the Church *is* "the pillar and ground or stay of the truth"? If any do, we need not argue. We have no basis on which to go. Our Lord's promise to guide His Apostles into all truth, on such a hypothesis, has failed, and we have no guide but our own sweet will.

As to the Church being an "interpreter" of Holy Scripture, Dr. Farrar's statements on the subject seem to me to be equally irelevant. He assures us the Church "has never laid down any rules of interpretation." Well, but who said it had? We must try, at least, not to misunderstand one another. We must lay down and defend, as best we can, certain elementary propositions. The different parts of the Church, for instance, Dr. Farrar seems to think, are agreed upon nothing! That, I think, is demonstratively false. There are many disagreements in the Church, but many points are settled. When one speaks of the Church "interpreting" Scripture, one means, of course, that in matters of doctrine or practice which have given rise to various interpretations of Holy Scripture, for a Churchman, the decision of the Church has settled the question.

For instance, Socinians interpret the teachings of Scripture so as to deduce from them the view that our Lord is not Divine in the sense of His real and essential Godhead. Will it be pretended that the Church has not been the interpreter of Scripture for us in this matter? Will it be pretended that it is open to any Churchman to treat the everlasting and essential Godhead of Christ as an open question, because the Church has laid down no "rules of interpretation" or "exegesis"? The Church *is*—and those who bind themselves to her creeds cannot but admit that she *is*—the "interpreter of Scripture" for us in all important matters. She *is*, whatever the text in 1 Tim. iii. 15 may mean, "the pillar and ground or stay of the truth."

Of course it would be readily acknowledged that a *custom* of the Church need not, ordinarily speaking, bind the conscience of a Churchman in the way in which a *doctrinal decree* would. Still a custom having reference to spiritual life and the deepening of reverence would surely be of grave importance in the eyes of all who are the obedient children of the Church. We can scarcely doubt this, if we trust in our Lord's promise to guide His Church into all truth, and to be "with her to the end." If a practice has had the approval of the Church —though it may not be a "deadly sin" to depart from it—it surely ought to command the deepest respect, and to disparage it would be a grave thing indeed. If the Church, then, has countenanced and encouraged and even *enjoined* Fasting Communion, then if Fasting Communion is a mark of "sacerdotalism," all I can say is, "sacerdotalism" is in that case a mark of the Church.

But before I go further, I am pulled up, my dear friend, to my astonishment, by Dr. Farrar's suggestion that in the word "Church" *latet fallacia*.

Now, of course, we know that the question *De Ecclesia*, the question, What *is* "the Church"? is *the* crux of controversy among Christians—Roman, or Anglican, or Dissenting. Quite so; but our present controversy is one which is within the frontiers of the Anglican Communion. When an Anglican priest thinks it his duty to assail his brethren for believing in "sacerdotalism," when they in answer point out that what he includes under the invidious title of Sacerdotalism is the teaching of "the Church," their meaning is, of course, of "the Church" *as the Anglican Communion interprets that phrase*. What is my astonishment, then, when this Anglican priest, my assailant, speaks as follows: "I wish he [that is myself] would tell us what he means by this [the Church]. Does he mean the Romish Church? or the Greek Church? or the English Church? or 'a congregation of faithful men in which the pure Word of God is preached, and the Sacraments are duly administered?' or what? If by the Church he means anything narrower than this, if he limits the word to any one fold in the universal flock, he uses the word in a sense which we repudiate"!

Very well; Dr. Farrar may be at rest. I do not "narrow it." By "the Church," I mean what the Anglican Communion teaches me and, I submit, teaches him to consider "the Catholic Church." And what is that?

Well, Dr. Farrar refers us to four statements on the subject which he is, apparently, prepared to accept as "the definition of the Church," to which he and I, as Anglican priests, are alike bound. I am prepared to accept them also, and the—I hope he will forgive me—rhetorical flourishes about "the Romish Church," "the Greek Church," and so on, might well have been omitted. It is a controversy between Catholic priests of the Anglican Communion.

Of these statements the first is in Article XIX., and runs as follows: "The visible Church of Christ is a congregation of faithful men, in the which the pure Word of God is preached, and the Sacraments be duly administered according to Christ's ordinance in all those things which are requisite to the same."

Now, here the teaching is with regard to the *"visible"* Church. What we learn about it is this: (1) that in it "the pure Word of God is preached," *i.e.* the teaching is in accordance with the Catholic Faith, which is, as we know from the Prayer-book, necessary for salvation; and (2) "the Sacraments be duly administered."

This latter clause (2) makes matters clear. We know that, in the view of the Anglican Church, for the due administration of the Sacrament of Holy Baptism it is necessary that water be used, and the holy words, "in the Name of the Father and of the Son and of the Holy Ghost." We know, again, that, in the view of the Anglican Church, for the due administration of the Sacrament of Confirmation there must be the laying-on of hands of the bishop. We know again, that, in the view of the Anglican Church, confessions must be heard and absolutions given by a priest who has received orders through the episcopate. We know, further, that, in the view of the Anglican Church, for the Sacrament of the Body and Blood of the Lord there must be consecration by a priest episcopally ordained. We reach, then, this meaning of the definition of the nineteenth Article: The Church is a Society which holds and teaches the Catholic Faith, and in which there is the Apostolic Ministry—Bishops, Priests, and Deacons.

It may be well to dwell upon this further, and here I cannot do better than quote a great teacher. "If Christ, the Eternal Truth," he says, "hath built His Church, Truth, transformed by the Spirit into Love, is become living among men. The Divine Truth, embodied in Jesus Christ, must thereby be bodied forth in an outward and living phenomenon, and become a deciding authority, if it is to seize deeply on the whole man, and put an end to pagan scepticism—that sinful uncertainty of the mind, which stands on as low a grade as ignorance. It is, then, the duty of the Church to preach the pure Word of God; to communicate, on the authority of God, that truth with regard to the nature of God and the destinies of creation which He has revealed; to impress upon the intellects of men the true doctrine of Christ,—by oral instruction, by the development of a school of theology, by symbolical and suggestive rites, by catechetical instruction, by preserving and interpreting Holy Writ."[1] I hope you will notice, in passing, that this profound theologian agrees with me —in contradistinction to the views of opponents— that the Church must in some sense "interpret" Holy Scripture. "Its emphatic office," he goes on, "so far as regards the *intellects* of men, is to impress upon the minds of men an abiding conviction of certain truths; which truths not merely *lead* to a holy life here and to salvation hereafter, but of which the mental accept-

[1] Bishop Forbes *in loc.*

ance is itself a part of the integral Christian life, one phase of that supernatural life, which, begun in this life, receives its fulness in the eternal world. Thus one department of the Church is to be an *Ecclesia Docens*. To the hierarchy, as distinguished from the great body of Christians, is committed the duty of handing down and communicating these truths; not merely as spiritual nourishment to those within the fold, but also to those without—to heathens and strangers—that they may be brought to share in the supernatural blessings which attach themselves to this blessed γνῶσις.

"But this is not all. When we come to consider the question of the sacraments, we shall see that these are the channels whereby the virtue that proceeds from Christ our Head flows into His Body in general, that is the Church Catholic, and into us the members in particular. From all antiquity the custody of the sacraments has always been attributed to the Church; in fact, they are, among other things, *tesseræ* of membership with her. And, given this custody, it is the duty of the Church to administer them. Next to the *teaching office* of the Church comes the *ministerial;* next to the appeal to the intellect and heart comes the appeal to the purely spiritual part of the nature, and this is made by the sacraments. A sacrament does not appeal to the intellect. It does not move the soul by any intellectual consideration. It only *per accidens* touches the heart. *It works solely by virtue of the institution of Christ.* It derives its power from Him; nay, in a primary sense He Himself operates in all the sacraments as the High Priest of the new law, using the earthly minister as the organ only.

"But the sacraments are so far influenced by the elements of the world that they have their proper matter and form; that is, there are certain conditions that must be observed, very simple ones indeed, but still definite, which go to give validity to each ordinance. Therefore the Article makes it a *note* (or mark) of the Church that in it the sacraments are duly administered according to Christ's ordinance; that all the necessary conditions to a valid sacrament are observed. Thus there is no true Baptism without the water and certain words; the water alone, or the words alone, are not sufficient; moreover, only certain definite words may be used with profit and effect. So to a valid consecration of the Holy Eucharist, in addition to a definite matter, that is, bread and wine, and a definite form of words, there must be the action of a priest, episcopally ordained, else the Body of Christ is not consecrated."[1]

Here is a fuller and more profound statement of the truth to which I have drawn your attention above, viz. in the view of the Anglican Church, *that* is part of the Catholic Church—of what I may call the *executive* of the kingdom of God—*and that only* which witnesses to the Catholic Faith, and in which there is the Apostolic Ministry of Bishops and Priests (I may add in view of the Ordinal) and Deacons, although *this* office does not come within the view *directly* of the Article.

Now, my dear friend, the Anglican Church may be right or wrong, but "the Church"—so far forth according to her teaching—is that Society, and only that, which teaches the Catholic Faith, and is officered by the Apostolic, threefold, ministry.

The second definition to which we are referred is that in the fifty-fifth Canon, which describes "Christ's Holy Catholic Church" as "the whole congregation of Christian people dispersed throughout the whole world."

[1] *Id., ut supra.*

Here, doubtless, is a recognition of the place of the baptized. It is true, of course, that all baptized souls, when they have duly received the initial sacrament, are baptized into the Catholic Church. If they live in "Dissent," or use a ministry not Apostolically appointed, they are indeed still children of the family, but under loss, since not living according to the rules of the family. They are children of the household, but erring children, and their varying organizations and ministries are not included in the organization and executive action of the Catholic Church. The English Church does not recognize any Communion which has not the threefold ministry coming down in succession from the Apostles as an integral part of the Catholic Church, *in such sense* that that community is a divinely appointed guardian and depository for the faith and customs of the Church. This is clear from the fact that while she requires no reordination in cases of those who may enter her ministry from the Eastern or the Roman Communions, any who seek to enter her ministry, coming from among her own "Dissenting" children, are disqualified from doing so until they have received the Sacrament of Orders from Apostolic hands.

When a custom, then, is said to be a Catholic custom, it is meant that it has been a custom sanctioned and approved by the Church of Christ, which has maintained the ministry in unbroken descent from Christ and His Apostles. In this sense Fasting Communion is a Catholic custom, and has the force of the approval of the Catholic Church.

To avoid this, it seems to me that men yield to the temptation of resorting to a misuse of words. That is, they use the word *Catholic* to mean *Latitudinarian*. This is the old trick of heresy, and it is an unworthy trick. Opponents, as Dean Hook says, "assume that under the general title of the Catholic Church must necessarily be included every sect and denomination of professing Christians, however different in doctrine, in discipline, or even in faith, from the primitive Church." This, he argues, is not just. "If," he goes on, "in the study of the literature, the philosophy, or the political economy of the ancients, we were to meet with a technical expression or a term of art, should we rest contented with the imperfect notions conveyed by either, in their first and literal sense? Should we not rather refer to the writings of the poet, the philosopher, and the politician, and adopt the term—whether agreeable or not to its strict etymological signification—in the precise sense to which it had been restricted by them? This, surely, is consonant with every principle applicable to the investigation of truth, and must, in justice, be adopted in analyzing any question connected with the first and greatest of all truths, 'the reason of the faith which is in us.'

"When, therefore, we adopt, and daily repeat, the Creed of the early Christians, we are surely bound to ascertain not only the *meaning* of their words, but the *precise sense* in which they were used, and in which those holy Fathers intended that we should receive them.

"By this test, then, we are prepared to abide; and we may, without presumption, challenge the opponents of our interpretation to point out one instance in which the term 'Catholic' is applied by the ancients in the indefinite and indiscriminate manner for which they contend. *They will invariably find it used for a purpose directly opposed to that which they profess.* They will find it used, to speak logically, as a word of the second intention—to distinguish the one true and

Apostolic Church, existing through all ages the same by the succession of its bishops, from the various sects, heresies, and schisms. . . . 'Christianus mihi nomen, Catholicus cognomen,' the former to distinguish him from the heathen, the latter from the heretics, was the motto not of Pacian alone, but of every orthodox member of the Church."[1]

Now, surely, my dear friend, no one can doubt that the Anglican Church looks upon the Catholic Church as that great Society, founded by Christ and His Apostles and *officered* by them with the three orders of ministry, holding their orders in direct succession from the Apostles. She further repudiates any desire to separate from the Churches of Italy, France, and Spain—in fact, from the rest of Western Christendom. She treats as parts of the Catholic Church the great Eastern as well as the great Western Communions, *i.e.* the Greek and the Latin Church. She does not consider that the interruption of external communion with them severs the bond; that though there have been serious "quarrels in the family" in the fifteenth and sixteenth centuries the family has ceased to be a family still. What is held *in common* by her with them is Catholic Faith or Catholic custom as distinguished from late and un-Catholic accretions in the Eastern Church, or Romish accretions in the Latin Church, or Protestant accretions in the Anglican. A custom handed on, with more or less exactness and uniformity, in these branches of the Catholic Church, would be Catholic custom, and would, in consequence of our Lord's promises to His Church, have a strong presumption in its favour that it is according to the mind of Christ.

It is no answer to this, then, for any one to say that

[1] "The Church and her Ordinances," Hook, vol. i. pp. 17, 18.

"in many branches of the Catholic Church—if that word is to mean 'the blessed company of all faithful people'—it is wholly unknown." I can only rejoin that, in view of what the Anglican Church recognizes on the subject, this statement is not accurate. The "faithful people" who constitute the Catholic Church as a witnessing body are, in the mind of the Anglican Church—as *action* even more eloquently than *word* shows — those who are faithful to the Apostles' "doctrine and fellowship, and the breaking of the bread, and the prayers;" those, that is, who hold the Creeds, and use the Apostolically-appointed ministry, and feed on a sacrament validly consecrated, and unite in the appointed worship of the Church. The English Church may be right or she may be wrong; but in a question as to loyalty to *her* teaching, when we use the word "Catholic" we must use it in *her* sense.

It is, surely, one thing to be thankful for goodness wherever it is found, one thing to believe that all baptized Christians have been baptized into the Catholic Church, one thing to recognize thankfully that where their separation is from prejudice, or mistake, or want of information, or in some way through no fault of their own, we may well believe that God will help them, as He helps all who seriously seek Him, and that they are what may be called crypto-Catholics—and quite another to look upon the *various communities* into which they have formed themselves, without Apostolic ministry and destitute of valid sacraments, and often holding a mutilated creed, as *integral parts* of the Catholic Body and witnesses to what is or is not Catholic custom.

I repeat, therefore, that the absence of this custom in all the various bodies of Christians who have separated from the Church is no disproof of the fact that it is, as

I said, the long-established custom of the whole Catholic Church. Do not quibble about the word "Catholic," or give to it a non-natural meaning, but understand it in the way in which the Church of England understands it, and the statement may be shown to be true that "Fasting Communion is the long-established custom of the whole Catholic Church."

At any rate, we have gone so far as this—that Holy Scripture teaches fasting as a spiritual exercise with almost as much emphasis as it teaches prayer. That we have seen already. Further, that the Church of England, whilst recognizing all baptized persons as having been baptized into the Catholic Church, recognizes as organized parts of the Catholic Church only those communities which have maintained the Apostolic succession of the ministry through the Episcopate, and therefore recognizes as Catholic custom only such customs as have been sanctioned in some sort by such communities. Such customs we may, I repeat, fain believe—if our Lord has kept His promise to His Church—are not at variance with the mind of our Lord.

Well, then, we now reach the consideration of the practice of the Primitive Church (3), and the teaching of the English Church (4). Forgive me if, for convenience' sake, I partly reverse this order, partly consider the two points together, as indeed they are closely connected. Now, how does the Church of England stand in relation to this practice herself? And how far can it be shown to be a primitive and a general practice in the early Church?

As to the Church of England—and what support *she* gives to the custom is, after all, the main question before us—she lays down no law on the subject *totidem verbis* in her Prayer-book. But, then, there are a great many things on which she does not lay down a direct law; and the reason is not far to seek. Being a part of the Catholic Body, she accepts the ways and teachings of that Body. She only mentions specifically things which needed to be emphasized, and which she was desirous strongly to enforce. Whenever anything is really Catholic, it is *of necessity* part of the heritage of an English Churchman. The Prayer-book warns the children of the Church of this, by teaching us to express our belief in "the Holy Catholic Church;" by telling us of the "sundry inconveniences" which ensue by changes being made in "things advisedly established;" and by assuring us of her disapproval of anything which strikes at any "laudable practice of . . . the whole Catholick Church of Christ.'

If a custom, then, is a Catholic custom, it is *ipso facto* a possession of every member of the English Church. That being the case, it is all the more certain that *this* custom is according to the mind of the English Church, because of the great emphasis she lays on *fasting generally*. No part of the Church has been more emphatic on this grave duty than our own.

(1) For there is no part of the Church in which Lent has been introduced with greater solemnity and even severity.

Think of the opening of the Commination Service—

"Brethren, in the Primitive Church there was a godly discipline, that, at the beginning of Lent, such persons as stood convicted of notorious sin were put to open penance, and punished in this world, that their souls might be saved in the day of the Lord; and that others, admonished by their example, might be the more afraid to offend.

"Instead whereof, (*until the said discipline may be*

restored again, which is much to be wished,) it is thought good, that at this time (in the presence of you all) should be read the general sentences of God's cursing against impenitent sinners. . . . Let us . . . return unto our Lord God . . . seeking to bring forth worthy fruits of penance," etc.

Then in the prayer at the close, " Be favourable unto Thy people, who turn unto Thee in weeping, fasting, and praying. . . ."

(2) The Table of Days of Fasting and Abstinence is precise and even severe. It is called, "A Table of the Vigils, Fasts, and Days of Abstinence, *to be observed in the year.* The Evens or Vigils before" certain Holy Days . and Saints' Days. Then there are "Days of Fasting or Abstinence;" and then the list is given beginning with "The Forty Days of Lent."

It is worth while to recall these statements of our Prayer-book, because curious and wild things have been said from time to time, sometimes, I believe, even by persons in high positions, as to the Church of England *not* teaching fasting as a Christian duty! If such sayings were not saddening (as an evidence how laxity will creep even into the Church itself), they would make one smile. No part of the Catholic Church has been more exact, and even severe, in teaching *fasting and abstinence* as practices of Christian duty and devotion than the English Church.

We reach these conclusions, then, so far—

(1) Fasting is taught in Holy Scripture as a devotional duty, and a fitting preparation for solemn occasions.

(2) The receiving of the Holy Sacrament *is* a specially solemn occasion, and therefore we should *expect* keeping the fast to be part of a due preparation for it,

especially as the Church of England makes an emphatic appeal to Holy Scripture.

(3) The Church of England teaches the duty of fasting as strongly as, if not more strongly than, any other part of the Catholic Church.

(4) The Church of England also claims as her own all truly Catholic teachings and customs, and this may be shown to be such.

That is what I now proceed to do.

(1) Before going back into the earlier habits of the Church, however, as witnessed by history, I must dwell upon some further teachings of the English part of the Catholic Church as *pointing in the direction* in which we are looking.

The Prayer-book orders, as you will remember, my dear friend, that when people desire to communicate they should signify their names to the curate "*at least some time the day before.*" It is true that this rubric has become to a certain extent obsolete, and naturally. At the time when it was written it was needful, on account of abuses. Communions had become infrequent. Reaction had made men, probably, careless both about Communion and about proper preparation. As time has gone on, we have acted in a larger spirit of liberty. God the Holy Spirit has mercifully revived among us a deeper desire for Communion, as well as a fuller sense of the privilege and blessing of Confession and Absolution as the appointed way—when needed—of preparation. The common sense of the living Church departs from *the letter* of such rubrics as this one, and the one as to the priest not celebrating unless there are "at the least three" communicants, because *in the spirit* they are fulfilled. People *do* now understand the duty of preparing for Communion, and—if they need it—of making their confessions. They *do* communicate so regularly that there is no need now of stopping the offering of the sacrifice unless a given number of communicants is first (by a somewhat inquisitorial process!) secured at the moment. Still these rubrics, if more widely interpreted by the common sense of the Church now, witness to the mind of the Church. If the one shows that she desires to encourage Communion, the other shows that that Communion should be made in the early hours of the day—otherwise, why send your name "the day before?"—in fact, at an hour when the custom of the Church of keeping the fast could be more easily observed.

Our Church never, indeed, as I have said, lays down an express law in her rubrics or post-Reformation Canons. But why? Why, because it never occurred to the minds of those who framed them that such a law could possibly be needed. To celebrate early was the universal practice, coming from the earliest times. There were few exceptions to this, and *those* were specified by authority. The thing was understood *because*, among other reasons, priests in celebrating and people in communicating were felt to be bound to keep their fast.

This fact is brought out to our minds by the horror very generally felt by the novel and scandalous practice of Evening Communion. I use the word *scandalous* in the strict sense of the term, for it *casts a stumbling-block* in the way of Christians. It is felt to be utterly *novel*. The defence put forward is the usual fallacy—imitation of our Lord, "after supper;" and expediency, for a help to busy people. As to the first, there was, as we have seen, a *special* reason for the time of the first Eucharist; but, indeed, there is nothing more remarkable than the way in which Protestant controversialists deal with these solemn questions. (1) Their manner is to discard the weight of the customs and teachings of the Catholic Church in which they profess a " belief," when these run counter to their private fancies; and (2) their habit is to treat our Lord and His Apostles as though *they* were ordinary people—no better and no worse, no wiser and no more foolish, than themselves! Their effort strictly to adhere to our Lord's example *to the letter*, in spite of the usage of the Church, implies that *they* know better what our Lord desired than His Church. If they are consistent, as I have said, they must keep Saturday, not Sunday, as the day of rest. Our Lord spoke with great exactness about certain essential points in the celebration of the Eucharist; He did *not* speak about the *time* of its celebration. He promised to guide His Church into all truth; and as to *the time* of celebrating, the Church *did* settle that, as we shall see presently, and accordingly the time so settled we may fairly believe is according to the mind of our Lord. But my point now is, that the fact that the practice of Evening Communions is felt to be *novel* (for it *is* novel), is another presumption in favour of the contention that fasting before Communion is according to the mind of the Church.

Before passing from this, however, it is quite worth while to remember that while the Primitive Church shrank with horror from late Communions, they must have had many strong reasons to which God had guided them. (1) First, of course, the feeling that as the Passover in the evening commemorated the evening deliverance from Egypt, so the Holy Eucharist in the morning, as the Lord's own service on the Lord's own day, commemorated the early morning deliverance of God's people in the Resurrection. This is no fancy, as you will remember, recalling the words of St. Gregory of Nazianzum and St. Cyprian.

St. Gregory says, "Christ instituted it [the Eucharist] in a supper-room and after supper, and on the day before His Passion. We celebrate it in Christian temples, and before taking supper, and *after His Resurrection;*"[1] implying that, since the Risen Life, all had a fresh meaning and a natural change, and that what was inevitable in passing from the old to the new dispensation, and in connecting the Eucharist with the Passover, and before the Lord's Passion, had a new aspect and implied new duties after the Resurrection.

St. Cyprian says, "It did behove Christ to offer about the evening of the day, that the very hour itself of Sacrament might show the setting and evening of the world. But we celebrate the Resurrection of the Lord in the morning."[2]

(2) And, knowing the custom of the Church, another reason probably was, the more easily to lead and enable faithful Christians to keep the fast.

The English habit, therefore, unbroken until quite recently in the shocking outbreak of Evening Communions,—the English Church habit of celebration in the morning seems to point in the same direction, viz. of remembering solemnly the Lord's Resurrection, and encouraging the keeping of the fast.

But now more specifically as to the Catholicity and Antiquity of the custom. There are persons who allow themselves to speak of the Church as if it had its origin in the convulsions of the sixteenth century. We can understand this in a Roman controversialist trying to make a point against our own part of the Catholic

---

[1] Orat. xl., tom. i. p. 659.   [2] Ep. lxiii., p. 156.

Church. It is difficult to understand it in those who have *ex animo* accepted the statements of the Prayer-book, or fairly examined history. We know that, though the English part of the Catholic Church has reformed herself from time to time, although possibly some of her reforms may not have been the best possible—for no single part of the Catholic Church is infallible—still they have been *reforms* in a long existing Church, not brand-new laws of a newly formed community. If any one really believes what we all profess to believe, that the Church is as old as the Day of Pentecost, then any arrangements, or customs, or teachings endorsed by her—unless these have been directly cancelled by the same authority at a later time —receive necessarily from such a one at the least respectful attention.

Well, the rule of Fasting Communion was at least of great antiquity. And it was sanctioned in our own Church certainly as early as A.D. 960. " We charge that no man take the Housel after he hath broke his fast, except it be on account of extreme sickness."[1] That such a law should have been in force, that no contrary statement should have been made at the reform of our Prayer-book and Canons, and that the Church clearly maintains the principle of fasting, and appeals directly to antiquity, goes far to show that those who seek to follow the guidance of the English Church would naturally accept with reverence the custom of Fasting Communion.[2]

For when we turn to Antiquity, certainly we find it

[1] King Edgar's Laws, n. 36; Johnson, vol. i. p. 419; quoted by Scudamore, "Notitia Eucharistica," p. 34.

[2] It may be added that as adults are expressly taught to prepare for Baptism by prayer and *fasting*, the Church would be likely to encourage such preparation for Communion also.

there; and to Antiquity the Church of England does appeal. Her appeal is to the whole Catholic Church of Christ and to the ancient Fathers. We are loyal to her, indeed, only because she *is* to us the expression of the mind of the Catholic Church. I repeat, when we find in pre-Reformation times that she allowed the law of Fasting Communion, that in Reformation times she never abrogated that law, that she insisted on the principle of which that law or practice is a natural and devout application, by so strongly witnessing to the duty of fasting —finding all this, we can scarcely help saying that Fasting Communion is a practice sanctioned by the English Church. But think, my dear friend, strong as this is, how much stronger it becomes when, I repeat, remembering the appeal of our Church to Antiquity, we find what Antiquity actually teaches.

Now, supposing it to be true that in the very first years of the Church the celebration — perhaps from some idea of imitating the circumstances of the institution—took place *after* the Love Feast; supposing that the abuse which St. Paul wished to correct arose in consequence;[1]—what we find is, that *in the very first fervour of devotion* a practice was permitted which, as the Church enlarged her borders, it was found impossible to permit. It will scarcely be contended that we in this age are so devout that we can safely abandon a restriction which in such very early days it was necessary to introduce. For it *was* found necessary. A change of hour from "after supper" to early morning was made, at any rate, pretty certainly in the first century. St. Augustine believed that it was made by St. Paul himself, in consequence of the abuses at Corinth. This is not improbable, because, although the early writers refer often

[1] 1 Cor. xi. 21.

enough to the Love Feast, there is no passage in which it is referred to as coming *before* the celebration after the passage in First Corinthians (if it do refer to it). There appears to be an allusion to the celebration of the Eucharist, *followed by* the Love Feast, a very few years later in the account of St. Paul's visit to Troas.[1] If this be so, we find the Love Feast *after* the Communion in the very heart of the Apostolic age.

Then we have the remarkable evidence of Pliny's celebrated letter to Trajan. That letter was written in A.D. 104. That is, it was written, according to some reckonings, *in the very year* in which St. John died; and, if not so, then a very few years after the death of the Apostle.

In Pliny's letter he informs the Emperor as to all he has been able to discover of the worship of the Christians. They were, he said, "accustomed to meet on a set day, before it was light, and sing a hymn together alternately to Christ as God, and to bind themselves by a *sacrament* (or military oath); . . . which things being done, they were wont to *depart*, and *to meet again* to take food—in common, however." When he wrote, he had examined persons who had been Christians many years before, and the natural construction of their language, as he reports it, would be that they had at that time been accustomed to have the Eucharist in the early morning and the Agape in the evening. Bishop Lightfoot admits that the time of celebrating the Eucharist was in the early morning *before* Pliny wrote; but I think it ought further to be admitted that, according to the evidence laid before Pliny, this was the case *long before*. He thinks that the change was made in order to avoid charges of horrible wickedness; but such charges might still be made so long as the Agape was held in the

---
[1] Acts xx. 7, 11.

evening; for although what was then eaten was not spoken of as the Lord's Body and Blood, malicious or stupid informers might to some real extent pervert the meaning of the Agape—at any rate, by charges of gross sins such as had, among others, been brought against Christians. Calumnies could not be defeated unless by an absolute suppression, instead of a merely temporary suspension of the Agape itself; and the Agape went on, certainly, long after the celebration of the Eucharist in the evening had become generally obsolete. The change of hour must have been made, then, on other grounds than the effort to avoid calumnious charges.

I venture also, with much respect, to differ from Bishop Lightfoot as to St. Ignatius's reference to the Agape in the Epistle to Smyrna (c. 8). He seems to think the Agape there a mere equivalent for the Eucharist already mentioned. It seems to me that the order of the words insists on the need of the bishop's sanction for *three* rites: (1) the Eucharist, (2) Baptism, (3) the Agape. Any one who takes the pains to examine the question can judge of this for himself. Then, as to Justin Martyr's account of the Eucharist, that will not, I take it, be thought to suggest evening celebrations as a usage, so I need scarcely dwell upon it.

St. Cyprian's language on the subject is interesting. He argues (Ep. 63) against Christians who, in order not to provoke heathen suspicion, used water only in the chalice. Some of them seem to have pleaded, "We do use wine when we celebrate in the evening; it is only in the morning that we use water only, lest when we go to our business the smell of wine should betray us; it was specially in the evening that Christ offered the mixed chalice, so that in the evening we can strictly follow His example."

To this St. Cyprian in effect replies: "(1) Your argument is *unpractical*; for we can't, in fact, bring all our people together when they are severally at their own domestic suppers. (2) It involves a gross departure from Church custom; it proposes to have two Eucharists on the same day, in order to comply thoroughly with the institution at the *second* of the two, whatever deviations you make at the *first*. But Christ had a *special reason* for celebrating in the evening, which ceased to apply after He had risen again in the early morning. The hour of His triumph fixes the right time for our celebration."

(1) We reach this, then, clearly, putting it at the latest—the Church did not celebrate in the evening or after a meal within some years of the death of St. John. (2) This is borne out by the testimony of Pliny, a dispassionate witness; of St. Ignatius; I submit, fairly considered, of Justin Martyr; and then of St. Cyprian.

Supposing, then, that owing to special circumstances, and in a time of special fervour and devotion, the actual precedent of the Last Supper was followed in the early Apostolic age; before that age closed, or *at furthest*, soon after the death of St. John, the Church saw fit to apply the rule of fasting before the receiving of the Communion of the Body and Blood of the Lord. Anyhow, the Agape took place in the evening, and the Communion was at an early hour.

Now I must say a word as to the testimony of St. Chrysostom, which to me is most interesting. He may be right or he may be wrong, but he believes that in the Apostle's time—in St. Paul's time—the Agape *followed*, did not precede, the Eucharist. When he states the reason of the Apostle's reproof, this is what he says—

"When the solemn service *was completed, after the*

H

communion of the Mysteries, they all went to a common entertainment, the rich bringing their provisions with them, and the poor and destitute being invited by them, and all feasting in common. But afterward this custom also became corrupt." [1]

Now, rightly or wrongly, St. Chrysostom believes that the corruption was in the Agape, in the Feast of Charity, *not* in the Eucharist.

St. Chrysostom may be mistaken, certainly. I have argued above on the supposition that he is mistaken, and that the Agape or Love Feast preceded the Communion. Let any one read his argument in his twenty-seventh Homily on 1 Cor. xi. 20 and the following verses, and judge for himself. I think he is right. It seems to me that the δεῖπνον Κυρίου, Lord's Supper, or Lord's breakfast, of which St. Paul speaks, is, as St. Chrysostom thinks, a very different thing from the Holy Communion.

I cannot do better in support of my own view than quote Mr. Keble on the passage. Mr. Keble is, at any rate, a weighty authority, and he writes as follows:—

"The whole drift of his [St. Chrysostom's] argument, or rather of St. Paul's, as explained by him, is, that such ill-behaviour at the Feast of Charity (the Agape), just after the Holy Communion, gave just reason to fear that men had not come with charitable and reverent hearts to the Holy Communion itself." [2]

[1] 1 Cor. xi. 17; Hom. xxvii.
[2] Dr. Farrar, I think, misunderstands me. He says (*Contemporary*, September, 1893, p. 354) that *I* quote "St. Chrysostom and Mr. Keble" as against *his* appeal to "Christ and His Apostles." No. I only say that St. Chrysostom's and Mr. Keble's *interpretation* of what "Christ and His Apostles" meant is, at least, as likely to be the right one as his or mine. Surely this is not an extravagant position. However, my argument holds, even if (as I have admitted is possible) St. Chrysostom and Mr. Keble are mistaken.

The point, then, is this, that as Mr. Keble—no mean authority—and as St. Chrysostom,—believed, the Agape, in Apostolic days, *followed* the Eucharist; that even so early as St. Paul's dealings with the Corinthian Church the fast was not broken before the receiving of the Holy Communion. This, as we have seen, was at any rate the case a few years after, at the time of the celebration at Troas.[1]

Whoever be right as to the Corinthian matter, this is certain. St. Chrysostom is *so possessed with the idea that Communion must be in the morning*, that he insists that St. Paul's δεῖπνον (supper) must mean *breakfast*. Then, again, he censures some persons—who fasted before Communion that they might seem in some sense fit to communicate, but immediately afterwards indulged in excess—*not because they fasted*, which he accepts as right, but because they allowed so scandalous a sequel to their Communion. He never supposes that such revelry took place *before* Communión. That was, to him, unheard of. The persons he has in view would never have dreamt of it. What *they* did wrong was to contravene the moral purport of their fasting by rushing into selfish and excessive indulgence as soon as the Eucharist was over.

This is clearly the drift of his argument. This has been, however,—I may say in passing,—somewhat daringly, or at least carelessly, misquoted in modern times so as to imply that he was thinking of some who came to Communion in a state of intemperance!

An exception is advanced as against the practice

---

[1] See Alford, *in loco*—"γευσάμενος, 'having made a meal.' The Agape was a veritable meal. Not '*having tasted it*' . . . usage decides for the other meaning." This is also quoted by Scudamore, "Notitia Eucharistica," p. 31.

from the testimony of Socrates as regards Egypt.[1] Whatever his testimony is worth, it is quoted (1) too absolutely, as if it took in *all* Egypt, whereas he limits it to *Upper* Egypt, and to the neighbourhood of Alexandria; and (2) whenever quoted, there should be added the expressions of disgust of the historian by way of comment, and the emphatic statement that such communicating was "contrary to the custom of Christians." Socrates really gives a much milder account of the practice. "In many cities and villages of Egypt, the Egyptians near Alexandria, and those who inhabit the Thebaid, *contrary to the custom received by all*, meet in the evening on the sabbath (on Saturday), and partake of the mysteries when they have already had their breakfast ($\dot{\eta}\rho\iota\sigma\tau\eta\kappa\acute{o}\tau\varepsilon\varsigma\ \ddot{\eta}\delta\eta$)."[2] He speaks of them as "having feasted and filled themselves with all manner of food." His testimony, then, is to *an exceptional practice, and one that was blameworthy*. The exception proves the rule. I think one may fairly speak of a custom being that of "the whole Catholic Church," when one reads of this gross exception, which meets with censure. But further, this practice could hardly have been recognized in Alexandria under the eye of the Archbishop Timotheus, for he (A.D. 380–385) had a case of conscience put to him, as to whether, if one had unintentionally swallowed a drop of water while washing the mouth, or in the bath—when keeping the fast in order to communicate—he ought or ought not to proceed to communicate. The answer is in effect, "Yes, you had better do so." The answer will be felt to be a wise one; but the question shows, I submit, what the custom of the Church, *as a rule*, was.

[1] *Contemporary*, September, 1893, p. 353, *n*.
[2] Soc., "Hist. Eccles.," lv. c. 22.

In the face of this, how is it possible for persons to assume that the custom was of *recent* introduction when St. Augustine wrote?[1]

Again, Tertullian writes, "Will not thy husband know what thou art tasting secretly before all other food?"[2] St. Basil, writing of priests, says, "It is not possible to venture on the sacred work [of celebrating] without fasting."[3]

St. Augustine's testimony, you will remember, is quite distinct. In his celebrated utterance on the matter he is not arguing as to Fasting Communion as his main point. He is really arguing as to the lawfulness of that special, well-known case, viz. the lawfulness of celebrating on Maundy Thursday *otherwise* than after a meal. There were some, St. Augustine seems to tell us, who, in order more exactly to imitate the Lord, offered and received after taking food "on one particular day in the year, to wit, that in which the Lord gave the Supper itself."[4]

It is plain from his statement that these very Christians who did, on one set day in the year, communicate *after* taking food, kept their fast on all other days. The Maundy was then, again, *the exception* which proves the rule. Only on one special day (*uno certo die*), and that for a special reason, was the breaking of the fast permitted (*tanguam ad insigniorem commemorationum*), which shows, according to the testimony of the great Father, that the highest importance was *universally* attached to the observance of the rule of fasting at other times. He does recognize the existence of the exception on Maundy Thursday, but he emphatically states that the custom of fasting—at

---

[1] "Mansi Concilia," iii. 1253.   [2] "Ad Lex," lii. c. 5.
[3] Hom. i., "De Jejuu."   [4] Ep. liv. c. 7.

any rate, at all other times—is a *universal* custom, and *he* is of opinion that it was Apostolic. He says the Church is not to be censured for her rule of Fasting Communion, since our Lord left no rule to the contrary; for he considers that this was just one of those points which our Lord left for His Apostles to settle. He is of opinion that when St. Paul said, "The rest will I set in order when I come," and since the custom is universal, it was one of the points St. Paul *did* "set in order." His inference may or may not be right, but his testimony is valuable, for it shows *his* sense of the *universality* of the custom, and *his* belief that the reason was—it had Apostolic authority. His words as to the view and practice of the Church are as strong as well could be. He grants that the disciples did *not* at the first Communion remain fasting. That all will grant. We have seen, however, that there was a special reason for this, as the early Church felt. He argues that, though this was the case, the Catholic Church is not to be blamed "because it is always received by persons fasting. For," he goes on, "therefore did it please the Holy Ghost, that in honour of so great a sacrament, the Body of the Lord should enter the mouth of a Christian before other food; for on that account is this custom observed throughout the whole world."[1]

The Council of Carthage sanctioned the Maundy *exception* in A.D. 397. The same council sanctioned the *rule* of fasting. The Council of Trullo, A.D. 691, abolished the exception. The rule had been felt, in fact, to be a good rule of the Church, and, as St. Augustine said, pleasing to "the Holy Ghost."

The nine-o'clock hour was a very universal one for the celebration for many ages. Even as to the Maundy,

[1] Ep. liv. c. 6.

St. Augustine says, "There is an offering in the morning because of those who dine, but at eventide for sake of those who fast."[1] In the East—at one time, at any rate—it appears that, lest the rigour of the fast should be relaxed by the receiving of the Holy Communion, the celebration was late on certain fast-days, at the ninth hour, "inasmuch as the faithful used to fast on those days."[2]

I am just now reminded, too, of another testimony worth recording.

"In the capitula of Theodulph, A.D. 794, which were much used as an Episcopal Charge in France and England (being translated into Saxon by Elfric in the tenth century), we have a similar rule for Lent: 'It is requisite that after Noon-song (Nones, at the ninth hour, or 3 p.m.) a man hear Mass, and after Mass his Evensong at the season . . . *and afterwards take meat.*'"[3]

Now, my dear friend, I venture to submit that from all such testimony there are certain conclusions which are inevitable. No one can doubt that self-discipline, in many ways, is a real need in the Christian life.

"St. Paul," says a great teacher (now, alas! gone from us), "opposes to the 'spirit of fear'—that $\delta\epsilon\iota\lambda\iota\alpha$, that meanness of heart, that coward and craven shrinking from responsibility and effort, which is portrayed in the unprofitable servant who could find nothing to do with his one talent—St. Paul opposes to this, that triple characteristic of all high action on human souls—'the spirit of power, and of love, and of a sound mind;'

---

[1] Ep. liv. c. 7. [2] St. Epiph., "Adv. Hersæs.," liii.
[3] C. 39, Johnson's "Canons," vol. i. p. 476; quoted by Scudamore, "Notitia Eucharistica," p. 35.

δύναμις, ἀγάπη, σωφρονισμός—energy, charity, *discipline* in its work and its results. . . . Vigour and activity are always in danger of becoming imperious or absorbing. Love may degenerate imperceptibly into self-pleasing dreaminess. Both need the corrective of a manly severity, at least with ourselves; of the spirit of sober self-command—what our version calls 'a sound mind.'" Then he goes on: "I have ventured to speak to you of . . . 'the sound mind,' which is the spirit and the fruit of self-discipline, and which is also the truest and most genuine form of manly and noble humility. For it implies the true acknowledgment to ourselves of our shortcomings and mistakes, and when they continue, as they so often do, the courage and patience to bow ourselves to the task of self-correction. Of all the work that we do, the work with our own spirits and characters is to ourselves the hardest to judge of: with some of us, the most disappointing. But the reality of all our work—I do not say the outward success—must depend on the reality of this. And if we go on with it in faith and honesty, surely it will not be in vain, even if less than we hoped for. For there is One Whose Divine help is promised and pledged to us, if we are honest and true; One Whose hand works in His own secret and wondrous way; Who is the Source to men of insight, and wisdom, and counsel, and strength—the Holy Spirit and Comforter. . . . Confiding in His help, our fathers trained themselves to be the guides, the pastors, the comforters, of His flock and people. The task of conquering ourselves, of governing ourselves, may now seem to us, as doubtless it seemed to them in their day, 'toilsome and incomplete.' 'Toilsome and incomplete' it seemed to them at the time, in the doing. But they now look back with other eyes on their efforts after self-discipline, from their place of rest." [1]

Here is a noble and generous statement of the need of a spirit of self-discipline, of which the practice we are considering is a tiny but, I think, valuable expression.

To look in a "legalist" or "rigorist" spirit upon such a detail is petty and wrong. Surely, however, it is a grave mistake, as life is a practical matter, in view of the need of this far-reaching spirit of self-discipline, to close our eyes to the wise and serious customs of the Christian Church.

The discipline of Almsgiving, of Fasting, of Prayer, has ever been put before men in the Church's work. Times have changed. Once the Church was severe, and perhaps too exacting in requiring of her children the grave exercises of penance, and the careful and exact restraints of holy custom. We treat matters of this kind with greater freedom (sometimes, we may fear, with an excess of levity) now. It may be better—anyhow, it is necessary—that responsibility for individual discipline of life should be more and more thrown on the individual conscience, and less and less on the Church. This is the wisdom of the Church of England. Conscience is required by her to do its own work more freely and with more entire responsibility. The Church as a body, the clergy as God's ministers, less and less interfere. There is freedom of Confession or of not using Confession, freedom even of Communion or of absence from the Table of the Lord (though this is very different), freedom of observing or neglecting the Fast. This is well, and at any rate it is inevitable. But,

[1] R. W. Church (late Dean of St. Paul's), "Cathedral and University Sermons," pp. 207, 217, 218.

surely, all the more it is right to keep before the minds of a relaxed and self-guiding generation the quiet but practical customs which the Church has sanctioned, as reminders of, and assistances to, a more disciplined life.

Just in proportion as we have passed away from the more searching and perhaps trammelling discipline of a vigorous Church system, such as prevailed in earlier days, so is it not necessary that the children of the Church—our common Mother—should be reminded of certain wise and practical modes of self-denial which she has sanctioned by her practice and authority? Trifles make up life, and some little things remembered as duties and acts of self-discipline are, though apparent trifles, not to be despised.

Again, it cannot but be well to keep before the minds of Christians the seriousness and blessedness of Communion in the Body and Blood of the Lord. Human nature is strangely capricious. If the pendulum swings far in one direction, it has a corresponding swing in the other. We are subject, all of us, to the law of reaction. The neglect of Communion was, and often still is, a danger against which we all have had to fight. Low views of that Sacred Mystery, a system of theology prevailing from Protestant teaching, which leaves no necessary or practical room for sacraments at all, led our people for long to treat Communion *rather* as the privilege of saints, or warm and enthusiastic professors of religion, *than* as a means of help and strength for weary and weak but penitent sinners. You, my dear friend, must remember the days—I do—when the young scarcely dreamt (unless possibly once after their Confirmation) of making their Communion at all. To a great extent those days are passed, and we thank God for it. The need of the Bread of Life is, through the reviving power of the Spirit of God, more widely felt—at least among those who profess anything like allegiance to the teachings of the Church. There are now more frequent Communions. We may indeed be thankful. Still, what we want and pray for, after all, is not so much *frequent* Communion as *good* Communion. The thing to be desired is that there should be *both*. Surely then, side by side with increased Communion, it is to be desired that, in an age and in a Church so free as ours, devout persons, and especially the young, should cling to some of these simple methods of self-discipline—such as Confession and Fasting Communion—that they may be helped to appreciate the dignity and enjoy the full benefit of that wondrous gift.

The fact that the Lord promised His guidance to His Church; the fact that He Himself insisted on fasting as a religious duty; the fact that the Church has so strongly approved—as I have shown that it has —of this custom, all point in the same direction. The custom, as we have seen, was a *very early* one. It was, we may say, *practically universal*. The exceptions noted only bring this into bolder relief. Are we so spiritual, so unearthly, so free from the bonds of the world, so impervious to temptation in this age, that we can afford to throw away a means so simple and so religious for helping us to rise to higher thoughts?

It is true, of course,—as I have admitted,—that the Prayer-book lays down no *positive command* on the subject; but, then, what does the Prayer-book do which leads us to feel that we have, in maintaining such a custom, the approval of our Church? This. It teaches us that the effort of our Church has been to reject all changes that were " of dangerous consequence, as secretly striking at some established doctrine or laudable practice of the Church of England, or indeed of the whole Catholick Church of Christ."[1] If our Lord encouraged fasting with prayer as a spiritual exercise; if He practised it Himself in preparation for His more solemn undertakings; if, in view of the awful solemnity of the Sacrament, His Church *very* early and *very* universally made the rule of fasting her way of preparation for her children for that Holy Sacrament; if the Church of England in years long passed positively enjoined the custom; if she has never revoked that endorsement of the habit of the rest of Christendom;—then we may be pretty sure that this is one of those "laudable practices of the Church of England, and indeed of the whole Catholick Church of Christ," to alter which she has meant to resist, or at least to discourage, as of "dangerous consequence."

The fact is, that, like many other things—like the *Gloria*, for example, before the Gospel—no positive order was given on the subject, because, like other good and well-known customs, it was taken for granted.

The Fathers of the sixteenth-century Reformation—no more than the Fathers of the many earlier reformations through which our part of the Catholic Church has passed—could never have dreamt of the strange habit of some in later times, who treat our Church as if it were an insular society started on a fresh basis by Cranmer and his coadjutors, instead of a part of the Catholic Church, which rearranged its Office-books, made certain readjustments for the benefit of its children, but remained in possession of all Catholic teachings and customs as by right her own. The truth is—to put it shortly—Fasting Communion is a wise detail of self-discipline which the Church has adopted:

[1] Preface to the Prayer-book.

it is a Catholic custom; and therefore, as the Church of England is one part of the Catholic family, it is *her* custom and *her* teaching for us all.

I do not, indeed, deny that about the habit of fasting, whether in this particular manner or generally, there are serious difficulties. A hurrying age, an age in which life is so full and so strained that the exhaustion of the nervous system is probably much greater than in an earlier and calmer time, makes these difficulties very real.

Then, again, the severities of our climate in the more rigorous seasons of the year may make a difficulty for the aged or the delicate not likely to be felt in the more genial temperature of the East. There are difficulties in all things. Customs have not the force of doctrines or of articles of the Creed. The Church is a *living* body. Souls have to act with a wise freedom, and under wise advice. "I will have mercy, and not sacrifice," is our Lord's teaching; *i.e.* "I will have sacrifice, but not without mercy." Bishops may grant—as they do more frequently—dispensations, when necessary, from the rigour of the Lent Fast, and, I suppose, from other fasts. The aged, the weak, those who are at great distances from their church, especially if they have been brought up without any teaching of this Catholic custom, we may well believe come under the head of those who are hindered from strict observance of the Church's rule by "reasonable cause." *Still, there the Church's rule is.* The testimony of ages is in its favour. The practice—I believe the uniform practice—of other parts of the Catholic Church support it. We can hardly plead that we are so spiritual as to be beyond the necessity of treating such a custom with respect.

I am sure of this, my dear friend—and I imagine

that your experience will bear me out—that it is most important, for a robust and practical religious life in the young, to teach them to grip and cling to certain tangible religious customs which often serve as anchors in dangerous days. We are ready enough, in these days of self-pleasing, to take a lower line. That scarcely needs much exhortation. The World, the Flesh, and the Devil are fairly strong. I am sure that definite self-denying customs, of a simple but practical character, are of enormous advantage to our young people in helping them to realize great principles, and to be loyal to religious obligations. It seems to me that those who have to do with the young, especially in our schools and parishes, incur a very serious responsibility if they do not give them the opportunity of early celebrations, so that they may, if they will, without detriment to health, observe the Church's rule.

Be that as it may, a simple and definite habit of self-denial in so solemn a matter cannot be far from the mind of Christ. To put God first is a good rule. "You English," said a Mahometan to me once in Jerusalem, "are the only people here who attend to the solemn things of your religion *after* you have had your breakfasts!" What has been so wide a custom in the Church, what has had the sanction of some of the greatest Saints and Fathers, can surely scarcely with justice be described as "materialism."

It is, it seems to me, a pious practice, greatly to be encouraged in a luxurious and self-pleasing age. We can scarcely doubt that, when done with prayer and religious principle, it must bring God's blessing; and if to teach it be "sacerdotalism," it is surely "sacerdotalism" of a truly scriptural and catholic character, helpful to souls in the life of devotion, quite in consonance with the teaching of the Church of England, and, what is of course the highest of all things, not out of tune with the mind of Christ.

II.

Eucharistic Worship.

I now turn, my dear Dean, to the third of those devout practices, which seems to be condemned by those who take a strong anti-Catholic line in the Church of England, as another indication of the "sacerdotalism" to which they object—that is, Eucharistic Worship, or what is called sometimes "non-communicating attendance," or sometimes—though this phrase is objected to on other grounds—"hearing Mass."

Whatever be the name employed, what is meant is clear enough. It is looked upon by some as being wrong, and objectionable, and out of tune with the teaching of the English Church, that Christians should ever be present at the celebration of the Holy Communion except on such occasions as they actually make their communion; whilst to others it appears—and I am myself, of course, among the number—a devout practice, much to be encouraged, and very necessary for these times.

The objections made to Eucharistic Worship are, I confess, to me, among the most unintelligible of all objections to Catholic practices. Of course, the deep meaning and real comfort and joy of such a practice is not reached if men do not hold the Catholic doctrine of the Eucharistic Sacrifice; but I should have thought that, even to those who unhappily embrace any one of the various lower views of sacramental doctrine, such a practice would have *some* meaning, and bring some real comfort.

It is difficult to discover why men should denounce with so much energy as they do, anything which seems to us so evidently religious and consoling. I cannot but think that their denunciations really arise from a strong antecedent prejudice, and not from well-weighed consideration of facts as they are. In any case, it is not waste of time if one endeavours to make clear why a "sacerdotalism" which encourages this is not an evil "sacerdotalism," but something not unworthy of a priest of the Church of England, and indeed of any serious servant of Christ.

Well, in the first place, I think we do well to remember that the great thought of *worship* has not been as well kept before us in England in these later days as it should have been. Perhaps I may remind you of the words of our dear friend Liddon on the subject. You will remember, of course, *his* view on the whole question before us; and, by the way, I remember well how, speaking of the strange objections raised to this practice, he said to me—I think I can quote his very words— "Surely, dear friend, this is at least a question of liberty for the faithful laity; and, in any case, they should not be precluded from presence at the great service if they please." But this by the way. His words on *worship* I venture to quote, because they are so entirely *ad rem.*

"When we assemble and meet together in church, it is, as we are daily reminded, to 'render thanks for the great benefits that we have received at God's hands, to set forth His most worthy praise, to hear His most Holy Word, and to ask those things which are requisite and necessary, as well for the body as the soul.' Of these four objects of assembling together in church, that of hearing God's Word, whether read or preached, is not now in question. But what is the relation of the other three, thanksgiving, praise, and prayer for blessings, to adoration? They all three differ from adoration in this, that in each of them the soul is less prostrate, more able to bear the thought of self, than in pure and simple adoration. Certainly, in praise we seem to forget self more easily than in thanksgiving or prayer, since thanksgiving carries the mind back to something which we have received, and by which presumably we have profited; and prayer, in the narrower sense of the word, asks for new blessings, whether for the body or the soul. Pure adoration has no heart for self; it lies there silent at the foot of the throne, conscious only of two things—the insignificance of self, and the greatness of God. And yet adoration must be the basis, so to put it, of true thanksgiving and praise and prayer; it is the fitting acknowledgment of our real relations with God which should precede them. It sometimes does, indeed, imply so paralyzing a sense of this our nothingness before God, that left to itself it would make praise, thanksgiving, and prayer impossible. But here, as we lie in the dust, the one Mediator between God and man bids us take heart as He utters that most consoling sentence, 'No man cometh unto the Father but by Me.' He bids us, as it were, take His hand, and thus with Him and by Him, not merely adore God, but praise Him, thank Him, pray to Him. Prayer, we know, is effectual when it is offered in His prevailing Name. 'Whatsoever ye shall ask the Father in My Name, He will give it you.' Praise is accepted when it is associated with Him, by Whom and with Whom, in the Unity of the Holy Ghost, all glory and honour is rendered unto God the Father Almighty. Thanksgiving is welcomed when it is offered in union with Him Who is the one Thank-offering of Christendom, no less than its one Propitiatory Sacrifice, especially when it is offered in that most solemn of all services that are possible on earth, in which we venture most daringly into the very presence-chamber of the heavens, because leaning on a strength and covered with a righteousness which most assuredly is not our own. But until our Lord and Saviour thus takes us by the hand, adoration, the most distant and the most lowly, of the Infinite and Almighty God is all that is, seriously speaking, open to such as we are. And when He has thus taken us by the hand, and has taught us to thank and praise and pray to God in virtue of the strength which flows in union with Himself, adoration still remains; it remains as the expression of our original and permanent relation as creatures at the footstool of the Creator. 'O come, let us prostrate ourselves, let us bend low, let us fall before the Lord our Maker,' is addressed to all human souls for all time."[1]

We have here, I think, my dear friend, a masterly and exact statement, such as would naturally be expected from so careful a thinker and so eloquent a speaker as Dr. Liddon was, of the meaning of worship and its relation to those other attitudes of the soul towards God described as thanksgiving, praise, and prayer. And here, also, we are reminded very rightly that it is in the Eucharist, above all things, that all these efforts of the soul find their highest opportunity, but especially the effort of worship. This thought has, of course, been greatly obliterated by the heresies of the sixteenth century, which—although they could not move her from her proper witness to the faith—have left a stain here and there on the teaching and practice of the Church of

[1] Dr. Liddon, sermon on "Adoration," preached in St. Paul's Cathedral, August 15, 1886.

England, and seem still to cloud the minds of some of her members who have no clear grasp of sacramental truth. But there is something besides this which has probably in later days hindered in this country a proper use of the mysteries as the great opportunity for worship, as the "Church's prayer-meeting," and as the sacrifice of praise and thanksgiving. It is probably this, that as our days are busy ones and what are called "practical," and as we are in some respects a somewhat materialistic people, there has been more and more of an inclination to remember our duty to our neighbour rather than our duty to God, and to look upon worship and thanksgiving as somewhat idealistic and sentimental, whereas they are in fact imperative duties. We are rather inclined to look upon the Church as an institution for doing people good, and especially social good. Every one, of course, acknowledges that the Church has social duties which she must be careful to perform, but as men are immortal beings, and their most solemn relation is their relation to God, *the* most important duty of the Church is to offer to God the worship which is His due from His creatures. The first duties of the Church are to men's souls in their relation to God. Her later duty —though not an unimportant one—is the extension of a philanthropy which will affect their bodily needs and their social condition. If we are to live at all as men should live who are immortal, and who have a God, we have first of all to learn the great duty of worship. It is of the last importance to our spiritual welfare. It keeps us face to face with God, and helps to prevent the commission of that grave sin which besets us all—the forgetfulness that we are creatures. It helps us to keep our eye fixed upon a future life, and exercises us this side the grave in that which will be a main occupation and happiness there. It impresses us with a practical sense of our immortality. It is an exercise also through which not only do we get light to our understanding and warmth to our affections, but by it the will itself is braced, for it brings us into closest touch with the great reality. All this is drawn out in careful detail by our dear friend in close connection with the passage I have just quoted, and it is always a saddening thing if religion tends towards such a *subjective* character that the soul not only is inclined to neglect a primary duty towards God, but also loses much of the strengthening force which helps it to robustness and vigour by a habit of real worship.

One great weakness, so it seems to me, in the imperfect statements of truth and duty which have always marked Puritan teaching, and are to be seen in the utterances of "Evangelicals" now, is the quite inadequate sense they have always revealed of the necessity of objective worship. From this there has come a certain weakness and absence of fibre. There has been a tendency to rest rather on words than on things, on phrases more than on facts; a tendency to emotional religion, and introspective self-analysis, which so often makes their system inefficient, or even destructive to the young. Their question has ever been—quite a proper question in its proper place, of course—"What must I do to be saved?" The favourite question of more practical and vigorous Catholic theology has been—"What can I do to glorify God?" God, not self, the Church has ever been teaching, is to be the centre of the life. Worship has, therefore, been a watchword of the Catholic Faith. In it the soul learns to forget itself, and not to think so much of what it can get from God, as of what it can give Him; and, knowing its own utter insufficiency in approaching Him apart from the one Mediator, finds that the truest and noblest opportunity for worship is that great service which the Lord Himself appointed, and in which, in a special manner, He places Himself at the disposal of His creatures, so that "by Him and with Him, in unity with the Holy Ghost," they may be able not altogether inadequately to laud and magnify God's glorious Name.

I think it is impossible for any thoughtful person to deny that the Eucharistic Service is *the* service of the Church, and gives the opportunity for the highest act of worship that the creature can offer to the Creator on earth. This is evident from the place it took in the mind of the Early Church. It is the one service of which we read in the opening days of Christianity. It is still more evident when we remember that it is the one service appointed by the Lord Himself. The wretched habits into which Christians have gradually drifted in these later days, in allowing their religious exercises to be confined, for the most part, to taking part in Matins and Evensong, and to attendance at a sermon, does not, the moment we think of it, allow of any defence. Our Lord did not say, "Say Matins, or say Evensong, or listen to a sermon in remembrance (or commemoration) of Me;" but He did say, "This do (or, this offer) in remembrance (or, in commemoration) of Me." And, indeed, the constant habits of closing almost every prayer in the Name or through the merits of Jesus Christ, which we have all learnt from the Church, our Mother, would naturally lead us to *expect*, I think, that those lesser memorials or reminders of the merits of His Passion would point towards some more solemn manner, in which the memorial or reminder should be made not in word only, but in act. In fact, the closing phrases of our every prayer would lead us to look for our great Eucharistic Service.

But now the *crux* of the question comes in, and some persons condemn in very severe terms the attendance of those who do not at the time make their Communions. In fact, " Eucharistic Worship," or " hearing Mass," or " non-communicating attendance,"—by whatever name men describe the presence of those Christians who at the time do not communicate,—is censured as if it were contrary to Catholic usage, and as if the practice of it were an act of disloyalty especially to the Church of England, and the encouragement of it an exhibition of evil "sacerdotalism."

As I believe that attendance at Eucharistic Worship is a distinct duty, which at certain times every instructed Christian ought to discharge, and the present neglect of it a most melancholy departure from duty, and injurious to the spiritual life, you will allow me, my dear friend, shortly to examine some of the objections which are made to it.

1. And, first, I would observe that it would seem a very strange thing, if you come to think of it, that our Lord should institute one service for His Church, that He should call even little children, as our Church teaches us, to come to Him by baptism, and to be made " members of Christ, children of God, and inheritors of the kingdom of heaven," and that these children of the Divine family should be excluded from joining in the worship which He appointed for that family. It is not merely a strange thing, it is an impossible thing. So strongly does the Church seem to have felt this that, as you know, for a time there was infant communion; but gradually it seemed to be felt—one cannot doubt, under the guidance of the Holy Spirit—that the close personal act of communion might be delayed with

advantage until a time when the soul was more fully alive to its personal responsibilities, whilst a share in the great act of worship of the Church might be taken by those who, being baptized, were not yet admitted to the full privilege of Communion.

The fact is—and one cannot help feeling it as one reads the history of the Church—there are two aspects to the use of the Holy Mysteries. On the one hand, they are for a "perpetual remembrance of the sacrifice of the death of Christ and of the benefits which we receive thereby." We are ourselves reminded of the love of our Lord in dying and rising for us, and, what is more important, we commemorate and show forth before God, and—if I may so say—*remind* Him of, that unspeakable gift. And when the Church does so, her baptized children, being members of the one body, take their part in the great act, and plead the merits of the sacrifice offered on the cross. On the other hand, it is *the* great opportunity for each soul that is communicating to *receive* the Body and Blood of the Lord for the "strengthening and refreshing" of the soul. Doubtless there have been times in the Church when so much attention has been given to one aspect of the Holy Mysteries, that the other aspect has been unduly lost sight of. Apparently, before the Reformation of the sixteenth century, there was more attention paid to "hearing Mass" than to making Communions. Almost the reverse was to be noted as the state of things some twenty or thirty years ago. I say *almost* the reverse, for although the duty of Communion was admitted, Christians so widely neglected attendance at the Eucharistic Service, that—as you and I very well remember, and as is notorious—the habit of communicating was very widely neglected also.

2. For, whilst it would appear obvious that every baptized member of the family of God should attend the Eucharistic Service even before the time comes when the intimate blessing of Communion is permitted, so it has proved to be a fact—of which there is plenty of indisputable evidence all round us, of which you and I have often had plenty of evidence before our eyes,—that it is just where the duty of Eucharistic Worship is encouraged, that the duty and blessing of communicating is most widely felt. Strangely enough, one of the favourite objections of those who oppose this Catholic custom is, that there is a danger of putting attendance at the Eucharistic Service *in the place* of making one's Communion. I have already admitted, my dear friend, that there are plenty of dangers everywhere for fallen man, and that there is nothing so good or sacred but that it may be abused or misused. If any one considers that attendance at the Eucharistic Service without communicating is precisely the same blessing as Communion, and absolves them from the duty of making their Communion at proper times, of course this is wrong.

But the objection is really devoid of any weight; it is purely unpractical. Facts knock it to pieces. As I have said, and as everybody knows, in our own days, when Eucharistic Worship was neglected, Communions were neglected; and since Eucharistic Worship has, by God's mercy, been revived in the Church, the number of communicants has enormously increased. It has been urged that before the Reformation men attended Mass and did not make their Communions, and that may happen again. If it was so—and to what extent it was so it is difficult to say; rather wild statements are made sometimes about " mediæval corruptions," and the iniquities of the " Dark Ages," which on closer inspection shrink considerably;—but granted it was so; well, the thing *might* happen again, which is another way of saying that *evils* recur among fallen men unless we are watchful and diligent and keep near to God; but it is hardly a sound argument, I think, to urge that you are to neglect one duty because, while fulfilling it, you may neglect another. If this argument is to be made operative, then—as far as the evidence before us goes—it would take us back to the times which we have personally known and which I have referred to, when the one duty was wholly neglected and the other *also* to a very great degree.

3. Those who oppose attendance at the Eucharistic Service will not deny this, that it is clearly a part of Christian liberty for a devout Christian to regulate the times and number of his Communions according to what he has conscientious reason to believe is best for his own soul, and most for the glory of God. The very persons who object to Eucharistic Worship have been the foremost to find fault with frequent Communions. In so high and solemn a thing as Communion it is surely right to be careful. For the young especially most persons would feel that the wise plan in order to secure, not so much *frequent* Communion as *good* Communion, is to increase their Communions carefully and by degrees. No one would advise every one *always* to communicate, whether they felt that it was best for them to do so or not, whenever they happened to be within reach of the service of Holy Communion.

Now, imagine a devout young fellow who is trying to serve God, and who is a regular communicant, but who, for very proper reasons of humility and carefulness which all religious persons would approve, communicates, say, once a month or once a fortnight; is he to be told that, as a Christian duty, and to avoid the "dangers of popery," he is under a religious obligation on the intervening Sundays, or week-days when the Holy Communion is celebrated, to lie in his bed, or go out for a walk, or converse with his companions, or gossip with his neighbours, but—whatever he does—to beware of being in church, and on his knees and joining in the prayers, when the Christian Church is commemorating the Passion of the Lord? My dear friend, the thing is monstrous; it is an infringement of Christian liberty, even if it were not an iniquitous checking of devout habits. The question of Christian people staying to be present throughout the Communion Service is *not* a question between communicating and not communicating, but it is a question between spending some time in meditating upon, giving thanks for, and commemorating before God, the Passion of our Lord, *and* deliberately departing from God's house in the middle of *the* service of Christ's appointment, and going to some ordinary secular occupation.

4. There is one very odd notion apparently hanging about the minds of many who discountenance the duty of Eucharistic Worship, which I think they certainly ought to guard against. They practically act as if, when you are in Church at the Communion Service, *though not at that moment communicating*, you are out of communion with our Lord. This is, of course, utterly untrue. As I have said, it may be, and often is, from the truest devotion and high and wise religious motives that persons do not communicate on any particular occasion. They are, of course, in communion with our Lord; but the very love and devotion and desire to please Him which restrain them from making their Communion, except in accordance with some wise and

regulated plan of their devotional life, would also lead them to be present and join in the Eucharistic Service, when for such proper reasons, and exercising their Christian liberty, they are not communicating.

Then again. Speaking in a *positive* direction, surely natural piety would lead us to suppose that the right thing for good Christians is to have the Lord's own service on the Lord's own day, while reverence and humility could not fail to lead many *not* to communicate always. The only way out of this is the Church's way for centuries—neglected, alas! among us in cold and dead times, revived again now by the mercy of God— viz. the Eucharistic Service always as *the* service of the Lord's day, and Communion made by each Christian according to his or her individual needs and sense of duty.

But further, wherever there can be the early celebration, and later the high celebration, or more dignified service, what an immense spiritual benefit, to speak of nothing else, must accrue to many! Take the case of communicants who, in the early morning, have made their Communions. Surely it is something for them, with the sense of nearness of our Lord so deeply felt as it would be, then to join in the Church's praise and thanksgiving, and realize more and more the life, the corporate life, of the whole Body of the Church. The Communion, which is the highest privilege, *and* the Eucharistic Sacrifice, seem to me to meet two longings in the soul—the longing for intimate intercourse, and the longing for worship.

And further, however much and rightly the Church may have set her face against abuses of the past, wherein the holy sacrifice became a real opportunity for profanation, from the formality or the sin of men, certainly, if prayer and intercourse with God be a daily privilege and a daily duty, surely then for the Church as a body there is need—when it may be so—of the Daily Sacrifice. And to many it is a blessed thing to associate themselves then with the one Sacrifice, even though they may judge it best and most reverent in their own cases to refrain from Communion at that special time. Surely no devout person can doubt, unless they are partially blinded by a prejudice, that for a quiet half-hour on an ordinary morning, it is good and helpful, and for God's glory, for an earnest man to be on his knees in church, thinking of, and thanking God for, and commemorating, and pleading,—the Passion in the Eucharistic Service of the Church.

Again, I repeat, if you consider that the Church is the family of God; that all who are baptized are God's children; that Christ is the great Elder Brother and the one Mediator; that to plead His Passion is everything; that this, the only service He ever appointed, is "the family prayers" of the Church;—is there not, my dear friend, something positively grotesque in the notion that the children of the family are not to come to "family prayers"? These are broad considerations, but they bring before us the common sense of the question. It is impossible to shut one's eyes to the fact that the Catholic Church is the home of common sense. When one meditates seriously upon things, however much one understands and allows for the various revolts of Protestantism, it is impossible to close one's eyes to the truth, that departure from Catholic custom and Catholic teaching is narrowing and unreal and untrue to common sense. Puritanism was so spiritual and so indignant at what it called error, that the multitudes were left out of account, and its methods became only practically useful for elect Pharisees. The Catholic Church, on the contrary, runs risks, I dare say, makes great ventures certainly, but at least she is Catholic. Our own part of that great Communion, however much she has suffered by the clouds and fogs of Protestantism, just as the Latin part has suffered by the clouds and fogs of Romanism, has still been true to the Catholic spirit of liberty. We have our great service appointed by our Lord; in the inner *penetralia* of its deeper meaning Christ's people make their Communion; in the fulness and power of its majestic expression of the relation of man to God through the presentation before God of the effectual commemoration of the unbounded merits of His Divine Son, our elder Brother,—it is *the* service, the only service, the prevailing service which any serious Christian would care to offer when he recognizes the true relation between earth and heaven. There are three classes of persons who—following the example of the early Church, and again following the teaching of religious common sense—may well be excluded from such a service: (1) The unbaptized (they are not in the family, and they have no right to come to "family prayers"); (2) the excommunicate (they, though in the family, have deliberately given up its privileges); (3) the demoniacs, those who have abandoned themselves to the powers of evil. For the rest, it seems to me to be simple common sense that the children of the family should be permitted to appear at "family prayers" if they please.

But further, there are other considerations which seem to show how we have blinded our eyes by fogs of prejudice and controversy, if we endeavour to forbid the attendance of Christians—except when they intend to communicate—from the Lord's own service on the Lord's own day, or on any other day when that service can be performed. It was all very well for the early Church—on the one hand dealing with heathen who were coming to Christianity, on the other hand dealing with penitents who were prepared to submit to severe penitential discipline—to exclude either of these classes from the mysteries. Times have changed. The Church is a *living* body. She deals with things as they are. Do these good people, who denounce what they call "non-communicating attendance," propose that we should return to the severe penitential discipline of the early Church? I presume not. Well, then, they accept the principle of liberty of the English Church. They assume that, according to the practice of the English Church, and the "principles of the Reformation," the stress of responsibility is laid upon individual conscience more and more, and less upon the Church and upon the priesthood. Are they going to be liberal with one hand and narrow with another? Are they not, by their opposition to "non-communicating attendants," practically asserting the Church's right to assume that, unless at a particular service a Christian is prepared to communicate, he is to be considered as *de facto* a heathen, or excommunicate, and unfit to join in the Church's great service, and that when Christian people are saying holy prayers and Christian ministers doing holy acts in commemoration of the love and merits of the Redeemer, they are so unworthy as to be unfit to join their prayers with the prayers of the Church, or to associate themselves in faith and love with her acts as performed by her ministers? The thing, I think, is monstrous. It is indefensible. People ought to be consistent. You have not the right, I submit, to turn Christian people out when Christian prayers are being said, and Christian acts done, because at that moment—though presumably in communion with their Lord—for reasons of real devotion, they do not make use of their highest privileges, or because—submitting to the rules of the Church—being not confirmed they are not yet eligible to take their part in the highest blessing of all. I submit it is their duty, in accordance with the principle of the Lord's teaching, to "do what they can." If it is not so, Christianity and Christian practice seem to me to be narrower than the teaching and the spirit of men. But more, as I have before implied, they are losing the opportunity of helping the young—who are baptized children of God, but not yet confirmed—to be trained in the great religious duty of *objective* worship.

So far, my dear friend, as to general considerations, according to which, as I conceive, and according to common sense in the present state of the Church, as guided by Divine Providence—may I not say, as guided by the Holy Spirit of God?—"non-communicating attendance" is a Christian duty. But now I am met by a grave objection which it is necessary to examine, viz. the custom and witness of the primitive Church.

I pause to remark that it is at least remarkable that those who lay stress upon this, in this particular matter, seem in so many other matters to treat the witness of primitive antiquity with contempt and even scorn. I am content myself, believing as I do that the Church is a living body, and that the Spirit of God is always guiding her, to rest my argument for non-communicating attendance upon such considerations as have already been before us; but it is well that the objection as to primitive custom, however inconsistent it be in the mouths of the opponents, should be seriously examined. Let us grant that non-communicating attendance was not a primitive practice. The question is, why? The answer is, that it was presumed that all "the faithful" would communicate every Sunday. It may be worth reminding you that the Council of Trent itself expresses a wish that the same state of things could still exist.[1] It is worth remembering this, although I know, from many not unnatural reasons, our opponents (although I think their action is somewhat unchristian) are in the habit of being angry if a wish is expressed for the re-union of Christendom in the Roman direction, and therefore are scarcely prepared to rejoice in any of the *better* features of Roman decisions. However, that by the way.

Now, the custom of attending at the Mass every Sunday without communicating, except at intervals, grew up from what we may call "the next best thing." That is, it grew up from what, humanly speaking, may be described as "common sense;" from what may, religiously speaking, be described as the guidance of the Spirit of God. When the influx of multitudes into Church fellowship and the consequent diminution of primitive fervour took place, it made it, I submit, impossible to secure the ideal standard with safety to souls, and with proper reverence for the greatness of the Holy Mysteries. Let us admit, then, that "non-communicating attendance," *when* recognized in the first four centuries was at first the peculiar privilege of the highest order of penitents, who were all but restored to the status of "the faithful;" let us admit that the aspect of a "high celebration" in the primitive Church at that time was different, so far forth, from the aspect of such a service

[1] C. T. Session 22, de Sacrificio Missæ, etc., 67.

in later days ; let us admit that in the first days there may have been no succession of early Communions, followed by a more solemn celebration at which a number of Christians were not supposed to communicate ; let us admit that the celebration on Sunday in early days—and we have plenty of evidence for this—was about nine a.m., and that the right thing then was that "the faithful" on the whole should attend and receive ; —admitting all this, it is necessary to insist upon the grave unfairness of quoting certain ancient canons or patristic sayings as if they told against the more modern service of a Catholic type.

For, first of all, I repeat again, times and circumstances change, and times and circumstances must be taken into account, as the Church is not a fossil or a repository of antiquarian precedents, but a living fact. But next, take for example the "Apostolical" and "Antiochene" canons which censure those "faithful," *i.e.* those Churchmen not under penance who did not "remain for the Holy Reception," or who did not "join with the rest in the [Eucharistic] prayer, but turned away in a disorderly fashion from the Holy Communion." There have been learned students of early Church history who have given reasons for believing that even this does not imply that the duty of "the faithful" was actually to *communicate* on these occasions, but that to "remain for the Holy Reception" meant merely to "remain during the celebration." They may be right or they may be wrong. Supposing that they are wrong, it is still evidently absurd to apply the censure of such canons to cases of attendance throughout the service *for purposes of devotion*. The censure is aimed solely at persons who (1) leave the Church before "the faithful" ought to leave it; and (2) who thereby exhibit disorderliness and irreverence. The position of "non-communicating attendants" in our time is, I submit, morally and in fact entirely different, so far as we are concerned to defend them. "Non-communicating attendants" are not disorderly and indevout people who scorn and insult "the Holy Reception." It may be true, of course, that there may be mere spectators among these "attendants" who have no real sympathy with the solemn service. There may be a risk of this. There is a risk in everything. We live in a world of "ventures." But if there be such at our celebrations of "the Mysteries," they have generally been Protestant controversialists and informers who are there, not for purposes of worship—we have all known of such cases —but to spy and find fault. These we may leave to the just censure of the ancient canons. But, after all, there is a risk of the presence of ungodly persons in any ordinary congregation—say at Matins or Evensong —though, of course, the risk, though real, is of a less grave kind. But if persons cite such canons as against Catholic practice in these days, one may fairly ask them this question: Do they or do they not wish, if possible, to restore the primitive conditions of Church fellowship? Do they or do they not wish to restore the primitive severity of penitential discipline? Are they prepared, as a *sine quâ non*, and under pain of excommunication, to *require* that *all* confirmed persons shall communicate every Sunday? If not, it is not logical, and it is evidently disingenuous to argue from one bit of a system without recognizing, or endeavouring to restore, the rest of that system.

But then we are confronted with St. Chrysostom's strong words in his third homily on the Ephesians. It is, I submit, equally disingenuous to argue against the

Catholic practice of modern times, and indeed of many ages, from the sayings of that great Father. Why? Why, because those whom he censures were in a totally different condition from those with whom we are concerned. *They* did receive on holy days, but "perfunctorily, without seriousness;" on other days they remained through the celebration without receiving, *and*—which is the point—simply as indifferent spectators, not worshipping, not in any devout mood. There is the case before St. Chrysostom. He treats it with a dilemma. "If you are not (as you are not) morally in a condition to communicate, you are not fit to stay through the service. If, not being under penance, you are ecclesiastically competent to remain, you are 'despising' the Eucharist by not receiving" (*i.e.* you being in this careless mood in which you are). He is not for a moment contemplating the case of persons who, though not under penance, might think—using their Christian liberty—that it was better humbly and devoutly to remain, rather than to wander out to secular occupations and amusements, but yet to deny themselves the supreme privilege of "the faithful," viz. Communion. Those whom he complains of have no such feeling or motive. They are not awed, nor moved, nor devout, nor wishing to make their intercessions, nor meditating upon the Passion, nor pleading the great sacrifice of Calvary; they seem to treat the matter "as a nullity."

Now, my dear Dean, I ask you, can you imagine anything more grossly unfair than to quote St. Chrysostom's censure of such persons as if it were directed against, or meant for those who *are* devout, and are only not communicating because either by the Church's rule they are not yet permitted to have that high privilege, or through devotion restrain themselves from exercising it—when the whole context shows that he is indignant at what he calls the "effrontery" of gross carelessness? This is the sort of unfairness which isolates or misstates serious sentences, conveying blame from the context which shows *why* the blame is conveyed. This I think dishonest. This is sophistry. In short, my dear Dean, the case of reverential "attendance"—such as I believe the Spirit of God has guided "the faithful" to, as time went on—was not before the Fathers at all, to whom reference is usually made. Canons or exhortations such as are quoted point to a different case. They point to a different state of things. If you cannot find in them any definite approval of the practice of later times, no more can you find in them any censure. New needs and new conditions emerged. The Church brought out things "new and old." Cases arose which were not contemplated by them exactly as they are now. "Yes," says an opponent, "but they lay down principles which condemn it." We answer, "Define what you mean by *it*." If you do that, they do not lay down any such principles. If people nowadays attend indevoutly, or without the fear of God, they are condemned by the principles of the Fathers for such attendance at the Holy Mysteries; yes, and for such attendance—if it come to that—at Matins or at Evensong. If people substitute attendance for Communion, when *they ought for their soul's good to communicate*, and when the Church's rule does not prevent them, then the principles laid down by the Fathers would condemn them; and so would we, and so would anybody. I quite grant that the highest privilege is *Communion*. I quite grant that, if people "hear Mass" in a merely perfunctory way, it is wrong. I think it quite possible that in the later Middle Ages there may have been an ignorant notion that to receive the hallowed Bread at Mass (the *pain béni* of the French Church) was practically as beneficial as to communicate. If so, this of course was wrong, and our Reformers were right in setting their face against it. This is certainly not our danger now. There are, as I have said, dangers now and always, but we do not avoid dangers by neglecting duties; and to say that we are either to encourage all our people to be always communicating, or else—though they are devout communicants at proper times, or though they are preparing to be such when they are permitted by the Church after Confirmation—to teach them that they are to stay away and rather to employ themselves in any secular occupation or amusement, than be present and join, as far as they may, in the one great service of the Lord's appointing, is to stunt the growth of their devout life, is to fall foul of the principles of our Master's teaching, is to neglect the custom—the devout custom sanctioned by the most prevailing usage of the Catholic Church—and is, as I think, a monstrous abuse. If to teach the duty of devout attendance at the Holy Mysteries, communicating when we can with benefit to our own souls and to God's glory, and when we cannot, still "doing what we can,"—if this, my dear Dean, be "sacerdotalism," then, indeed, I think Christians ought to be "sacerdotalists."

But now as to the Church of England. There seemed to be a danger, some years ago, that, under stress of a Puritan attack upon Catholic practice, Convocation might have been induced to commit us all to a terrible innovation, and cut up the service of the Holy Communion, and sanction with authority the terrible habit of Christians "going out in the middle of the service." That danger, one would hope, is overpassed. The Church of England is the land of freedom. People, using their rightful liberty, should certainly be permitted to leave their church when they please. I have maintained that it is a *principle* of the action of our Church that responsibility should more and more be thrown upon *conscience*, and less and less on the Church and the priest. It is most desirable to break through many of our merely conventional ways; most desirable to do what Catholic-minded men, on the whole, have struggled for in the Church of England—while keeping reverent ways and rules, still to avoid mere stiffness, and to set people free. But *authoritatively to sanction* the abuse of using bits of the Communion Service, without the chance of offering the great oblation, or giving "the faithful" the opportunity of communicating, would have been serious indeed! A Communion Service without the offering of " the Sacrifice of our ransom " would have been like a baptism without a baby, or a marriage service without a bride and bridegroom, or a funeral without a corpse. We were, thank God, as we have been so often before, by the Divine mercy saved from such a catastrophe.

But the fact that such a proposal was made, is itself a witness to the truth that the Church of England has been true to Catholic custom and teaching and tradition; that her Prayer-book, as it stands, recognizes the true meaning of the celebration of the Mysteries; that "non-communicating attendance" is contemplated, as by all other parts, so by our part of the Catholic Church.

Well, the question really is this:—Are true members of the Church justified in turning their backs upon the great service in commemoration of the Passion of Christ at such times as, for good reasons, they do not desire to communicate? Or is it their duty, if they are faithful members of the Church, to be devoutly present at the celebration of the Holy Mysteries, even at such time when, as I repeat, for good and serious reasons, they do not intend to communicate?

I think they *are* justified, according to the teaching of our Church. I think, if they understand their privileges and duties, it is their duty to be present at the celebration of the Mysteries—at least on Sundays and Holy Days, if they can. I think our young people should be taught the duty. I think it is a real help in spiritual life, and I think it is in accordance with the teaching of the Church of England; and if this be "sacerdotalism," then "sacerdotalism" is the teaching of the English Church.

(1) Now, the Church of England contemplates the attendance of her people at Holy Communion as she does at no other service. Why? At no other service are *public notices* ordered to be given. As to Matins and Evensong, they, though adapted for the use of the people, are to be said "either privately or publicly." That is not the case with Holy Communion. *It is the one service at which the Church of England invariably contemplates the presence of the congregation.*

(2) Now, it is evident that in every assembly of Christians there must be many who cannot *communicate*. There are the unconfirmed. There are those who for devout reasons are right in not communicating at *every* opportunity. Do opponents say that baptized children who are unconfirmed may not be present? The Church of England distinctly teaches godparents that children are to "hear sermons;" and she has appointed

no preaching of sermons except *in* the Celebration Service. It is clear that she contemplates the presence of baptized but unconfirmed children, who therefore cannot, according to her rules, communicate; and of those—for she leaves her children *free*—who may not wish to communicate at any given celebration.

(3) For not the smallest hint does the Prayer-book give that any one is to "go out in the middle of the service." She *requires* her children to communicate at the least three times in the year, and Easter is to be one of these times. If she only *requires* this, however she may wish for more; if she requires her children to be present—for, as we have seen, children, if her commands are fulfilled, must be there—if she gives no hint of leaving in the middle of the service, one thing is clear, the Church of England contemplates "non-communicating attendance."

(4) This is still more clear when we remember that she considers "communicants" to be a special division. *They* are to be "conveniently placed." She gives no permission to any one to leave before the celebration of the mysteries, and she does *not* require all—as I have shown—to *communicate*. So far, we see, the teaching of the Church of England is "non-communicating attendance."

(5) The service suits *both* classes—those who then and there are to *communicate*, and those who are engaged in Eucharistic Worship. For example, the Prayer of Humble Access suits *any* Communion—for a faithful Christian as well as the Communion made at that moment. The Prayer of Oblation offers petition for those who communicate *and* for those who offer the sacrifice. If the Thanksgiving be used, it suits all who communicate at any time; and if the young who have

not yet been admitted to Communion are present, they may well pray for those who have.

The Church of England is clear on the subject. She expects her people to be present at the service. She expects unconfirmed children to be present. She *requires* no one to communicate more than three times in the year. She gives no permission to leave before the end of the service. Whatever evil habits may have crept in and grown up, one thing is clear—the Church of England, our Mother, contemplates and *expects* from her Prayer-book—to which all of us are bound—" non-communicating attendance," or Eucharistic Worship. Those who denounce this Catholic custom are not supported by the Prayer-book.

This is, after all, *the* question in dispute. Who is loyal to the Church of England? Those who oppose Eucharistic Worship, those who are indignant that Christians should "hear Mass," or attend without communicating, whatever other plea they have, they are not true to their Prayer-book.

I beg you, my dear friend, to consider the case apart from the mere denunciation of controversialists. Remember, I say again, (1) the Church of England only *requires* her children to communicate three times in the year; (2) she *expects* her children to be present at that service, for at that alone she provides for necessary notices; (3) she *contemplates* the presence of the unconfirmed, for she orders that they shall "hear sermons," and *only* in this service does she provide for sermons; (4) she remembers *two* classes, those who communicate and those who do not, for the communicants are to be "conveniently placed;" and (5) she gives no sort of hint or encouragement for any one to leave the church during the celebration of the Holy Mysteries. I might add that in the eighteenth Canon she is somewhat stringent in her directions *not* to leave in the middle of the service.

If "non-communicating attendance," if "Eucharistic Worship," that is, is only encouraged or taught by "sacerdotalists," then "sacerdotalism," like devotion and common sense, are, I contend, when rightly understood, the teaching of the Church of England.

I am sure, if men would open their minds, they would see that it is a reasonable and sensible thing. All this suspicion, all this anger, all this hardness and scorn, come, I think, from a furious prejudice. Partly the roots are good. They imagine that those who teach Catholic practice are putting services *in place of Christ.* Fancy it!

Imagine putting anything *in place of your Redeemer!* Why, we love *His* service because *He* is there! We love it because *He* appointed it. We think it narrow and unloving to keep His children from gathering round His sacred Feet. We cannot but feel that Eucharistic Worship deepens devotion to Jesus Christ.

I am, my dear Dean, yours affectionately,

W. J. KNOX LITTLE.

THE COLLEGE, WORCESTER,
October 13, 1893.

PART III.

THE REAL PRESENCE AND THE EUCHARISTIC SACRIFICE.

MY DEAR DEAN,
    I now turn from practices to doctrines. All action must ultimately rest upon conviction. The practices which I have defended—which unbelievers or half-believers, or opponents serious or careless, have found fault with—are only, I maintain, the natural and, indeed, necessary outcome of real loyalty to the Church of England, and a true grip of the Catholic Faith.

We turn now, therefore, to much deeper questions. These are questions on the truth of which the devout practices—which I have asked you to remember are in agreement with the teachings of the Church—literally *depend*.

No one in their senses—that I entirely grant—would keep their fast before Communion; no one would be likely to take the trouble, at least for any length of time, to be present at the service; in fact, it appears to me no really thoughtful person would take pains to communicate, unless there be in the Eucharist something very serious and very awful, something implying deeper Truth than ordinary Protestant theories seem to recognize.

If, on the other hand, the teaching of the Catholic

Church be true; if the Holy Sacrament be *the* meeting-point between Earth and Heaven; then it is worth while keeping your fast; then it is worth while—when not communicating—being present and "pleading the Passion;" then it is in accordance with true piety to prepare for the "Holy Mysteries" by Confession, if need be, from time to time, and by prayer and fasting.

To justify my contention as to the wisdom of Fasting Communion, then, and as to the duty of Eucharistic Worship (or "non-communicating attendance," to borrow a somewhat objectionable phrase), and indeed as to the need or wisdom of Confession, I am bound to two things—

(1) To vindicate the teaching of the Church as to "the Real Presence."

(2) To vindicate her teaching as to "the Sacrifice of the Altar."

The Real Presence.

Now, before I enter upon this part of the subject, my dear Dean, I have three observations to make. In an investigation of this kind it is important to investigate with care—

(1) What is the teaching of Holy Scripture?

(2) What is the mind of the early Church?

(3) What is the view of all the rest of the Catholic Church besides our own part?

(4) What is the teaching of our own part of the Catholic Church, *i.e.* of the Church of England?

This last (4) in the present controversy, I repeat, is *the* point. Whether the Church of England be right or whether she be wrong, *the* thing to determine as to our loyalty to her is—*What* does she teach?

If her teaching be contrary to Holy Scripture and

to the early Church, it might be our duty to abandon her ministry; but we are *her* loyal children so long as we teach what she teaches, whether it be right or wrong.

Then, again, to go back to my original thesis, the accusation of opponents is that we are guilty of "sacerdotalism." In trying to discover what "sacerdotalism" means, we find it means belief in "the Real Presence," and—to borrow the phrase of a great Father—"the Sacrifice of our Ransom." If, then, we plead guilty to this part of the charge—as I unhesitatingly do—we are concerned to show that *these* doctrines are true, and that the "sacerdotalism" in which *they* are included is The Truth, and that those who condemn them are —whatever else they are—not in a position to speak of *us* as other than good Catholics, and loyal children of the English Church.

Now we know where we are. The issue is plain.

It is asserted that there is practically no "Real objective Presence" at all. Whatever "the Presence" —if that word is to be used of it at all—it is not *extra usum*; it is not, in fact, there at all, unless you *receive*, and unless you receive in faith. The fact of the Presence—if Presence it can be called—depends on *your* act and condition, *not* on the Lord's act and promise.

This Presence, I say, the Church teaches is *real;* it is *objective*, i.e. it is, whether you have faith or not, whether you receive or not; it depends *not* on *your* act and condition, but on the Lord's act and promise.

I, on the other hand, assert that the teaching of Holy Scripture, of the early Church, of the whole living Catholic Church now, and—above all, for *that*, I repeat, is our point of our own English part of it—is that there is "the Real Presence of the Body and Blood of the Lord"—therefore of Himself, His Soul and Divinity—" under the form of Bread and Wine" in the Sacrament of the Altar. (2) And I further add, that if it were not so the whole thing would be scarcely more than a more or less picturesque and pleasing ceremony, hardly—to my mind—deserving the attention of a serious man.

(1) Now, first of all, it is well to consider this.

Few things in religion—to an outsider, say, viewing the subject philosophically—are more striking and extraordinary than the Blessed Sacrament in the Catholic Church. To remember that for nearly nineteen centuries this extraordinary rite has been observed; that the same "creatures" have been used; bread and wine—generally mingled with water—that the same words have been recited; that only men ordained to a special office have been permitted to celebrate the rite; that certain motions of the hands (or "manual acts," as we say) have been required; and that all this has been asserted to have a close connection with the Death and Resurrection of Christ;—this is remarkable!

Well, the Catholic Church has always felt from the first that this was a "Holy Mystery." The supernatural instinct, so to speak, led her to this. How could it, indeed, be otherwise? Think of it. It is a strange thing. In lowly rooms; in excavated chapels underground, where men were driven under stress of persecutions; in quiet village churches—sometimes reverently, sometimes, as time went on, in a slovenly manner; in stately cathedrals, east and west, and north and south, with simple services or with impressive rites, this strange thing was done, is done, has been done, for well-nigh nineteen centuries. Bread has been blessed, wine—mostly mixed with water—has been blessed, *always* by ministers consecrated to the office of the priesthood, *always* with the same awful words used by the Lord "the same night that He was betrayed:" "This is My Body," "This is My Blood." Always this has been, and it is. I ask you first to remember, my dear friend, this remarkable fact, and—in passing—to remember that we are required now to believe that those who think it means *anything corresponding in fact* to the words used and the acts done are "sacerdotalists," and to be considered disloyal to the English Church, and, indeed, to Christianity! Anyhow—for any thoughtful person —here is a remarkable thing. It is a strange thing. It is an odd thing. It is not a common religious ceremony. It means something very serious, *or* it is a foolish piece of sentiment which ought, by persons who are in earnest, to be swept into the sea of forgotten delusions.

It seems to me "the Sacrament," the blessing and receiving of the bread and the wine, is either, at least, *something* mysterious, majestic, overwhelming, moving, sublime, or—forgive me—it is rank nonsense.

Now, here I pause to inform you of an interesting fact. I knew a man, by no means devoid of intelligence, who, amidst the cross-currents of modern controversy, and having a taste for German speculation, lost his faith. One thing held him. He was arrested and amazed at the startling fact of this rite, this blessing of the bread and of the wine, so unlike anything else in the world. He examined it; he followed the clue thus given, and he returned to the Christian Faith. This by the way. Still, this matter of bread and wine (and water), blessed by one order of men, and received as a solemn thing all these centuries, *is* an arresting fact, whatever we are to make of it.

Now, what has the Catholic Church made of it? Well, unquestionably it has, I repeat, ever been treated as a " Holy Mystery."

I must dwell upon this. "Mystery," even though it occurs in the Bible and the Prayer-book, is—if I may so say—a suspected word. An Englishman is—each one of us Englishmen is—a suspicious animal! Our dear friend Liddon used to say that the word " mystery " roused in the average Englishman a certain amount of " mental discomfort." He imagines that it implies some want of straightforwardness. This is like us English, but notwithstanding, when we come to think of it, it is absurd. "Mystery" which existed—as an expression for solemn and half-revealed things—was adopted by the Apostles, and has been used ever since by the Church. It does not mean a fancy, a sentimental notion; it means pre-eminently a truth, but a truth which in its completeness is more or less veiled. Well, the Sacrament of the Lord's Body and Blood is a "Mystery." It is a truth, a solemn and awful truth, which in its completeness is more or less veiled.[1]

Now, again, I pause, my dear friend, to observe this. Any religion which comes to us pretending to be Divine and is *not* full of mystery, we may be sure is an imposture. That is why, I think, all reasonable men, whatever they hold, ought to hesitate before they commit themselves to any—professedly Religious—system, which, while it pretends to be a positive religion, shuns and discourages faith in unseen realities. For it is untrue to human nature; it is untrue to Divine revelation; it is in danger of becoming a debasing superstition or a hollow form of veneered worldliness, or a corrupted

[1] See Dr. Liddon's sermon on " The Mysteries of God," preached in St. Paul's Cathedral.

form of unbelief. If it discards mystery, it is, therefore, and so far forth, untrue.

Nature—I must dwell upon this—is one vast mystery. We know by experience the change of seasons, the growth of grass, the blowing of the flowers, the bursting of the leaves, and their yearly change to autumn crimson and gold. We know it. Do we know *how* or *why?* Certainly not. In spite of our almost immeasurable conceit, we are in a land of mystery. We know the fact of human life and human growth. We are surrounded, in obedience to God's laws of love, by those who take their lives from us, and whom we love. *Why* they come we know not; *how* their bodies and their minds develop we cannot tell; but there it is. We are in a world of mystery. Again, to us ourselves, in the inner circle of our very own lives,—changes come. Our minds develop; our convictions are formed; new experiences leave their traces upon us; years go on, and we, who feel that life is fleeting, and that *each* thought and act is leaving its mark behind, are becoming aware that we are moving on to eternity. We are creatures of mystery. Let any man offer such a being as man a religion which is *not* a religion of mystery,—it is an insult. *That* is the—one might even say—impertinence of systems which have attempted to take the place of the Christianity of the Church of Christ. They have the impertinence—I can use no other word—to offer to a being so wonderful, so mysterious, so great as man, a petty, shallow Philosophy instead of a Religion.

This is nowhere more evident than when you touch on the sublime mystery of the Blessed Sacrament. For the theories which are placed in opposition to the teaching of the Catholic Church have an unhappy affinity—

it seems to me—to such systems. My dear Dean, I beg you, at any rate, to notice the salient points of the theory which even some Catholic priests have actually put before us as the teaching of the English Church.

Strong words have been written against those who teach the truth of the Real Presence (sometimes, I dare say, in scarcely exact phraseology).

1. I do not want to lay too much stress upon them. I think the words must have been written in haste. They are too passionate, I think, for any sober-minded theologian. Expressions of opponents which are certainly not exact in theology, but which, like a great deal of the language of enthusiastic devotion, have to be discounted with fairness of mind, are described as "abject heresy." We are told that St. Peter, St. Paul, and St. John would have "revolted with horror and indignation" against these statements. We are told that the "adoration of the elements" is now "openly recommended," and is "a degrading idolatry."[1] I do not desire, as I have said, to dwell on these statements. I think their author in calmer moments would regret them. They are surely somewhat unbalanced; they are, I think, exaggerated; they are, I think also (though doubtless unintentionally) not quite accurate. But what I must call attention to is this. It is declared that "there is no possibility to hesitate or to doubt respecting the doctrine of the Church of England. It is," so it is stated, "and always has been, absolutely and transparently clear. She rejects Transubstantiation formally, expressly, unmistakably, indignantly; she rejects no less clearly Luther's doctrine of Consubstantiation; she rejects also Zwingli's doctrine that the Lord's Supper

[1] *Contemporary Review*, July, 1893, p. 66.

is a commemorative act alone." And now we come to what she is said to teach.

"She teaches with absolute precision that the Lord's Supper is not a sacrifice; that the Lord's Table is not an altar; that the Body and Blood of Christ are received spiritually alone, and only by the faithful; that the Presence of Christ is in the heart of the true worshipper, and not, in any sense of the words whatever, in the hands of the priest, or locally on the Lord's Table; that there is no Presence whatever *extra usum*."[1]

Well, there is one thing satisfactory, and only one, about such a statement; it shows us the worst, I think, that can be said against the Anglican Church, and it is always well to know the worst. In such a statement there is, I think, a mixture of truth and falsehood; but, on the whole, it is, I am sure, unfair to the Anglican Church. I do not think that any Roman cardinal, trying to make out the worst case against us, could have said anything more damaging, if indeed it were true. I do not believe it to be true, as I shall try to show, but in great measure false with a fascinating varnish of truth. Realize, my dear friend, for a moment, what this amounts to. The Romans are wrong, the Lutherans are wrong, the Zwinglians are wrong—I may add, the New Testament is wrong—but the Anglican Communion is absolutely right. She differs from the existing Catholic Communions—for the Easterns also hold the Real Objective Presence—she differs apparently from the views of other Christian Bodies. She alone is right. Having realized this—which, I submit, makes the truth of such a proposition, to say the least of it, improbable—I beg you to realize the details of the proposition. (1) The Anglican Church, it is said, "teaches with absolute pre-

[1] *Contemporary Review*, July, 1893, p. 66.

cision that the Lord's Supper is not a sacrifice." This I hope to show, by-and-by, is entirely untrue. If it were true, the Anglican Church would have departed from the teaching of the Catholic Church. (2) The Anglican Church teaches that "the Lord's Table is not an altar." This, again, I hope to show is entirely untrue. Again, I say, if it were true, she would have departed from the teaching of the Catholic Church. (3) The Anglican Church teaches that "the Body and Blood of Christ are received spiritually alone." This is true, and it is the teaching of the whole Catholic Church, only we must be sure as to what it *means*. I have to reiterate that "spiritually" does not mean "unreally;" that, on the contrary, it means "really;" that there is no fact more "real" than a "spiritual" fact, and that to think accurately is at least to remember that "*real*" does not mean "*material*." (4) That the Body and Blood of Christ are received "only by the faithful." On this I have to say, that *in one sense* it is quite true, but it must not be forgotten that it is juggling with words to use "the faithful" otherwise than as the Church uses the expression. It is meant, I imagine, here that the gifts are only received by those who are "full of faith." The Church means nothing of the kind when she speaks of "the faithful." In her language, "the faithful," as can easily be shown, is an expression which implies "Church-people," without inquiring as to their exact spiritual condition before Almighty God. Communicants—as I shall show—who are members of the Church, receive the gift, whether they are "full of faith" or not; but only those who are "full of faith" receive it *to their soul's benefit*. (5) "That the Presence of Christ is in the heart of the true worshipper, *and not, in any sense of the words whatever*, in the hands of the priest." This proposition, as I shall hope to show, is in great measure false; though here, again, truth and error are so mixed up, that it is difficult to disentangle them. (6) That the Presence is not "locally on the Lord's Table." This proposition has a mixture of truth and falsehood about it, as I shall hope to show. It is, in one sense, perfectly true, but it may be used so as to imply what is false. (7) "That there is no Presence whatever *extra usum.*" This proposition is, as I shall also hope to show, untrue. Taking the statement on the whole, here is *almost*, though not quite, the Zwinglian heresy in an approximately accurate statement: it is, I think, untrue to the highest thoughts of human nature; untrue to Scripture; untrue to the belief of the early Church; untrue to the witness of the whole Catholic Church; untrue to the Church of England— a form of half-bred unbelief. If this, indeed, were the interpretation to be put upon the teaching of the Church of England, no man, I grant, who holds Catholic doctrine, who has respect for the morality of language, for the sanctity of conscience, or for the revelation of God, ought to serve her in the priesthood for another half-hour. But this is not her teaching. It is neither more nor less than somewhat diluted Zwinglianism.

But consider again, from another point of view, the salient points, I say, of this teaching.

(1) According to it, our Lord does *not* mean what He says. If He says, "This is My Body," "This is My Blood," He *means* that it is nothing of the kind.

(2) When Apostles talk of the bread they break being the "Communion of the Body of Christ," and so on, they are talking at least in riddles. That bread is *not* so. Whatever Communion there is, has really nothing to do with that; it is a matter of the faith of individuals.

(3) When they talk of men being "guilty of the Body and Blood of the Lord," if they receive the Holy Sacrament without right dispositions, they are allowing themselves in rhetorical exaggeration, for there is no " Body and Blood " to be guilty of!

In fact, in this as in so many things, Puritanism and Protestantism, I fear, discard mystery, deny the Bible, and are false to Revelation. Surely this kind of thing is perilously near to becoming a watered-down Rationalism. "Sacerdotalism" is found fault with because "sacerdotalism" is true to Revelation, true to Mystery, true to the Gospel of Christ, true to Reality.

Such systems of teaching mean, dear friend, moonshine and fog and half-truth.

The Catholic Faith is Reality.

Of course, I do not mean that all men who call themselves "Protestants" consciously abandon themselves to this. There is a vast difference between a *system*—as such—and good persons who call themselves by a name. What I mean is, that here we have in the Christian religion a striking rite; that one modern system practically empties it of any meaning at all, that another and more ancient system accounts for it in a serious and practical way; that the latter is the system of common sense and of the English Church, and that we are not to be stigmatized as "disloyal" to the Church if, as her priests, we adhere to her system.

Well, then, what is denounced as "sacerdotalism," what I maintain is the teaching of Christianity, the teaching of Antiquity, the teaching of the English Church, as well as of the rest of the Catholic Church, is this—that in the Holy Sacrament of the Altar, after consecration by an episcopally ordained priest, there is, *apart altogether from the faith or unfaith of those who are present*, the Real Presence of the Body and Blood of Christ, His Soul and Divinity to be adored and loved of all His faithful people under the form of bread and wine.

Further, I assert that this, being the teaching of the Anglican Church, is *not* Transubstantiation. Further, I contend that if—*per impossibile*—this Catholic doctrine were not true, the Sacrament would be painfully like a more or less picturesque, but not very instructive, commemoration, possibly affecting the *sentiments* of some, but likely in the long run to be ignored by reasonable people.

On this, it seems to me, priests of the English Church, as of every other part of the Catholic Church, may well be prepared to stand or fall. If the Christian religion is good for anything, its watchword is *Reality*. If Christ our Lord is to be trusted, He *meant* what He *said*. If His expressions have to be explained away, so that, *e.g.*, when He said, "This is My Body," He *really* meant, "This is *not* My Body," then all I have to say, as a plain man, is—the less we have to do with His teachings the better. *Reality* is the watchword of the Catholic Faith. *Subjective Sentiment* may be the watchwords of any other systems. The English Church—as part of the Catholic Body—teaches *real* regeneration in Holy Baptism, *real* forgiveness in the Sacrament of Penance, *real* ordination, with gifts of grace, in the Sacrament of Ordination, *real* grace of the Holy Ghost in the Sacrament of Confirmation, and the *Real* Presence in the Sacrament of the Lord's Body and Blood.

The Catholic Church, and the English Church as part of her, is the home of *reality*.

Now, before I go further, the odd thing which I must notice is this. There are pious persons who, from prejudice or misunderstanding, are quite horrified at the Catholic doctrine—who yet would not dream of denying that there is "a Presence" in the Sacrament, only it must not be a "*Real* Presence." Now, I ask you, my dear friend, what sort of a Presence is an "Unreal Presence"? Your friend is *with* you or he is *not*. You cannot have him present, but not "*really* present." Either our Lord *is* present in the Sacrament, or He is *not*. If He is *not*, there is no presence at all, and there is the end of it, there is a Real Absence; there is a ceremony more or less edifying but very much out of proportion, in its meaning, to the language used in it. Or He *is* present, and then it is a *Real* Presence. If this is "sacerdotalism," I as a plain man, having an idea what *reality* means, and what *unreality* means—what Presence means and what Absence means—find it difficult to understand what is meant when both are asserted as a state of fact *at the same time*. The Sacrament is, it seems to me, a more or less picturesque and edifying and sentimental piece of ritualism, *or* it is a most august and awful and solemn fact. If our Lord is *not* there, it is the former. It is the latter if there is the Real Presence of His Body and Blood under the form of bread and wine.

For, before we go further, surely we ought to realize this.

(1) Good people sometimes say, "Yes, I cannot believe the Real Presence, I believe a *spiritual* Presence." What is implied in such a statement, so often made? This; "Spiritual" means "unreal." Is it not evident, my dear Dean, that people who speak in this way commit themselves to this absurdity? Why, dear friend, what is so *real* as a *spiritual* fact? Are granite mountains, or public buildings, or pyramids, or rolling oceans, or strata of rocks, or travelling stars, more *real* than a

living soul, a splendid character, a trial of deep and penetrating sorrow? We are a materialistic nation, I am afraid, and we grow to think that there is positively not such a thing as a *spiritual fact*. This spirit of unconscious materialism goes far, I think, to account for half the things that are said against the truth of the Real Presence.

We come to this. The Sacrament is emptied of its most serious meaning unless there is *the Presence*. If there is the Presence, it *must* be Real. If real in this august Mystery, it must be *spiritual*.

(2) Then another class of pious persons say, "Yes, He is there if you have faith; all depends upon your faith." Is it possible, I ask you, to conceive anything reasonable, and indeed, I think, less consistent with a spirit of reverence? Apply such a notion to ordinary life. "I am coming, dear friend, to visit you. If you are kind and good-tempered, and glad to receive me on my arrival, I shall be there; if not, I am not present." Did you ever hear—one may say without rudeness—such nonsense, such genuine nonsense? Our Lord's coming or not coming must depend upon His word and promise. The amount of blessing it brings to *us* must depend upon the disposition in which we receive Him.

If He promised, He will perform. Whether *we* are fit or unfit to profit by it, in the Blessed Sacrament there is—surely according to all reasonable principles—there is, I say, to be expected, the Real Presence.

So far, I have dealt with broad principles and common sense. I assert that so wonderful, so mysterious, so prevailing a rite as the Blessed Sacrament coming into religion at all, can only be accounted for reasonably by the Catholic doctrine of the Real Presence.

Now, dear friend, let us do two things. Let us state

the Other view again, then let us state the Catholic Doctrine. Then let us examine witnesses.

(1) Well, there are, of course, shades of variation in the Protestant view, but practically, I think, they all come to this—

The Sacrament is a ceremony in which we remember the death of Christ. We eat bread in it, which is common bread, and drink wine, which is ordinary wine. We use words which Christ used in doing so. They are strange words, Eastern words, metaphorical words; they are from " Semitic modes of thought," we must not attach too much importance to them. They don't *really* mean what they appear to say. If we have pious dispositions, and, so, go through this strange ceremony, we have some sort of blessing. But, on the whole, the ceremony is *embarrassing*. It is in the Bible, so we can't leave it out. On the other hand, if you are "converted" and good, you are " saved," therefore *really* there is no need for it, and no room for it, properly speaking. It is—very extreme persons have gone the length of saying—rather " carnal." It is a " broken cistern." We must not "lean" upon it. Protestant truth would have been better without it. It is a difficulty. We could almost wish it had never been started. It really in itself means nothing. Some people think it means something. They are " sacerdotalists." They " savour of Rome." This is practically the general Protestant view of the Blessed Sacrament, put in short words.

I pause for a moment to recall to you that nothing in the world can be imagined more unlikely to *remind* you of the sufferings and death of a good man than eating bread and drinking wine! I can't imagine—on this half-believing theory—anything more inappropriate for its supposed purpose, than the Sacrament. Christ is nailed up to a cross as a malefactor, and—according to this most strange hypothesis—we Christians, in order to *remember* this fact, kneel down and eat bread and drink wine ! *Could* anything be more entirely inappropriate ? I can imagine a command being given to Christians to meet and gaze on a crucifix, or look at a picture, or read over together the story of the Crucifixion, in order to *remember* that Christ was crucified; but that they should be commanded to meet together, and eat bread and drink wine in order to *remember* that awful fact— dear friend, this is strictly inconceivable. The Sacrament would surely, I say again, be a singularly inappropriate memorial *unless* it is an awful and majestic mystery, and that because of a Divine, a Blessed, a Supernatural, a Spiritual, a Real Presence.

Now for evidence.

The question—as I have often said—in the immediate discussion is, "What does the Church of England teach ?" Whether she is right or whether she is wrong, to be true to her teaching is to be loyal to *her*. That must, I think, always be kept clearly before us. None the less, the opponents of Catholic teaching appeal to Scripture, and to the early Church. What Scripture *means*, in such a matter as this, is settled for us Churchpeople, of course, by the decisions of our Church, by which we are bound. We are not at liberty, while we remain in her ministry, to interpret Scripture, in such matters, so as to contradict her decisions. Her appeal, however, *is* to Holy Scripture and also to the Catholic Church. So that to examine Scripture, and to examine the teachings of the early Church, is important, because the evident teachings of both illuminate the decisions by which, as ministers or children of the English part of the Catholic Church, we **are** bound.

I. Now first as to Holy Scripture. As to the Old Testament, on that we need not dwell at any length. Speaking broadly, then, we are given to understand, that whereas men *then* were in shadow, and subject to figures and representations, the time was coming when, instead of shadow, they would have substance; instead of figures and representations, they would have *the real thing*. If there be no Real Presence in the Blessed Sacrament, then the men who had the Shechinah were better off than we are, and, what is more, the not very apposite argument about "the localization of the Deity," which is a favourite weapon of opponents, tells—to say the least of it—as much against the revealed fact of the Shechinah than it can against the Real Presence.

But now as to the New Testament. When you turn to that, it seems to me that nothing but some sort of shuffling and Jesuitry, and casuistical assigning of non-natural meaning to words, can get over the mass of evidence here.

The earliest record that we have of our Lord's mention of the Blessed Sacrament is to be found in the sixth chapter of St. John's Gospel. It is a striking fact that *this* Evangelist—the eagle-eyed teacher who saw most deeply into the mysteries of his Master's work— is the one who goes into the deep meanings of the Sacraments. In the second chapter of his Gospel, he records the miracle of Christ changing *water* into wine; and then in the third chapter he gives our Lord's instruction to Nicodemus on the Sacrament of Holy Baptism. So also in the sixth chapter is recorded the miracle of *feeding* five thousand; and then, following upon that, comes the discourse on the mystery of the Blessed Sacrament. Some five times in that discourse our Lord declares that His "Flesh and Blood," His glorified and sacred and life-giving Humanity, must be partaken of by us as our very Food, in order that we may live by Him. He calls Himself the "living Bread," and tells us that men are to eat thereof in order not to die. The striking thing is that whilst the other Evangelists give the account of the *institution* of the Blessed Sacrament, St. John—who seems to supplement their teachings and to record what they had omitted—gives no account of the institution, but records this wonderful discourse which throws light upon the mystery. Think of St. John's words: "Except ye eat the Flesh of the Son of man, and drink His Blood, ye have no life in you;" and again, "My Flesh is meat indeed, and My Blood is drink indeed."[1] Now, if we believe the Catholic doctrine of the Real Presence, this, I submit, my dear friend, though mysterious, is intelligible. It is felt to be a tremendous difficulty by those who deny the Faith of the Church, as is shown by the astonishing shifts to which they betake themselves in order to—what I can only call—"wriggle out of" its plain teaching. Sometimes they say that eating the Flesh and drinking the Blood only mean attending to His teaching, as we might say that a man "drinks in a sermon," or "devours a book."[2] This evasion is discredited at once when we remember what happened on the occasion. The Jews, and among them His own disciples, like all Eastern people, were perfectly used to the language of metaphor and allegory, and such language would have presented no difficulty to them. They felt, however, that our Lord meant a great deal more than that. Numbers of them were offended, and even devoted followers left Him in consequence, and all of them thought it a "hard saying," and some—which

[1] St. John vi. 53, 55. [2] Cf. Littledale, "The Real Presence."

makes the thing quite plain—asked point-blank, "How can this Man give us His Flesh to eat?"[1] This mode of evading our Lord's teaching must evidently be abandoned. It cannot honestly be maintained.

But, further, it was certainly in accordance with our Lord's usual manner, and what may be called His "sweet reasonableness," to make things clear where it was possible, if men misunderstood His sayings. It was not His way wantonly to encourage misconception. How easily could He have said on this occasion, "You have quite misunderstood Me; I have only meant that My teaching would enlighten you"! Does He do so? Nothing of the kind; even though they "strove among themselves, saying, How can this Man give us His Flesh to eat?" He proceeded to repeat His statement without any change. But more than that; when His very disciples were staggering under the hardness of the saying, He warns them that they will have to prepare their minds to realize the astonishing properties of His Sacred Body; that they will have to be awakened to the truth; that in that very Body of Flesh which they saw He would ascend to heaven. "Doth this offend you? What and if ye shall see the Son of man ascend up where He was before?"[2] He does not withdraw one word of His astonishing statement, but He *does* go on to throw light upon the mystery by explaining the *power* by which it was to be effected. It is quite clear, then, that our Lord spoke of a mysterious but *real* giving of His Body and Blood, and that such attempts at evading His statements are not really capable of being justified to unprejudiced reason.

But, then, others, who are as much staggered as the Jews or the disciples at our Lord's teaching as to His

[1] St. John vi. 52.   [2] St. John vi. 62.

Real Presence, get out of their difficulty in this way. They say, "Doubtless there is some kind of presence of Christ connected with the Sacrament, but it is only a spiritual one in the hearts of believers;" and they support this by quoting our Lord's explanatory saying, "It is the spirit that quickeneth; the flesh profiteth nothing: the words which I speak unto you, they are spirit, and they are life."[1] This, I suppose, is what has been called the "virtualist" view. It is a wonderful view. It is, I think, one of those examples of the ways in which Puritanism has managed to juggle with words. Its dogmatic statement would amount to this: "Our Lord is not *really* present, but He is *virtually* present." This, I imagine, from the quotation I have given above, would be the view of opponents who stop, at least in words, just short of Zwinglianism. It seems to me that bare Zwinglianism itself is less contrary to right reason than a notion of this sort. It empties the Sacrament of any real meaning at all. For consider, according to this, to receive the Body and Blood is, after all, only to receive grace. The Sacrament is no longer a thing *sui generis;* in it people receive grace which—for some unexplained reason—is *called* the "Body and Blood;" but they receive grace when they pray heartily or form good resolutions.[2] Where, then, is the meaning of the Sacrament? The unique position assigned to it in the practice of the Church at all times has no reasonable justification. It is a work of supererogation. It is, as we have constantly seen in practice, a real embarrassment and difficulty in a system of religion of this sort. One can, to a certain extent, understand a Zwinglian who joins

[1] St. John vi. 63.
[2] Cf. Littledale, *ut supra*, tract, "The Real Presence;" and Carter, "Letter on the Blessed Sacrament."

in a commemorative banquet in honour of the Founder of his religion, and looks upon it as a commemorative banquet and nothing more. He is thoroughly unscriptural, and he has no support from the Church; but he is intelligible. But it is difficult to understand a "virtualist," who is by way of resting his convictions on the teaching of the Church, and who makes much of Holy Scripture, when he explains such a phrase as "the Body and the Blood" to mean nothing more than a presence of Christ in the souls of those who have faith, seeing that he cannot deny that *that* is equally true—as I have said—of any faithful person who says his prayers earnestly, or makes good resolutions. Our Lord is really present or He is not.

A Zwinglian says He is *not*, and thereby breaks with Scripture and the teachings of Christ and the witness of the Church. A Catholic says He *is* really present, and thereby gives an intelligible meaning to our Lord's statements and to the Church's witness. A virtualist says He *is* present, but He is *not* present, and thereby assigns the most impossible and, I must say, senseless meanings to such a phrase as "the Body and the Blood." "Virtualism" seems to me to be one of those miserable subterfuges to which men betake themselves when they cannot deny a truth altogether, and yet will not commit themselves to it with all its consequences. I cannot but say, in passing, that if we allow ourselves to use such a phrase as "the Body and the Blood" in non-natural senses of this kind, we are indulging in a lax treatment of sacred words which is logically sure to lead to wider application, and to induce men to deal in a similar fashion with texts and statements relating to the Incarnation itself. But, in saying all this, *the point* that I desire to dwell upon at the moment is, that such teachers are given to rest their contention upon our Lord's words of explanation to His disciples: "It is the spirit that quickeneth; the flesh profiteth nothing: the words that I speak unto you, they are spirit, and they are life." From this they endeavour to deduce that there is no *Real* Presence, *for* it is always *spiritual*. Now, first of all, we have this usual and really astonishing confusion of thought. Of course it is *spiritual*. The whole question is a question of *spiritual things*, although connected with their *material expressions*. But *spiritual*, I repeat, does not mean fanciful, or imaginary, or unreal. Whenever these people use the word *spiritual*, they apparently mean something that has *no reality at all*. It is this absurdity, it is this rooted prejudice, it is this form of materialistic thought, it is this want of faith in the *reality* of the Unseen, which is at the bottom of so much heresy. A *spiritual fact*, I repeat, is as *real* a fact as a granite mountain, or the dome of St. Paul's. Our most real and important part is our spiritual and immortal nature. Angels are spirits, but they are as real as we are, if the Bible and the Church speak true. St. Paul himself says, "There is a natural body, and there is a spiritual body;" and the presence of our Lord's Sacred Body and Blood is, of course, *according to the laws of spiritual substances*, not according to the laws of materialistic things; but it is a *Real* Presence all the same, and our Lord's explanation to His disciples merely explains that it is so.

What He means is evidently this: His Humanity by itself would have no power; but by the power of His Godhead (the Spirit, as He calls it) that Humanity becomes a sacred and powerful and life-giving Force. "I do not speak to you," He seems to say, "of My Flesh and Blood in a carnal or natural state, nor of these by themselves alone; but I speak of them in their mysterious union with My Divine Nature. By the power of that Divine Nature they will ascend, and after what I call My 'Ascension'—which will give you some idea of the mysterious powers of My Sacred Body —they will be communicated to My people through the power of My Spirit in the Holy Sacrament, and become to them a source of everlasting life."

We may *put aside* St. John's testimony if we please, but we cannot *satisfy* the conditions of His statements —to use a phrase of mathematicians—unless we accept the Catholic doctrine of the "*Real* Presence of the Lord's Body and Blood under the form of bread and wine." So much for the testimony of St. John.

Now we turn to the testimony of the others. If St. John teaches us what may be called the philosophy of the Holy Sacrament, the three other Evangelists teach us definitely the Institution. Of these, one was present when the Institution took place, and the definiteness and exactness of the other two is all the more remarkable because they were *not* present themselves. Now, what took place? "On the same night that He was betrayed," He explained many things to His disciples. Last words are solemn words. We in the Anglican Church, at any rate, believe that our Lord, the Man, is very God. His last words, in His earthly life, are more than ever solemn words. He tells His disciples about His betrayal, about His death, about His going back to His Father. They are human, they are loving; they are filled with sorrow and with fear. They have a sense of being deserted, and a sense of their own incapacity, when He Who was their Strength was gone. He comforts them by assuring them of the coming of the Holy Spirit. But He goes further;

He says, "I will not leave you orphaned" (that is the meaning of His word); "*I* will come to you." According to the moral law of Divine teaching, such words have a *wide* fulfilment, in the constant inward communion that Christ has, through the Spirit, with His people; but they have this *wide* fulfilment *because* they have a *special* fulfilment in the Great Mystery. This, after speaking these words, He proceeded to institute. The three Evangelists record the words of Institution, and in each case He says, "This is My Body," "This is My Blood." If the *Real* Presence be not true, these words must be explained away. Remember the force they have from the *time* at which they were spoken, from the *previous statement* of St. John which we have considered, and from the *unbroken custom* of the Church, from then until now, to use them in the consecration of the Holy Sacrament. It is strange, indeed, if our Lord and His Church have gone out of their way to mislead men on so grave a subject when it would have been so easy to make all things plain. They have *not* gone out of their way to do so. What they have said, and say, is truth. Instead of Jesuitical and casuistical and non-natural twistings, if we only will simply and straightforwardly *believe*, then there is nothing to explain away; for when we do what He has commanded us to do, we can trust Him to keep His promise. This *is* His Body; this *is* His Blood; there *is* His Real Presence under the form of Bread and Wine. Now, I think, my dear friend, I must remind you on what tortuous paths—in order to escape the force of straightforward truth—Protestant prejudice or unbelief has trodden. It has been asserted that our Lord only meant, "This *represents* My Body," and that it is parallel to His statements, "I am the Vine," "I am the Door," "I am the Good Shepherd."

When men say these things, it is really difficult to believe that *they* believe what they say. It is difficult to believe that they can be the victims of such an extraordinary confusion of thought. The statements have no likeness to one another whatever. They could only have that likeness, if our Lord, putting His hand upon a vine tree, had said, "*This* vine is Myself;" or, taking hold of a door, had said, "*This* door is Myself;" or, laying His hand upon a shepherd, had said, "*This* shepherd is Myself." In the one case, He is alluding to certain things or persons fulfilling functions, fulfilled by Him in ideal perfection; in the other case, by His Divine authority He is using certain portions of a creature of His own creation as a vehicle to convey His Divine and Human life. He did *not*, in the institution of the Blessed Sacrament, speak about *bread in general* at all, but He spoke about a particular thing—apparently *only* bread —as becoming, by Divine power, *also* His Body.

When our Lord spoke, His words were "with power." To the outward sign, which was a part of His own creation, He added the inward part or thing signified. The words He used denoted the higher or nobler part. By His own power He united earthly and heavenly substances, and made them one through Sacramental Union. The Bread did not cease to be Bread, the Wine did not cease to be Wine, but through the consecration of Christ, and by the power of the Holy Ghost, they became the Body and Blood of the Lord. The substance of the one was not changed into the substance of the other, but a fresh spiritual force was, by the power of Him Who created them, given to the Elements, so that they were transformed into Holy Mysteries, and became sacred Tabernacles of a heavenly Presence, and so justly received the names which indicate their supernatural dignity. The Elements, to the eye and touch of man, became the outward sign of those awful and unseen realities on which the soul fixes its attention by faith. Take the words of Institution as the Evangelists have recorded them, as the Church has received and used them ever since, and you have the record of a Divine and blessed fact, and the witness to our Lord's fulfilment to His own promise. Take them with all the glosses of—what might be called —Protestant Jesuitry, and casuistry, and shuffling, and twisting, and unreality, and you are lost in an unconsoling and, indeed, chilling fog. As far as the testimony of the four Evangelists go, you have, I submit, the most direct evidence from Scripture of the Real Presence of the Lord's Body and Blood, under the form of Bread and Wine.

And now we turn to St. Paul. St. Paul, as you know, my dear friend, is supposed by extreme Protestants to be their stronghold when they are staggered at any part of the Catholic Faith. His testimony, therefore, ought to be received by those who deny this doctrine with special respect; and that testimony, I submit, is exceedingly strong. First of all, he tells us that he also had *received* that which he delivered on the subject of the Blessed Sacrament. We know that he was exceedingly sensitive as to any supposition that he received the truths which he taught *through* others, and not *directly* from our Lord Himself. The Blessed Sacrament, then, must indeed have been a matter of supreme importance, since our Lord thought fit *Himself* to reveal it directly to St. Paul. " For *I have received of the Lord* that which also I delivered unto you." And then he proceeds, like the Evangelists, to inform us that our Lord's statement as to the Bread and Wine, when consecrated, was, "This is My Body," "This is My Blood."[1] He is a further witness, then, to this fact of the Real Presence, and a witness directly illuminated by a revelation from Christ our Lord. His witness, besides, goes directly to an important point, there can be no mistake here as to allegory or metaphor. He does not speak of bread in general or wine in general as typifying the life-giving qualities of our Blessed Lord; he speaks of *the* Bread and *the* Wine, consecrated according to Christ's command in the Sacrament. "The Cup of blessing *which we bless*, is it not the Communion of the Blood of Christ? The Bread *which we break*, is it not the Communion of the Body of Christ?"[2] His testimony goes further still. He shows beyond all question that the Real Presence of the Lord's Body and Blood in the Sacrament *does not depend in any way whatever* upon the faith or unfaith of communicants. Notice his words: "Whosoever shall eat this Bread and drink this Cup of the Lord unworthily, shall be *guilty of the Body and Blood of the Lord;*"[3] and, "He that eateth and drinketh unworthily, eateth and drinketh condemnation to himself, not discerning the Lord's Body."

Put side by side with this statement of the great Apostle, the assertion quoted above, that "the Body and Blood of Christ are received . . . only by the faithful," and that "the Presence of Christ is only in the heart of the true worshipper." Can you, my dear Dean, imagine a more flat contradiction? How *could* any man be "guilty of the Body and Blood of the Lord," if that Body and Blood are only present in his heart when he is full of faith and love? How *can* any one eat and drink to his own condemnation when he does not "discern the Lord's Body;" that is, when he does not

[1] 1 Cor. xi. 23. [2] 1 Cor. x. 16. [3] 1 Cor. xi. 27.

discriminate between common food and a supernatural and awful Presence, if that Presence can never be there unless *he* is such a person, so full of faith and love, that " unworthily " receiving is to him impossible ? The fact is, my dear friend, that the teaching of all four Evangelists, and above all the teaching of St. Paul, becomes, I submit, unintelligible, becomes almost nonsense, contrary to the plainest axioms of right reason, unless you accept the Catholic doctrine of the Real Presence of the Lord's Body and Blood under the form of Bread and Wine. If you accept that, the teaching of Scripture is plain and reasonable and consonant with common sense. You then, I think, and only then, *satisfy* the conditions of the statements.

What I think, then, should be fairly remembered is this, that if the Catholic doctrine of the Real Presence be true, all these statements of Holy Scripture are intelligible, and that this action of the Christian Church, both in using such words as she has used, and in doing as she has done in regard to the Mysteries, is reasonable and sensible ; but that if you are to ride off upon any of the shifty explanations which one after another have arisen from the fertile hotbed of Protestant heresy, you empty Scripture of its meaning—and as for the action of the Church,—the less, then, said about *it* the better.

Turning from Holy Scripture, then, we necessarily examine what the early Church has believed and done in relation to this Holy Mystery.

I must pause for a moment to remind you, my dear Dean, that although we have examined the statements of Holy Scripture, and although we have seen that, according to right reason, they are only *satisfied* by the Catholic doctrine of the Real Presence; still, that for all believers, *what* Holy Scripture means in relation to any doctrine is decided by the Church. "I believe in the Holy Catholic Church," is a statement which we are all repeatedly making, with great solemnity, before God. I think I have shown that there are reasonable grounds for believing that Holy Scripture teaches the Real Presence. I now go on to show that that *is* the interpretation put upon the statements of Holy Scripture by the "Holy Catholic Church."

Still, however, there are several points which require to be stated before we pass to the *direct* teaching of the Church.

(1) In the first place, you cannot forget that the Church has always felt how the mystery of Easter morning has illustrated the mystery of the Real Presence. There are, of course, those—especially in this age of narrowness and materialism—who would consider that the one is about as foolish as the other. With people of that sort we have nothing now to do. A soul entirely guided by the canons of what is called *practical*—i.e. materialistic—philosophy, it is impossible to approach with the mysteries of the Christian Faith. To those, however, who have still their eyes wide enough open to believe that there *is* another world, and that there *are* such things as spiritual facts, it may not be wasted time to reassert the mysterious revelation of the Resurrection Body of our Lord.

Now we know, if we believe the Gospels (cf. St. Matt. xxviii. 2-6), that our Lord had risen from the dead *before* the appearance of the angel who rolled away the stone. He came—that blessed messenger—to *tell* the holy women that the Lord "*was* risen, as He said." This, as you will remember, is emphasized by St. Chrysostom [1]

---

[1] St. John, Hom. 85, § 4, p. 764; Oxford Trans.

and St. Jerome.[1] So—to remind you of the commentary of St. Gregory of Nyssa—"the angel said, 'He is not here; He *hath* risen (ἠγέρθη).' . . . For had this not been so he would have said, 'Lo, He riseth (ἐγείρεται),' pointing to what was then taking place. But since it had preceded, he said, using the past tense, 'He is not here; He hath risen (ἠγέρθη).'"[2]

I would weary you, my dear friend, and all my readers, if I were to fill my pages with the innumerable references there are to this: viz. that the early writers of the Church felt the mysterious but *real* fact of the spiritualized Body of the Lord, witnessed to by the historical truth that, *without the door being opened, there* was that real Body and Blood present to the disciples in the Upper Chamber; and, *without the stone being rolled away, there* was the Lord's *real* self—Body and Blood—on the morning of the Resurrection; and that, *therefore*, His Real Presence under the form of Bread and Wine is far enough from being contrary to revelation and contrary to reason, but is, as a matter of fact, consonant with both.

The fact is, my dear friend, that those who deny the Real Presence are the victims of a materialistic imagination. They are carried away, I think, by a notion that we *must* mean something gross and material, but surely all this is to "walk by sight," and not "by faith." If we seriously believe Christian revelation and Christian history at all, if we are not the victims of *à priori* theories, and do not so far break with common sense as to say a thing *can't* be because *we* are *not used to it*, then the appearances of our Lord, in spite of closed

---

[1] St. Jerome, "Epist. ad Hedip.," 9, 6.
[2] "In Christi Resurrec.," Orat. 2, t. iii. p. 401. See Pusey, "The Doctrine of the Real Presence," Note C, p. 57.

doors, in spite of the unrolled stone—nay, as the Fathers have said, though *that*, for obvious reasons, I do not dwell upon—in spite of the mystery of His birth, by the *illæsa virginitate*—all point to the wonderful powers of that divinely gifted body which makes it *not* surprising, after all we have considered of the teaching of Holy Scripture, that it should be given "under the form of Bread and Wine."

You can't get out of the Lord's words, "This is My Body," "This is My blood." They are wonderful words, but what *so* explains them as the Catholic doctrine of the Real Presence? I am wrong. You *can* get out of His revelation, *if* you rationalize, if you do not *believe*. A system of denial is often unrestrained human nature —on the one hand clutching at religion, on the other refusing to "walk by faith." Protestantism in its extreme forms is neither more nor less than "walking by sight." And it is a real *help* to well-meaning and devout Protestants to be reminded that the doctrine of the Real Presence is the only doctrine quite in tune with the teaching of Holy Scripture as to the Resurrection Body of the Lord.

(2) Then, again, it is worth while to remember—is it not?—what has been said, in fact, by a very great teacher—that mankind generally has felt that it is a fundamental principle of law, that in testaments the plain, the direct, the simple, and evident meaning of words is not to be departed from.[1] "It is not right," says a great teacher on law, "to depart from the meaning of words, save when it is manifest that the testator meant something else." Then, again, says another great legist, "If the testator meant the contrary, there was no difficulty in so disposing it."[2]

[1] Pusey, "Doctrine of Real Presence," Note D, p. 60. [2] *Id., ut supra*.

Now consider; here we have a "New Testament." The "Testator"—being Divine and all-powerful, as well as human—leaves His testament. He foretells that He *will* give His Body and Blood. He institutes a rite by which He declares that, using His own creatures, He *does* give His Body and Blood. He orders His followers to carry on the rite. His followers do so, and tell us that this rite, as carried on by them, and those who follow them, *is* the Communion of His Body and Blood; and, after all that, His professed followers are positively angry with us if we venture to say that He, the Everlasting Truth, meant what He said, and does what He has promised!

If the Real Presence is not true, then the promises and the sayings of Christ our Lord have in a measure failed; then His Testament is *not* to be interpreted, as every testament is, according to the plain meaning of words; then, instead of being honest men, we are, in a matter of serious gravity, to play fast and loose with language, and we are to say in effect, "This is My Body," "This is My Blood," means, "This is *not* My Body," "This is *not* My Blood." "Don't be so stupid as to believe one word I say!" This may be that immorality in the use of language too common with sinful man, too usual in diplomacy, when words seem to be used to *hide* men's meanings, not *express* them; one thing it is not— this is *not* consistent with Christian morality, this is *not* in accordance with the simplicity of Christ.

Men must juggle with language; men must affix non-natural senses to it; men must allow themselves to drift, by prejudice, or temper, or some other evil "undertow," far into the ocean of doubt and half believing, before they can say, "This is My Body," "This is My Blood," means anything except the Real, true, objective

Presence of the Body and Blood of the Lord under the form of Bread and Wine.

(3) I need not detain you on what I may call "the figure theory, because I *have*, to a certain extent, dwelt upon it already; still, I touch on it again, to make things clear. Those who deny the truth of our Lord's saying call it "figurative language." Now, here—just to recur to the matter for a moment, because it is one of those fallacies, I think, which tend to lead even good men from the truth—I can't be wrong in reminding you of the wise saying of a great teacher, who says that a figure must lie either in what is spoken of, *or* in what is said about it, *or* in the word or phrase which connects the two. I can't quote his words, but I am sure this is the gist of them. Anyhow, no reasonable being can deny that this is *a fact*.[1]

Well, to go back again to the usual assertions that our Lord's statement as to the Real Presence is paralleled by His phrases, "I am the Door," "I am the Good Shepherd," "I am the Vine." Compare the sayings. Clearly there *is* a figure in these sayings—as one would expect—in the final word, *i.e.* in the predicates. There is a "figure" in "Door," "Vine," "Good Shepherd." These statements, then, are "figurative." You can't, however, have a figure in a *whole* sentence if you haven't a touch of it *in any part* of the sentence. That is clear. Any one who denies *that*, is outside argument. Where, then, dear friend, I ask you, is the "figure" in this great saying of our Lord, "This is My Body"?

Certainly there is no "figure" in "This." The word indicated a definite portion of His creature of bread, then and there to be consecrated.

With equal certainty there is no "figure" in the

[1] Pusey, "Doctrine of the Real Presence," Note E.

word "is." This word is simply a copula—a word of use to join two parts of a sentence; a word which in the Hebrew idiom may often be omitted; a word which is qualified by a negative, before which we insert the word *not*, if the two parts of the sentence do not correspond.

I need hardly say, "My Body which is given for you" is no "figure," but expresses the fact of a real, definite, sacred Body nailed to the Cross for us sinners.

The fact is, as far as the argument from *language* goes, there is not a shred of strength in the anti-Catholic contention. If this kind of immoral use of language is permitted—for I can call it nothing else—then, of course, the Incarnation itself goes. Anything may mean anything else. You are out on an open sea of uncertain and unmeaning verbiage. "The Word was made Flesh" may mean "The Word was not made Flesh," and the Docetæ may be as right or as wrong as the Christian Church. You have to deal in Scripture either with evident and well-understood picture-language, *or*—when figures are used, Scripture tells you they *are* figures; but not a single instance can be shown in which names which represent an actual thing are used—without the slightest notice given—used in a perfectly *unreal* sense. Men have seriously to ask themselves, when they juggle with our Lord's words in this way, "Did our Lord come to give us another 'shadow' in addition to the many 'shadows' of the Old Law, *or* did He come to give us an absolute and blessed Reality?" Is it conceivable, further, that, using the strongest language He *could* use in declaring that He gave us a *Reality*, all the time He was not giving a gift at all, but only adding—and adding in a way terribly to confuse us—to the land of shadows? It seems to me, dear friend, there can be but one answer to a thoughtful

Christian: He, the Great Reality, gave, as He said He did, His own Real Presence, His own Body and His own Blood.

(4) Again, people have raised an objection—an objection again, I think, simply coming from "shortened thought," from a *want of real faith*—when they say, "How *could* the Lord, being present in the body before the very eyes of His Apostles, *also* give His Body to them under the form of bread and wine?" We answer at once *we do not know, and we do not profess to know;* we do not know everything as to the mystery of His sacred Humanity. Even "virtualists," however, believe that *somehow or other* He does give some grace or gift which He calls His Body and Blood—otherwise the Sacrament is an unmeaning and roundabout way of giving what is given in answer to *any* prayer—and yet He is now present *in His Body* in heaven. Think in answer to this objection—which is an objection of pure unbelief—of Bishop Jeremy Taylor's saying—

"When we say we believe Christ's Body to be 'really' in the Sacrament, do we believe 'that Body, that Flesh, which was born of the Virgin Mary, that was crucified, dead, and buried'? I answer that *I know of none else that He had or hath*. There is but one Body of Christ, natural and glorified; but he that says that Body is glorified which was crucified, says that *it is the same Body, but not after the same manner: and so it is in the Sacrament;* we eat and drink the Body and Blood of Christ that was broken and poured forth; for there is no other Body, no other Blood of Christ; but though it is the same which we eat and drink, *it is in another manner . . . it is not eaten in a natural* [or carnal] *sense.*"[1]

---

[1] Bishop Jeremy Taylor, on the Real Presence, vol. ix. p. 431.

On these points it is necessary emphatically to dwell. We are, of course, as a Catholic believes, in presence of *a real fact*, but also of *a majestic mystery*. Once grasp, once believe in the overwhelming mystery of the Incarnation, and *this* mystery which follows from it presents no difficulty at all *to faith*. Still, for our present purpose, we must deal with questions *of evidence*.

II. Well, after the teachings of Holy Scripture, and after such considerations as these, we must turn for a moment to the testimony of the early Church. If the early Church is against us, we of the English Church may find ourselves in difficulties, for the appeal of the Church of England is emphatically to Holy Scripture and to the early Church.

It may, perhaps, be worth while again to call attention, in passing, to this fact. The real question before us is, What does the Church of England teach? Opponents declare that she denies the Real Presence in the Sacrament. I affirm that, rightly or wrongly, she asserts this as truth. Now, that being so, it is worth while to remember the words of her canon, passed by the very Convocation which passed the Articles—

"They [that is, preachers] shall in the first place be careful never to teach anything from the pulpit to be religiously held and believed by the people, but what is agreeable to the doctrine of the Old or New Testament, *and collected out of that very doctrine by the Catholic Fathers and ancient Bishops.*"

Now what, on this solemn subject, do "the Catholic Fathers and ancient Bishops" say? We have seen what has been said by Holy Scripture; we have seen that only by *explaining away* the Holy Scripture, and by affixing non-natural meanings to its statements, can any plain man get rid of the doctrine of the Real

Presence: what, then, as to the teaching of these other authorities to which we are referred?

The difficulty here is to write within any reasonable limits. The evidence for this majestic truth, as it is plain from Holy Scripture, so it is overwhelming and superabundant from the witness of the early Church.

This I may introduce by quoting weighty and true words: "The words 'This is My Body,' 'This is My Blood,' have been . . . the subject of long, still-continued, and often very bitter controversies. There was, however, scarcely a dispute concerning them for a thousand years after they were uttered." [1]

The fact is, men who held the Christian Faith at all, took for granted, during that long reach of time, that what our Lord *said, that* He *meant*. Well, let us see.

One or two examples amongst the vast mass of evidence are all that one need mention now. St. Ignatius, as you will remember, who, if any man, must have known the mind of the Apostles, and who was martyred about A.D. 107, writes as follows: "They [that is, the heretics who denied the reality of our Lord's human Body] abstained from Eucharist and Prayer, because they confess not that the Eucharist is the Flesh of our Saviour Jesus Christ which suffered for our sins, which the Father in His mercy raised again. They, then, who speak against the gifts perish while disputing: good had it been for them to love it, that they might rise again!" [2] In another place he writes, "Haste ye, then, to partake of our Eucharist. For there is one Flesh of our Lord Jesus Christ, and one Cup for the uniting of His Blood." [3] And yet again he writes, "Breaking one Bread, which is the medicine of immor-

---

[1] Carter, "Letter on the Blessed Sacrament."
[2] Ep. ad Smyrn., n. 7. [3] Ep. ad Phil., n. 4.

tality, the antidote that we should not die, but live in Jesus Christ for ever."[1]

You will remember, of course, the celebrated passage in St. Justin Martyr's "Apology." St. Justin was converted in A.D. 133 and martyred A.D. 165. In describing the Eucharistic Service, he says this, among other things: "This Food is amongst us called Eucharist. . . . We do not receive it as *common* bread or as *common* drink; but, in what way Jesus Christ our Saviour, being through the Word of God Incarnate, had both flesh and blood for our salvation, so also have we been taught that the Food, over which thanksgiving has been made by the prayer of the Word which is from Him (from which [food] our blood and flesh are by transmutation nourished), is the Flesh and Blood of Him, the Incarnate Jesus."[2]

I do not want to weary you; and others also would be tired out if I were to quote anything approaching to the vast mass of testimony which comes from the early Church; still I think it is well to remind you and others of the words of such a man as St. Irenæus. Perhaps it may be interesting to some—although, of course, *you* remember it—to recall what St. Irenæus himself says about his experiences, apart from the question immediately before us.

"I remember," he says, "the things of that time [viz. when he was young with St. Polycarp] better than recent things (for those which we have from boyhood, growing up with the soul, are made one with it), so that I can even name the place where the blessed Polycarp sat and conversed, and his goings-out and his comings-in, and the character of his life, and the appearance of his person, and his discourse with the multitude, and his

---

[1] Ep. ad Eph., n. 20. [2] "Apol.," i. 65–67.

familiar intercourse with John, which he used to tell us of, and with the rest who had seen the Lord; and how he used to recall their sayings, and concerning the Lord, what things he had heard from them, and concerning His mighty works, and His teaching, as Polycarp, having received them from the eye-witnesses of the Word of Life, used to relate them; agreeing in all things with the Scriptures. These things at that time also, through the mercy of God towards me, I heard with diligence, and noted them down, not on paper, but in my heart, and ever, by the grace of God, I meditate truly upon them."[1]

Now, can any man in the early Church be more valuable as a witness to the mind of those who had been with the Lord Himself? Well, discussing various Gnostic speculations and absurdities in connection with Dualism, he goes on—pointing out the absurdity of thinking of any creator but the one Creator, and any father but the one Father—as follows:—

"How shall they know for certain that that Bread over which thanks are given is the Body of their Lord, and that the Cup is the Cup of His Blood, if they do not acknowledge Him as the Son of the Creator of the world, *i.e.* His Word, through which wood yields fruit and fountains flow, and the earth yieldeth, first the blade, then the ear, then the full corn in the ear?[2] But counselling also His disciples to offer to God firstfruits from His creatures, not as though He needeth ought, but that they might not be unfruitful nor ungrateful, He took that which of His creation is bread, and gave thanks, saying, 'This is My Body;' and likewise the Cup, which is of that our creation, He confessed *to be His Blood*, and taught that it is the new oblation of the New

[1] Fragm., Ep. ad Florin., in Euseb., H. E., v. 20. [2] iv. 18. 4.

Testament, of which among the twelve prophets Malachi thus presignified: 'I have no pleasure in you, saith the Lord of hosts, neither will I receive an offering at your hands; for from the rising of the sun unto the going down thereof My Name shall be great among the heathen, and in every place incense shall be offered unto My Name, and a pure offering: for My Name shall be great among the heathen, saith the Lord of hosts;' most clearly signifying by these words that the former people indeed shall cease to offer to God; but in every place sacrifice shall be offered to Him, and that pure; and His Name shall be glorified among the heathen."[1] And again he says, "If the Lord belong to another Father, how was it just that taking bread of this our creation He confessed that it was *His own Body*, and He affirmed that the mingled drink of the Cup was *His own Blood?*"[2]

Now, here, dear friend, we have, so to speak, exemplary testimonies to the Real Presence from those who sat at the feet of Apostles, and to whom, above all, the Church of England appeals. It would be, as I have said, utterly wearisome to go on quoting testimony after testimony of the early Church. No one who takes the trouble to examine the writings of these early teachers can doubt for one moment—unless they twist their language into non-natural senses—that they held a simple and straightforward faith in the great fact of the Real Presence. I might, as you know, quote St. Melito (A.D. 170), and Tatian (A.D. 172), and St. Clement of Alexandria (A.D. 192), who says, "He is both Bread and Flesh, and giveth Himself, being both, to us to eat." I might quote Tertullian, who says, "When the Body of the Lord hath been received and reserved, both are saved, *i.e.* both the partaking of the Sacrifice and the

[1] iv. 17. 5. [2] iv. 33. 2.

fulfilment of the Service."[1] And again, "The flesh feeds on the Body and Blood of Christ, that the soul may be enriched from God."[2] I might quote, as you know, the sayings of heretics who jeered at the Faith of Catholics, and who all witness to the Faith of the Church in the Real Presence. You remember the striking inscription at Autun, at the close of the second century, in which occurs the words—

"Receive the honey-sweet Food of the Holy Things of the Saviour; Eat, drink; having ΙΧΘΥΣ in thy (or two) hands."[3]

Then I might quote St. Hippolytus, the disciple of St. Irenæus (about A.D. 220): "He gave us His Divine Flesh and His Precious Blood, to eat and to drink for the remission of sins."[4] Then, of course, Origen (A.D. 230), in innumerable passages; and St. Firmilian (A.D. 231), a most illustrious bishop; and St. Dionysius the Great of Alexandria; and St. Cyprian (martyred A.D. 258), a real witness for the African Church, even though I fear that Dr. Farrar does not approve of him; and so on, and so on: so that it is impossible to find any of those "Catholic Doctors and ancient Fathers," to whom the Church of England appeals, who do not bear the strongest testimony to the great truth of the Real Presence.

Now, here, my dear friend, surely it is well to pause and consider this. Mere naturalism, mere "walking by sight," mere following the usual ways of the natural understanding, mere efforts to be guided by the ordinary, easy-going ways of men, could never lead people to imagine that, in this strange world, so

---

[1] "De Orat.," § 19, p. 312; Oxford Trans.
[2] "De Res. Carn.," c. 8, p. 384.
[3] Quoted by Pusey, "Doctrine of the Real Presence," p. 338.
[4] In Prov. ix. 1. 1, 282.

strange a thing had been done, as that the Eternal Son of God should not only come down from heaven to take flesh, *but also* should *feed* us with His Sacred Humanity, in order to renew our sinful, human nature,—I say, nothing so strange could have come into the minds of men unless it had come by Divine Revelation. Well, then, we find a distinct assertion of the fact from the lips of Him Who is Eternal Truth; we find the same from the direct teaching of His Apostles; we find an unvarying testimony to the same truth from those who sat at the feet of the Apostles; we find that, for about a thousand years after the great Institution, no one ever dreamt of denying this blessed truth; we find that, in order to deny it, modern and new-fangled heresies have to twist and torture the Word of God, the teachings of Apostles, and the teachings of the ancient Fathers who knew best what was the Apostolic mind. We are justified, then, in saying that we will have nothing to do with these new-fangled heresies; that the Catholic Church has always accepted this blessed truth; that the English Church—being part of the Catholic Church—has therefore accepted it; that as she especially appeals to Holy Scripture and the ancient Fathers, she is *specially* bound to the maintenance of this doctrine, to which *both*—as I have reminded you—bear such emphatic witness; and that, therefore, if under the head of "sacerdotalism" is included (as it seems to be) the teaching of this doctrine, then "sacerdotalism" is certainly the teaching of the Church of England, as she by her appeal to Scripture and the Fathers evidences plainly that she holds the doctrine of the Real Presence of the Body and Blood of the Lord in the Holy Sacrament under the form of Bread and Wine.

III. But two questions require to be dealt with in this

connection, in order to make things clear on this solemn subject. It is contended by opponents that when we assert the doctrine of the Real Presence, we are in fact teaching Transubstantiation, and that Transubstantiation is directly contrary to the teaching of the English Church. Out of this, I say, there arise two important questions which ought to be considered. (1) Does belief in the Real Presence involve belief in Transubstantiation? (2) Does the English Church, in denying Transubstantiation, deny the doctrine of the Real Presence? I answer emphatically "No!" to both these questions, and I proceed to show cause why.

(1) Turn, then, to the first. I repeat the question again—Does belief in the Real Presence involve belief in Transubstantiation?

Now, here I may remark that, if one did not know the violence of passion which has been aroused by controversy, it would be almost unintelligible the fierceness of anger raised in the minds of some by the bare *word* "Transubstantiation." This way of explaining the mystery of the Real Presence as to its *mode* or *manner*, I do not believe to be a way justified by either philosophy or revelation. Still it is, after all, only the expression of an opinion as to *the manner* in which the Lord is present. Now, suppose it to be a mistaken way of *explaining* the fact—as I think it is—why, I wonder, should men be so furious about it? If members of the Roman Church believe—as I suppose they do—that the *manner* or *method* of the Lord's Presence is by Transubstantiation, the worst you can say of them as to their belief is, that they explain a *fact*, which is certainly true, by *a method of* which they have no proof, and for which they can adduce no evidence. If *this method* had been advanced—as our own Archbishop Bramhall called it—

as "an *opinion* of the schools," no fault could be found. Reasonable men would say, "I don't hold that opinion," "You cannot assert it as an article of faith," and there would have been the end of the matter. But what really has occurred, my dear friend, amounts to this—

(*a*) The word "Transubstantiation" has been used in *a popular* and *unphilosophical* sense. I suppose in *this* sense the popular imagination before the Reformation was impressed with some fancy which was gross and carnal; that after Consecration there was in no sense any bread and wine, but only flesh and blood. There seems to have been a notion that that "Substance," in the ordinary meaning of that term, had passed away; that there was no "outward sign;" that there was only "the thing signified," and *that* in a gross and materialistic manner. Now, against *this* meaning of Transubstantiation the Church of England protested in her Article. She affirmed that Bread and Wine must be *there*, otherwise the "nature of a Sacrament" is destroyed. If a Sacrament is a mystery with "an outward sign" *and* "an inward part," and if you take away "the outward sign"—as this popular notion did—and leave only "the inward part," you of course "destroy the nature of the Sacrament." Against all this the Article protested, and rightly. It did *not* protest against the Decree of Trent, and for this very good reason, that the Article was written before the Decree of Trent was framed.

(*b*) Again, there is the other sense in which the word "Transubstantiation" is used. This is *the philosophical* sense, and this is the sense of the Decree of Trent. There is nothing gross, or carnal, or heretical about it. It is "an opinion of the schools;" it is an *opinion* which people might hold if they liked, so long as they did not assert it as an article of faith.

It is based on that form of speculative philosophy which represents all things as having two parts—*substance*, or the thing *in itself;* and *accident*, or the thing as it *appears* to our senses.

According to this philosophy of the substance, or *substantia*, or οὐσια, or *thing in itself*, or *that which makes it to be what it is*, we know nothing at all. What we *do* know is the "accident," *i.e.* what it *appears* to our senses. Now, the Decree of Trent takes for granted the truth of *this* philosophical theory. It asserts nothing gross or carnal about the Presence. What it assumes is, that all things consist of *substance* and *accident;* i.e., as I have said, of what they are *in themselves*, in their very fundamental being, *and* of what they *appear* to the senses—of their *phenomena*, in fact. The Decree assumes the truth of the philosophy, and then lays down as an article of faith, that after Consecration the *substantia*, or οὐσια, or *substance* of the consecrated elements, become the Body and Blood of the Lord, while the *accidents* are still the *accidents* of Bread and Wine.

This meaning of Transubstantiation is a totally different one from the gross and carnal and materialistic meaning according to which it is condemned in the Sacrament; what we really have to quarrel with in the Decree of Trent is this—

(1) It is framed by a mere section of the Catholic Church, being the Latin section, and not by the whole. It is an example of those unhappy assumptions of the Roman or Latin *part* of the Catholic Church, whereby she has unfortunately taken upon herself to legislate as to faith and morals, without the agreement of the rest of

the Church in her action, and so has emptied her decree of value. The Articles of the Anglican Church may be excellent; the Decree of Trent may be excellent; but neither one nor other are infallible truth, for the simple reason that they are the outcome of the mind of *a section* of the Divine Family, and not of *the whole.* The first objection to Transubstantiation is that it is decreed *as an article of faith* by a mere section—the Latin section—of the Catholic Church, and no such decree can hold with binding authority unless it comes from the *consensus* of the *whole* Church.

(2) Another objection to the Decree of Trent as regards Transubstantiation is this. It—passed, as I have said, by only one section of the Western Church, and therefore *not Catholic*—pretends to sanction, as of Divine Revelation, a philosophy which, to say the least, is open to question. Men may quite reasonably doubt whether all things *are* divided into *substance* and *accident*. They may consider the philosophy which so dealt with things as an exploded philosophy, or they may believe in it; but it is—to say the least of it—to be regretted when one single section—the Latin section —of the Catholic Church deliberately accepts that particular philosophy as being a Divine Revelation, and deliberately frames a decree as to the *mode* of the Divine Presence, which *assumes* the absolute truth of that philosophy.

If men will only remember, my dear friend, that "Transubstantiation"—the gross, popular, carnal notion —condemned by our Article, has nothing in common with "Transubstantiation" as decreed by the Council of Trent; if they will remember that the Decree of Trent rests upon the philosophy which I have touched upon;—this, at least, I am sure, will follow—

(a) They will not lose their tempers over the word "Transubstantiation," as if it meant a belief in something gross, carnal, abominable, and only fit for the depraved and for fools!

(b) They will, while they regret the unhappy assumptions by the Roman Church, and her unfortunate way of issuing decrees, as if *she* were *the whole* of the Executive of the kingdom of God, instead of only one department of it—they will, I say, feel that "Transubstantiation," as the Decree of Trent teaches it, is "an opinion of the schools," a speculation as to *the manner* of the Divine Presence, in no sense *a heresy*. Men *may* hold this opinion as to *the manner* of the Presence if they please, so long as they do not teach it as a matter of faith.

I differ from any who do so think. The philosophy in which such an opinion is founded is, anyhow, a doubtful philosophy; but, no matter what *I* think, or *you* think, this *opinion, as an opinion,* men may hold if they like, so long as they do not put it forward as a matter of faith; one thing is certain, if any *do* hold this opinion of *the mode* of the Divine Presence, you and I may not agree with them, but they certainly do not contravene the Article, which is aimed at a totally different *sense* of Transubstantiation, which we should all—which I imagine the Roman part of the Catholic Church would herself—condemn.

(c) And then this is *the* thing to be remembered above all. *Holding the doctrine of the Real Presence has nothing whatever to do with holding the doctrine of Transubstantiation.* Nothing whatever! There is no more sense in saying that it has, than in saying that when a man declares that he is going from London to Edinburgh, he thereby declares that he *must* go by the

Great Northern Railway! The Catholic Church, like Holy Scripture, has *always* taught the majestic truth of the Real Presence of the Lord's Body and Blood under the form of Bread and Wine. She has never committed herself to any statement as to *the manner* of that Presence. The Latin Church has unhappily committed herself to a statement of the "how," of *the manner* of the Presence. She may be right or she may be wrong. She is certainly wrong in pretending to make decrees without the assent of the rest of the Catholic Church. But, right or wrong, one thing is certain—that from the first and now "the Holy Church throughout all the world" has been faithful in teaching the Real Presence, while only the Latin section has unfortunately attempted to say *how* that Presence is. To believe in the Real Presence is to hold a truth held and taught from the first—to deny which is to deny the plain teaching of Holy Scripture and the Fathers;— to believe in Transubstantiation is to believe a philosophical doctrine of very doubtful validity, adopted in comparatively recent times by one department of the visible Church. If a man denies the Real Presence, he must explain away Scripture and the teaching of the Church in all ages in the interest of a rationalistic prejudice. If a man denies Transubstantiation, he denies—to say the least of it—a very questionable philosophical theory, and a comparatively modern pronouncement of *one* section of the Church. I must say I think it astonishing, then, when opponents are so carried away as to say that to teach the Real Presence is to teach Transubstantiation. It is nothing of the kind.

Here, my dear friend, one cannot help noticing a wonderful illustration of the old saying that "extremes meet." Violent Romanists—anyhow in the past—ran perilously near a denial of the "outward sign" of the Sacrament. Violent Protestants at present, even among ourselves, run perilously near a denial of "the inward part or thing signified." The Holy Sacrament has two parts. If we drift towards the Zwinglian heresy, our religion becomes a matter of subjective impression, and such a rite as the Blessed Sacrament an almost unmeaning, and certainly an embarrassing, accretion. Accept frankly the Catholic Faith as Holy Scripture has taught it, as the Church long before her "family quarrel" witnessed to it, and you have *real* Bread and Wine an "outward sign," without any philosophical hair-splitting or confusion, and you have also, after consecration, and according to the terms of the Divine promise, the Real Presence of the Body and Blood of the Lord under the form of Bread and Wine.

The question, however, I again repeat, before us is this—not so much what is or is not taught in Holy Scripture, not what is or is not according to right reason, but what is the teaching of the English Church. Let us see how far we have gone. Surely so far as this—

(1) Holy Scripture—unless it be mangled or manipulated in an unfair and, indeed, Jesuitical manner—teaches the doctrine of the Real Presence.

(2) The Fathers of the Church, who had special opportunities of knowing the mind of our Lord and His Apostles, with one voice do the same.

(3) The doctrine of the Real Presence and the doctrine of Transubstantiation are by no means the same thing. One does *not* involve the other.

(4) The Church of England, by her appeal to Holy Scripture and to the Fathers, asserts the truth of the Real Presence in accordance with the rest of the

Catholic Church, while she condemns the carnal notions once represented by Transubstantiation, and leaves the philosophical notion—unhappily endorsed by the Latin Church—as a matter quite untouched, and for discussion in the schools, not for a decree as to faith.

Two further points, however, require to be touched upon. The one is perhaps of no grave importance, after all that we have already considered; the other is, however, the *pièce de résistance* of our discussion.

I. The first is, What do the ancient Liturgies say on this solemn subject?

This is, of course, important, for "Lex orandi, Lex credendi" is, as I have said before, a rule of serious and necessary and general application. The early Liturgies are the early Communion Offices of the Church. There are, as you remember, five important families of these. (1) The Liturgy of St. James, *i.e.* of Jerusalem; (2) of St. Thaddeus, *i.e.* of the East; (3) of St. Mark, *i.e.* of Alexandria; (4) of St. John, *i.e.* of Ephesus; (5) of St. Peter, *i.e.* of Rome. As to the dates of these Liturgies; at least they are of great antiquity. That of St. James was *venerable* when St. Cyril's Catechetical Lectures were delivered, *i.e.* in A.D. 340. These Services for Holy Communion, though we cannot of course say that they were *composed* by the Apostles whose names are connected with them, yet, we have every reason to believe, contain their teaching, and are, as they have been called, "the legitimate development" of what *they* handed on regarding the Christian Sacrifice. The words even in many portions of them appear to have been handed on, unchanged, from authors at least of the Apostolic age. The Liturgy of St. James is certainly in the main earlier than A.D. 200. The Liturgy of St. Mark is nearly as old. The Liturgies of St. Basil and St.

Chrysostom really, in greater measure, appear to come from these saints. St. Basil died A.D. 378, St. Chrysostom died A.D. 407.

In the Liturgy of St. Mark we have these words: "We pray and beseech Thee . . . to send down . . . the very Paraclete . . . that He may . . . make this Bread the Body . . . and this Cup the Blood, of our very Lord, and God, and Saviour, and Universal King, Jesus Christ."

In the Liturgy of St. James we have these words: "Send . . . upon these proffered gifts Thy Most Holy Ghost, the Lord and Life-Giving . . . that coming upon them with His holy, and good, and glorious Presence, *He may hallow and make this Bread the Holy Body of Thy Christ . . . and this Cup the Precious Blood of Thy Christ.*"

In the Liturgy of St. Clement are these words: "Send down Thy Holy Spirit . . . *that He may make this Bread the Body of Thy Christ, and this Cup the Blood of Thy Christ.*"[1]

I need not go further. The thing is manifest, and cannot be denied. Men may, if they please, say that *they* know better than those who were much closer to Apostolic times and more likely to know the mind of Apostles; or they may twist and distort the language of St. John and St. Paul to what looks very like non-natural senses; or they may despise the witness of the Communion Services of the early Church, and prefer the modern and more new-fangled theories of Zwingli or of Calvin; but if they will simply and straight-

---

[1] Cf. Dr. Neale, Letter to Bishop of Brechin, "Earnest Plea for the Retention of the Scotch Liturgy," pp. 9, 10, 13; cf. also Dr. Neale in "Ante-Nicene Christian Library" (T. & T. Clark, Edinburgh), Introductory Notice to Early Liturgies, p. 4; also "On the Holy Eucharist" by Lord Forbes, who quotes these.

forwardly study the teachings of the Apostles, and of the ancient Liturgies which came anyhow from near their times, then there is little room for question, as it seems to me, that the Church held *then*, as she holds *now*, the blessed truth of the Real Presence of the Lord's Body and Blood in the Sacrament under the form of Bread and Wine.

IV. And now, my dear friend, we come to the *direct* testimony of the Church of England herself.

As I have reminded you before, if a doctrine is a doctrine of the Catholic Church, it is, of course, and *therefore*, a doctrine of the Church of England. The Church of England is in one sense as old as the Day of Pentecost; and in this island, and with her special mission from God, as that part of the Catholic Church sent to work in and for England and the English people, she is older than the English kingdom or English Parliament, which in fact she formed. It is enough to know her history to be sure, then, *any really Catholic doctrine* is hers. Since, however, the convulsions and troubles of the sixteenth century, since "the quarrel in the family," in consequence of which the Roman and Anglican parts of the Church have been so unhappily standing apart, we are sometimes challenged to show from our translated Office-books—from our present Prayer-book, in fact —that the Church of England is still true to her earlier traditions. This, in regard to *this* doctrine which we are just now discussing, is not, I submit, difficult to do.

I repeat, indeed, that if there were the slightest shade of doubt in her utterances as they stand in our present books, these would be dispelled by reference to early witnesses to whom I have already referred; being part of the Catholic Church, *all* her teachings must be interpreted in a Catholic sense. But there is not, I think, a shade of doubt on the subject.

(1) The Church, first of all, is an *Ecclesia Docens*, a teaching Church. We turn naturally, therefore, first to her Catechism to learn what, on so serious a subject, she teaches the young. Here we are left in no sort of doubt. There is no room for mistake. In order to evade the truth, we must twist and mangle the Church's language; otherwise the Church is clear on the Real Presence.

" *Q.* What is the inward part or thing signified ?

" *A.* The Body and Blood of Christ, which are verily and indeed taken and received by the faithful in the Lord's Supper."

Now, notice the inward part is *not* merely a grace, or a blessing, or a benefit. It is more; it is the Author of grace; it is—no words can be clearer—" the Body and Blood of Christ."

This is direct; this is plain. There is no getting over this, whatever Jesuitry we may be tempted to employ. The Church of England—rightly or wrongly —*that* is not the point now—says the inward part of the Sacrament is "the Body and Blood of Christ." They, then, who teach the Real Presence of His Body and Blood under the form of Bread and Wine are certainly not disloyal members of the Church of England.

Then the Catechism goes on to say, these are "*verily and indeed taken and received* by the faithful in the Lord's Supper."

On this I have first to observe, if "*verily and indeed*" does not mean "in real and actual fact," then language is useless to express ideas, and we may abandon the use of it in despair ! And again I ask you, for plain and straightforward people, how *can* anything be "*taken*" if it isn't there to "take"? How can a thing be "*received*" if it isn't there to "receive"? The thing is absurd. Supposing—*per impossibile*—that our part of the Catholic Church had departed from the Faith, and embraced some of the Zwinglian or Calvinistic theories, which some of her members apparently teach, in the teeth, as it seems to me, of their undertakings to the contrary,—I say, suppose for a moment she *had* abandoned the Faith on this point, and *had* denied what appears to be our Lord's teaching as to His Real Presence, how, I ask, could she have expressed herself in a manner less calculated to convey her real meaning than she has done in the Catechism?

Imagine for a moment that *you* are a framer of the Catechism, and that *you* hold, with some of our opponents, "that the Presence of Christ is in the heart of the true worshipper, *and not, in any sense of the words whatever*, in the hands of the priest,"—I say, supposing *you* held this view, how would you frame that answer? I undertake to say your answer would be something of this sort: "The inward part or thing signified is a grace from God. I have to remember that it is, above all, *not* the Body and Blood of Christ. These are never taken or received, for they are not there, and as, 'in no sense of the words whatever,' are they 'in the hands of the priest,' he can't give what he hasn't got, I can't 'receive' from him what he can't give, therefore he does not give, I do not take, and I can't receive the Body and Blood of Christ."

Now, my dear friend, this would be the true answer in the Catechism if those who deny the Real Presence had had the framing of it. What is the answer? Again I say, she may be right or she may be wrong, but what we want to know is, What does the Church of England teach? This: "The Body and Blood of Christ ... are *verily and indeed taken and received.*" Can there be a more explicit statement of the Real Objective Presence? I say there cannot. If the Real Presence be *not* true, then the less we have to do with the Church of England the better, for certainly she has done her best to teach us that it *is* true. If it *be* true—as it is—no part of the Catholic Church has been more distinct and emphatic in the matter than the Church of England.

But the tortuous resources of opponents to her teaching are almost inexhaustible. I am ashamed to allude to such an absurdity, but it is, I believe, a fact, that there are men who try—if I may so say—to "wriggle out" of the teaching of the Catechism by saying, "Yes, they are received by '*the faithful* in the Lord's Supper,' *i.e.* by those only who are full of faith."

Well, (1) granting this—what is doubtless not meant to be, but which looks very like a—bit of shuffling; well, even so—even by those who are "full of faith"—*that* cannot be "taken and received" which is not *there*. But (2) you know as well as I that "the faithful" is a technical expression for professedly devout Church-people, without inquisitorial investigation as to their exact condition before God. Everybody knows this, and to ride off on a "stick" of this sort shows to what straits people are brought in trying to saddle the Church of England with uncatholic teachings.

The Catechism is explicit. In the Sacrament of Baptism it deals with "the outward sign" and "the inward grace." In the Blessed Sacrament it no longer asks, "What is the inward grace?" but "What is the inward part or thing signified?" The answer is, "The Body and Blood of Christ." *Then* come the question and answer as to the "benefit." "The thing signified" is something distinct from the "grace" or "benefit;" the "Res Sacramenti" from the "Virtus Sacramenti." *All* Church-people who communicate receive the "Res Sacramenti," i.e. *all* "the faithful" receive the Body and Blood of the Lord; but those who receive it "worthily" are the only ones who receive the "Virtus Sacramenti," to the "strengthening and refreshing of their souls;" those who receive "unworthily," *i.e.* without faith and repentance, "eat and drink condemnation." But the reason, in the one case of blessing, in the other, of condemnation, *is* that "the Body and Blood of the Lord" *are there*. You *could not* be guilty of desecrating something that was not there.

There is, it seems to me, no getting out of this teaching of the Catechism; it is plain and exact, and teaches "the Real Presence of the Lord's Body and Blood" under the form of Bread and Wine.

Objections, as you know, have been made to this on the ground that the Twenty-ninth Article contradicts it by denying the reception by the wicked. Now (1) if the Article in question *appears* to deny that unworthy communicants in some sense receive the Body and Blood of the Lord, it must be interpreted according to the Prayer-book. It cannot mean to deny it, even *if* it appears to do so. But (2) the Article, of course, cannot mean this. If it did, it would contradict Holy Scripture. St. Paul, again I remind you, said, "Wherefore whosoever shall eat *this* Bread and drink *this* Cup of the Lord unworthily" (*i.e.* without penitence and earnestness and faith—in fact, in a bad worldly spirit), "shall be guilty of the Body and Blood of the Lord. But let a man examine himself, and so let him eat of that Bread and drink of that Cup. For he that eateth and drinketh unworthily, eateth and drinketh judgment (κρίμα) to himself, not discerning the Lord's Body."

Now, I repeat, if the Bread and Wine be not the Body and Blood of the Lord, it is not possible for an unworthy communicant to be "guilty of the Lord's Body and Blood." If the Sacrament were only the pious rite for which opponents to the Catholic Faith contend, then an unworthy communicant might be ungodly, or sacrilegious, or profane, or irreverent, or neglectful—as he might be by being careless or thoughtless in his prayers—but "guilty of the Lord's Body and Blood" he could not be. The Sacrament has—the Church and surely also the Bible teach—the "outward part," "Bread and Wine;" it has the "inward part," "the Body and Blood of the Lord." This "inward part" is "verily and indeed taken and received by the faithful," *i.e.* by professing believers and Church-people. If any of them receive it "unworthily," they are "guilty of the Body and Blood of the Lord." Why? Because it is there, and *they* receiving it are not in a state ready for so great a gift. If they receive no such gift, of course they *can't* be guilty of receiving it *in a wrong way*.

But further, St. Paul goes on to point the way to avoid such a danger. "Let a man examine himself." The way is the use of real penitential discipline. Past sin is cleansed through repentance. Self-examination, and all that *that* implies, is the way to avoid the danger. The danger, I repeat, then, is real; it is the danger of eating and drinking "judgment," because unworthy communicants do not "discern the Lord's Body." My dear friend, there *could*, I repeat, be no fault in not "discerning" what is not there. St. Chrysostom, commenting on St. Paul's words, says, "Not discerning, not searching, not bearing in mind as he ought, the greatness of the things set before him—not estimating the weight of the gift; for if thou shouldest come to know accurately *Who* it is that lieth before thee, and Who He is Who giveth Himself, . . . thou wilt need no other argument, but this is enough for thee to use all vigilance."[1]

The matter, if you think of it, really comes to this—

(1) Unworthy communicants *either* receive something more than Bread and Wine, *or* they do not.

(2) Well, *if they do not*, they may be acting sinfully, but no more sinfully than in being careless about prayer or any other religious service, and St. Paul's words about being "guilty of the Body and Blood" would be, to say the least of them, singularly inappropriate.

(3) But their sin stands by itself; it is a *much more* serious sin; it is a guilt in regard to the Body and Blood of the Lord.

(4) What *they* receive, then, is something more than Bread and Wine. It is the Body and Blood of Christ.

(5) For you can't, I repeat, have an Absence *and* a Presence. Our Lord is really Absent or He is really Present—one or other. Present He must be, then, for such sin to be possible.

Besides, again St. Paul reminds us that the sin is "not discerning the Lord's Body," *i.e.* not distinguishing or discriminating between it and all other food—μὴ διακρίνων τὸ σῶμα τοῦ Κυρίου. Now, there could be no possible sin in not making such a distinction between the Body of the Lord and all other food if the Body of the Lord be not there!

---

[1] Hom. 28, 1 Cor. v. 29, sec. 2.

Either this is so, or it seems to me language has no meaning, and we may play fast and loose with the clearest statements of Scripture, so that they may be made to mean anything or nothing, according as it suits our taste.

The Article XXIX. *cannot*, then, mean to deny the reception by the wicked; for if so, it would contradict Holy Scripture, to which the Church appeals.

But (3) the Article really is meant to teach a truth *which depends upon the Real Presence*. In the Holy Sacrament is (*a*) the outward sign, (*b*) the thing signified, (*c*) the benefit. There is (*a*) the *signum*, (*b*) the *Res Sacramenti*, (*c*) the *Virtus Sacramenti*.

The penitent, and those who approach in faith and earnestness, receive all three. Unworthy communicants receive *not* the last. They receive, indeed, the Body and Blood of Christ, but not to "the strengthening and refreshing of their souls," but to condemnation. Christ, in fact, is in the Sacrament—in some cases to bless, in others to judge; but Christ is always *really* there.

This is still more clear if we compare Article XXV. with this. There, speaking evidently of the Holy Communion, the Article says—

"In such only as worthily receive the same, they have a wholesome operation; but they that receive them unworthily, purchase to themselves damnation [*i.e.* condemnation], as St. Paul saith."

When, then, Article XXIX. speaks of the wicked being "in no wise partakers of Christ," it means by "partakers of Christ" what Article XXV. means by saying there is "a wholesome effect or operation." That is, Article XXIX. does *not* deny the reception of the wicked, does *not*, therefore, deny the Real Presence; *does* affirm, along with Article XXV., the absence of benefit in such reception, and indeed *the sin* of it, which depends upon the *reality* of the Presence.[1]

So far we have seen that the Catechism and Articles teach this truth.

We turn now to the Communion Service itself, and here again the plain statements of the Prayer-book must be *explained away*, it seems to me, unless we hold this truth.

In the first Exhortation we are reminded that " in that Holy Sacrament " Christ is " our Food." " Spiritual food and sustenance " is the expression. I need hardly repeat that " spiritual " does not mean " unreal," but the reverse. It is not " grace," or " blessing," or " benefit," or good things coming from Christ, which are declared to be given to us, but *Christ Himself*, to be " our Food in that Holy Sacrament."

Again, in the Exhortation just before receiving, the Church tells us how worthy communicants not only receive the *Res Sacramenti*, but also the *Virtus Sacramenti;* not only receive the Body and Blood of the Lord, but receive it *so that* they are united to Him.

If we " receive that Holy Sacrament with a true penitent heart and lively faith, *then* we spiritually eat the Flesh of Christ, and drink His Blood; then we dwell in Christ, and Christ in us; we are one with Christ, and Christ with us." Here is the Real Presence, and—to a worthy communicant—all its benefits. These words are also valuable, for they show that the Church of England, like the rest of the Catholic Church, holds the great discourse in the sixth chapter of St. John's Gospel to refer to the Blessed Sacrament. It is *that* chapter which

---

[1] Cf. Pusey, " Doctrine of the Real Presence in the Church of England," chaps. ii., viii.; also " Theological Defence " of the Bishop of Brechin.

supplies to our Church authority for saying that *then* "we eat the Flesh of Christ, and drink His Blood." The words of this Exhortation are almost a repetition of His own blessed words, "He that eateth My Flesh, and drinketh My Blood, dwelleth in Me, and I in him."[1]

Blessed, surely, it is to know that if, by His help, we bring only "a true penitent heart and lively faith," there He is—not created by our faith, but waiting for us; and we *receive* all that we can desire because of the *reality* of that Presence, by His own power and love.

Again, in the Prayer of Humble Access the same is clearly taught—

"Grant us therefore, gracious Lord, *so* to eat the Flesh of Thy dear Son Jesus Christ, and to drink His Blood, that our sinful bodies may be made clean by His Body, and our souls washed through His most precious Blood, and that we may evermore dwell in Him, and He in us."

Now, here, dear friend, it is clear that if we pray "*so*" to partake of His Body and Blood that the effect may be blessed, it is evident that it *may* be partaken of *in another way*. In either case the presence of the sacred gifts is assumed.

Again, there is no mere general allusion to being saved by faith in Christ's death. Here is a cleansing of body and soul, through contact with the blessed Body and Blood of the Lord, so clearly and strongly put, that one cannot but feel that if such words were *our* words, and not the words of the Prayer-book, opponents would probably rebuke us for what they are so inclined to call "materialism," but what, when

---

[1] Cf. Pusey, *ut supra*.

you avoid confusion of thought, you perceive to be *spiritual fact and reality.*

Again, in the Consecration Prayer, the priest is praying over God's "creatures of Bread and Wine." They are "His creatures" then, and *only so*, at that moment, as not yet consecrated. They remain—these elements—even after consecration, "His creatures in their natural substance;" but now, if they are received "according to our Saviour Jesus Christ's holy institution," *i.e.* if they are consecrated by His own words, and in His own power, then we pray that if we so receive them according to His will and way—what may happen? That we may have a blessing, or some grace given? Not at all; but that we may "become partakers of His most blessed Body and Blood."

The words with which the consecrated elements are given, state the great truth emphatically: "The Body of our Lord Jesus Christ which was given for thee . . . the Blood of our Lord Jesus Christ, which was shed for thee, preserve thy body and soul unto everlasting life." Is it conceivable, my dear friend, that the Church in such a moment could put such words into the mouth of her priests if she meant something totally different? It is not conceivable. It would be to juggle with language on a most sacred subject and at a most sacred moment, if she allowed herself so to speak of the Body and Blood of Christ, when she *really* meant that there was no presence of the Sacred Humanity! The thing would be monstrous, and, in the interest of the morality of language, if the Real Presence be not true, the use of such words is wrong.

And yet these same words, with slight variations, but always as strong, have been used in the Church at all times. The Church has formed them out of our Saviour's promise; and in the Church of England herself, ever since her earliest days, such words have been used. Every one held the Real Presence then. It is trifling with language to pretend that now they are to bear some different meaning, when their meaning has always been well understood, and are to be subjected to non-natural interpretations in order to make them do duty for a meaning the very reverse of what has always been affixed to them, and what they were meant to express.[1]

These words are important, it seems to me, to dwell upon, for they are a *direct* address to *each* communicant. Two or three points about them require to be thought of.

(1) The second clause added *takes nothing away* from this. The second clause enforces a duty. The duty is to be grateful to God for His blessed gift, to be earnest and spiritual in receiving it, and to remember that the Holy Eucharist is *also* a remembrance, and has a commemorative aspect.

(2) With some such words as these, as it has been truly said,[2] in every Liturgy or Communion Service of the Christian Church, the Body and Blood of Christ have been given by the priest to the communicants. "With such words of blessing the consecrated elements were delivered to every communicant in every church in our land. What these words meant during nine centuries, what they meant in the reign of Henry VIII., *that* they must still have meant, when, at the very beginning of Edward VI.'s reign, the old words of benediction sounded to us again in our own tongue." Every one knew what they meant. The same they meant, of course, in Edward's First Book. The same

[1] Cf. Pusey, *ut supra*.   [2] Pusey, *ut supra*.

they mean now. They meant then, and now they mean, that the priest does not give the communicant common bread and common wine, but, in giving the consecrated bread and consecrated wine, he gives the Very True Body and Blood of the Lord Jesus Christ, which He took of the Virgin Mary, not in a carnal manner, but in a mystery according to the laws of a spiritual Body, but *really* and certainly "under the form of Bread and Wine."[1]

(3) So completely was it known that these words taught the Real Presence, that when evil influences of heresy were at work they were dropped out. And no more striking proof can be given of the deliberate purpose of our Reformers to maintain the doctrine than their deliberate reintroduction of these words. To deny the Real Objective Presence is really, it seems to me, to violate "the principles of the Reformation" in the English Church.

The quantity and weight of testimony in this matter is so great, that it would be out of the question to dwell on it all; but these further considerations, I think, ought to be remembered before I close this part of our subject. Nothing, perhaps, more clearly expresses the Catholic doctrine on the subject as taught in Scripture, as held by the undivided Church, and as witnessed to by the Church of England, than the phrase used at the end of the First Book of the Homilies—" of the due receiving of His Blessed Body and Blood under the form of Bread and Wine." This precisely expresses the doctrine of the Real Presence as taught by the Church, *apart from* and to be distinguished from that 'opinion of the schools," as Archbishop Bramhall called

[1] Pusey, "Doctrine of the Real Presence," pp. 178, 179.

P

it, as to the *manner* of the Presence, which is called Transubstantiation. I repeat, that to teach the Real Presence is to teach a Scriptural doctrine as our Church interprets Scripture, and a Catholic doctrine, and one authorized and endorsed by the Church of England; while to teach Transubstantiation is to teach a special *mode* of the Presence, which has no authority, except the authority in later times of the Latin section of the Catholic Church.

Those who oppose Catholic doctrine have, oddly enough, argued against this phrase of the Homilies, as if it had no authority, and I believe that some of them have gone so far as to say that the phrase was *withdrawn*. This, of course, is not the fact. It is worth while, in this connection, to quote the learned words of the late Sir Robert Phillimore, in his judgment delivered as official Principal of the Arches Court of Canterbury, in the celebrated case of Sheppard *v.* Bennett. The words of the learned judge are as follows: "This form of expression has been used in our formularies as applicable to the substances of Bread and Wine remaining unchanged. They were so used in the Articles of 1536, and in the 'Institution of a Christian Man' in 1537. In the Six Articles a direct statement of Transubstantiation took their place. They do not appear in the 'Necessary Erudition' of 1543. After a lapse of four years, they reappear under the auspices of Cranmer and other bishops at the end of the First Book of the Homilies, where it is said 'Hereafter shall follow sermons of the Nativity, Passion, Resurrection, and Ascension of our Saviour Christ; of the due receiving of His Blessed Body and Blood under the form of Bread and Wine.' And it is not unimportant to observe that, early in the reign of Elizabeth, the bishops advert to this statement; for, in their title to the Second Book of the Homilies, they speak 'of such matters as were promised *and entituled* in the former Book of Homilies.' And in Queen Elizabeth's Primer of 1559, we find the prayer which begins, ' Our Saviour and Redeemer, Jesus Christ, Which in Thy last Supper with Thine Apostles didst deliver Thy Blessed Body and Blood under the form of Bread and Wine.' The First Book of Homilies has undergone two revisions, and the statement 'under the form of Bread and Wine' *remains unchanged up to the present time.*"[1] The judge then goes on to point out that pretty much the same form of expression had been used by Ratramnus, who is quoted with approval by Bishop Burnett. He reminds us also that under the inhuman statute enforced in the reigns of Henry IV. and Henry V., the followers of Wickliffe and the Lollards suffered for teaching this very doctrine, "the Sacrament of Christ's Flesh and His Blood in form of Bread and Wine," and refusing to acknowledge that after the words of Consecration, material bread and wine no longer existed. Sir John Oldcastle, Lord Cobham, suffered in 1414 for asserting the very same doctrine of the Real Presence, but not believing in Transubstantiation. The learned judge also reminds us that in the First of the Six Articles *which went back to Transubstantiation*, this expression had to be varied, and the statement was, "that in the Eucharist is really present the *natural* Body of Christ *under the forms* and *without the substance* of bread and wine." This is a plain enough evidence that the phrase of the Homilies does *not* teach Transubstantiation, but *does* teach the Real Presence. Ridley, he reminds us, was certainly in accord with, and would have adopted

[1] Judgment, p. 71 [The italics are mine.—W. J. K. L.]

the language of, Ratramnus, and have induced Cranmer to do so.

It is well known, also, that the Confession of Augsburg teaches the same, and uses the very same expression; and it is worth remembering that at the time the Jerusalem bishopric was formed, the instructions to the English bishop sent from Lambeth and London were, to ordain Prussian subjects who had subscribed *the Confession of Augsburg* as well as the Thirty-Nine Articles of the English Church. There can be no doubt, then, I submit, that the expression, "the Body and Blood of the Lord under the form of Bread and Wine," as it is a statement of the doctrine of the Real Presence, and *not* of Transubstantiation, so it expresses the mind of the English Church.[1]

Again, it is worth while to call attention to the fact that no one who dwells upon this Blessed Mystery desires to use such language as that "the elements *locally* contain in themselves the Presence of Christ's Body and Blood." Attention has been drawn recently to two passages which it is worth while to quote in this connection.[2]

(1) "Christ is present in the Sacrament only in substance, and substance does not require or imply the occupation of place, but if place is excluded from the idea of the Sacramental Presence, therefore division or distance from heaven is excluded also; for distance implies a measurable interval, and such there cannot be except between places. Moreover, if the idea of distance is excluded, therefore is the idea of motion. Our Lord, then, neither descends from heaven upon our altars, nor moves when carried in procession. The visible species

---

[1] Judgment, pp. 72, 73.
[2] By Canon Bodington, *Guardian*, Oct. 18, 1893.

change their position, but He does not move. He is in the Holy Eucharist after the manner of the spirit, *we do not know how;* we have not parallel to the 'how' in our experience. We can only say that He is present, not according to the natural manner of bodies, but sacramentally. His Presence is substantial, spirit-wise, sacramental, an *absolute mystery.* Not against reason, however, but against imagination, and must be received by faith." [1]

And (2) "the opinion of those . . . seems to be most safe and most right who think—nay, who most firmly believe—that the Body and Blood of Christ is *truly, really, and substantially* present, and taken in the Eucharist, but in a way which is *incomprehensible to the human understanding,* and much more beyond the power of man to express, which is known to God alone, and not revealed to us in Scripture." [2]

The fact is, my dear friend, that in speaking of the Real Presence we are dealing with a great and solemn Mystery; that is, we are dealing with a Divine Fact, but a Fact partly veiled from us, and of the *manner or mode* of which we know nothing at all. Unfortunately for the peace of Christendom, the Roman Church undertook to define the manner or mode, and called it Transubstantiation. Unfortunately, various Protestant teachers not only refuse to believe in this *mode,* but actually deny the *fact.* Some of them, like the extreme Zwinglians, followed by a number of Protestant Dissenters in this country, make the Sacrament into a mere sign of the love that Christian people ought to have for one another. With them the nature of a

---

[1] "Via Media," vol. ii.
[2] Bishop Forbes, "Considerat. Modest. de Eucharist," lib. iii.

sacrament is destroyed, for there is no *inward part* at all, and it becomes a mere ceremony of questionable appropriateness, in the use of which persons, if devout, may expect some blessing from God, just as they might expect it from any other religious act devoutly fulfilled. Others rise a step higher, and seem to believe in some kind of presence or gift, given to persons who *receive* the Sacrament devoutly and with faith. According to these, there is no sort of Presence of Christ *extra usum*. According to them, whatever Presence there is, is the consequence of *their* faith.

All such views, I submit, are inconsistent, as we have seen, with the teaching of Scripture as our Church interprets it, with the Faith of the early Church, and therefore with the teachings of the Church of England. The important point to remember is, that the *consecration of the elements* by a properly ordained priest, *not* the faith of the receiver, *nor* the fact of his receiving, is the characteristic circumstance upon which the validity of the Sacrament, and the reality of the Divine, mysterious, and blessed Presence, depends. Think, my dear friend, as I draw to a close of this part of our subject, of the words of St. Augustine: "Our Bread and our Cup is not any one" (that is, any specimen of such food in its ordinary condition), . . . "but it is a mystical one, *which is produced by a fixed consecration*, and does not come by growth. That which is not produced in this way" (that is, by consecration), "though it may be bread and a cup, is a means of bodily refreshment, not a Sacrament of religion."[1]

Think, again, of the words of St. Ambrose: "Before the blessing of the sacred words, another species is named; after consecration, the *Body* is signified. Before

---

[1] "Contra. Faustum," xx. 13.

consecration, it is called a different thing; after consecration, it is called Blood."[1] Or, again, of his words as follows: "Sacraments, by the mystery of holy Prayer" (that is, by consecration) "are transfigured into the Flesh and Blood."[2] Think, again, of the strength of belief in the Real Objective Presence shown in the many statements of our own great divines. It would weary you, and require too much space, to quote one-tenth of such utterances; but think of one, as an instance, from Sherlock's "Practical Christian"—

"Grant, Holy Jesus, that as I have now received in faith Thy precious Body and Blood, veiled under the species of Bread and Wine, I may hereafter behold Thy Blessed Face revealed in Heaven."[3]

"He discerns not this Body of our Lord, who sees not with the eye of faith *Christ really present under the species of Bread and Wine,* though he conceive not the manner thereof . . . not curiously questioning, much less pragmatically defining, the way and manner of His Presence, as being deeply mysterious and inconceivable."

"These old verses, expressing the Faith of the wisest of our first Reformers, may satisfy every modest, humble, sober-minded, good Christian, in this great Mystery of godliness—

"'It was the Lord that spake it,
He took the bread and brake it;
And what His Word did make it,
So I believe and take it.'

*   *   *   *   *

"And he that receives Christ's Holy Body and Blood into his soul, not first emptied of all his sins by holy faith, and all the sacred offices of true repentance, doth

---

[1] "De iis qui initiantur Myst.," c. xi.
[2] "De Fide," iv. 10, n. 124, t. ii. 544.
[3] "Practical Christian," part ii., chap. x.

with Judas betray His Master into the hands of His enemies—even those very enemies which crucified Him; for those were our sins. And therefore it is said of such unworthy enemies that they are guilty of the Body and Blood of Christ."[1]

To draw to a close, then. It is a comfort, of course, to remember that persons, who unhappily deny the Catholic doctrine of the Real Presence, often, in their heart of hearts, are *holding* what in words they deny. They really mean—we may well believe—to deny some carnal or material notion which they imagine to be implied in the Catholic doctrine. It is a comfort to think how these devout persons approach the Sacrament with loving faith, and receive the inestimable blessing of that Divine Presence, which in words and through misunderstanding they would deny. Still, there is always some loss, we cannot but feel, in the want of a clear view of truth where it may be had. Once let us believe the Lord's own words, the teaching of His Apostles, and the voice of His Church, we no longer are driven to juggling with language, and torturing our minds and spirits by such notions as those of Zwinglianism or Virtualism, which perplex us by using the sacred words that assert a Real Presence, while yet they practically insist upon a Real Absence. Once hold the majestic doctrine of the Catholic Church, and you have all that you can need. For think of its simplicity and consolation. Simplicity—for what the Lord says, *that* we know He does—*how* He does it we do not know, nor do we care to inquire; consolation—for think of the joy in loneliness, in sorrow, in the trials of absence, in the loss of friends, to find ourselves before the Holy

---

[1] "Practical Christian," part ii., chap. i., quoted by Phillimore, Judgment, p. 75.

Sacrament in the very Presence of Divine Compassion, and in closest touch with Him, Who is there, not by virtue of any faith or feeling of ours, but in fulfilment of His own promise, and by virtue of His own power. *Reality*, as I have ventured to say before, is a watchword of the Faith. It is too sad to think how Christian men have struggled over this awful and blessed Mystery; but surely many of their struggles and disagreements would pass away, if they only got the length of feeling and acknowledging that however mysterious and awful and inexplicable this great Mystery of the Holy Sacrament may be, it is—because Christ is—as I have said, quite apart from our faith or feelings, quite apart from explanations *how*—a most certain, a most blessed Reality.

II.

THE EUCHARISTIC SACRIFICE.

Closely connected with the doctrine of the Real Presence, you will remember, my dear friend, is the doctrine of the Eucharistic Sacrifice. In endeavouring to discover what is meant by "sacerdotalism" in a bad sense, I find that there seems to be included under that title a belief in the "Sacrifice of the Altar." Opponents of Catholic doctrine state that the Church of England "teaches with absolute precision that the Lord's Supper is not a sacrifice; that the Lord's Table is not an altar."[1] This statement is, I think, about as wide of the truth as it is possible to imagine. A great deal which relates to this question is involved in the question of the priesthood, which must be treated of by-and-by.

[1] *Contemporary Review*, July, 1893, p. 66.

Something, however, ought to be said here and now on the doctrine of the Sacrifice itself. My contention is that the Church of England teaches that the Eucharist is in a true sense a Sacrifice, and that if such teaching involves "sacerdotalism," then to be true to the teaching of the Church of England is to be a "sacerdotalist."

Well, there are two remarks to be made on the threshold of such a subject—

(1) Whilst the Holy Eucharist may be said to have two aspects—the one that of *Communion*, i.e. the *receiving* the Body and Blood of the Lord for the health of the soul, the other that of *sacrifice*, i.e. the *showing forth* before God the Passion of Christ, and thereby the pleading of the merits of that Passion—it is quite probably true that the former aspect is more prominently put forward in our Prayer-book than the latter. The reason is twofold : (*a*) that the doctrine of the Real Presence, which is, as we have seen, emphatically taught, *involves* the Sacrifice ; and (*b*) at the time of the Reformation, *Communion* having been somewhat neglected, it seems to have been felt desirable to lay great stress upon it.

(2) Another point which ought to be remembered, I think, is this. The denial of the truth of this doctrine in some quarters seems to arise from a misunderstanding. Opponents have often imagined *either* that it is meant that the sacrifice of the Cross was insufficient, and therefore had to be supplemented, *or* that it is repeated, *or* that something is substituted for it. Of course this is an entire misconception.

There is but one sacrifice for ever for the sins of the whole world, and that is the sacrifice of Jesus Christ, true God and true Man, upon the cross. Just, however, as there were numberless sacrifices ordained by God in the earlier dispensation, which are called "sacrifices" because they were types and shadows, or *foretellings*, of the one great Sacrifice; so in the New Dispensation there is the "perpetual memorial of His Death and Passion," as the commemoration *or showing forth before God* of the one Sacrifice.

What the Catholic doctrine means is in fact this— that, as we have seen, *by virtue of consecration*, there is the real, true, but mysterious, sacramental, and invisible Presence of the Body and Blood of the Lord on the altars of the Church; so consequently we have something besides our prayers to present to the Father— something beyond and out of ourselves, the Body and Blood of His Son, which were broken and shed for us, and which He in His words, "Do this in remembrance of Me," or, as they mean, "offer this for a memorial of Me," taught us to present and plead to the Father. The Catholic doctrine is, further, that this sacrifice is not a separate one from that of the Cross; it is the same substantially (that is, *in respect to its substance*, viz. the Body and Blood of Christ) as that of the Cross. *The manner* of the offering is different. The offering of the Cross was in blood-shedding and sorrow and death. The offering of the Altar is sacramentally and in mystery. But in the two cases *there is an essential identity*, for there is the offering of the Body and Blood of the Lord.

What is meant, then, is, that as our Lord offered Himself once for all in the great sacrifice of Calvary, and, as bearing His human nature with Him in heaven, He by His very Presence there "ever liveth to make intercession for us," by ever showing forth and pleading the merits of His Passion; so His Church on earth, which is united to Him as the body to the head, and in which He is ever working, is doing precisely the same. She is doing on earth—or rather He, by her, is doing—that which He does in heaven.

This majestic doctrine is so stately and so wonderful, and so falls in with the analogy of faith, and with the highest yearnings and needs of man, that when once it is taken hold of, it seems to me we cannot but feel that it could not be an invention, it must be a revelation; and far from derogating from the merits of the Passion, it presents before our minds a vivid picture of the splendour and extent of those merits, and we see before our mind the Great High Priest, uniting with Himself all His children, and *showing forth* that one sacrifice once offered, which is a "sufficient sacrifice, propitiation, and satisfaction for the sins of the whole world."

As I have said, such a doctrine is so closely connected with that of the priesthood, which we shall have presently to consider, that there are only a few points in relation to it which need be touched upon now.

1. It ought never to be forgotten, surely, that in all times sacrifice is the great act of religion. It is by it that man offers something to God in a solemn manner, and freely, in token that he recognizes the duty of obedience, and his place as a creature, and his duty of thanksgiving, and the necessity of penitence, and his desire to make propitiation for sin towards his God. We read of this in the very opening teachings of the Bible, and before the Mosaic Law was given. Sacrifices then consisted, for the most part, either of animals who were slaughtered and their bodies burnt on the altar, or of the fruits of the earth, such as corn and wine. Man, as we know, had an instinctive feeling, reinforced by revelation, that in his fallen state he was unfit to appear before the All-Holy God; he had also an instinctive sense that it was

his duty to offer some acts of acknowledgment that all things come from God, and acts of thanksgiving for all God's gifts. Hence these two classes of sacrifices. There can be no doubt, to those who believe in the Bible, that whether or not sacrifices were first revealed from God as a duty, they were certainly sanctioned by Him under the Mosaic Law. And here I cannot do better than quote words which put this part of the subject excellently, and with which you are probably not unacquainted—

"The chief public sacrifices under the Law were: (*a*) The *Passover*. This was a lamb slain, roasted, and solemnly eaten, partly in memory of the deliverance by the children of Israel from Egypt, and partly in memory of the destroying angel passing over the houses which had the lamb's blood on the door-post (Exod. xii. 27). (*b*) The *burnt offering*, presented daily in the temple, morning and evening, consisting of two lambs, with flour, oil, and wine (Exod. xxix. 38–42), and with increased amounts on sabbaths and festivals. (*c*) The *meat offering*—not of flesh, but of bread or flour—sometimes along with the burnt offering (Exod. xxix. 38–42), and sometimes by itself, as the shewbread, which consisted of twelve cakes placed on a table in the tabernacle, and changed by the priests every sabbath day (Lev. xxiv. 5, 8); and as the firstfruits (Lev. xxiii. 10-20; Numb. xv. 20; Deut. xxvi. 1-11). (*d*) *Sin offerings*, on the chief festivals (Numb. xxviii. and xxix.), and on the great Day of Atonement (Lev. xvi.). (*e*) *Incense*, sometimes offered by itself (Exod. xxx. 7, 8), but more generally in union with other sacrifices. Besides all these, there were private offerings, made by the people separately, as thanksgivings, or as acts of penitence, to obtain pardon for sin."[1]

---

[1] Littledale, tract. "The Christian Sacrifice," p. 1, v.

In speaking of the great Day of Atonement, the same writer goes on—

"Only the High Priest could perform it, and its most solemn portion took place in the Holy of Holies, within the veil. The High Priest, dressed in white, brought a bullock as a sin offering for himself, and two goats and a ram for the people, to the door of the tabernacle, where lots were cast to find which goat should be slain, and which should be the scapegoat.

"Then he killed the bullock in the Holy Place, and, taking a smoking censer and some of the blood within the veil, he sprinkled the blood on the mercy-seat. He returned to the Holy Place, slew the goat, and passed once more to the Holy of Holies, doing as before. Then he came out to hallow the Holy Place, and made atonement for the sins of the people, and for the pollutions of the temple. Next, he laid his hands on the scapegoat's head, confessed the sins of the people over it, and gave the animal in charge to a man to carry into the wilderness. Finally, he put on his priestly garments, and came out to offer the burnt offering in the presence of the people.

"In Lev. viii. the order and rank of the sacrifices is clearly laid down. First must come the sin offering. Till that, the chief act of expiation and penitence, is ended; the burnt offering, which denotes self-surrender to God, cannot be offered; far less the peace offering, or thanksgiving, which is, as it were, only a part of the burnt offering. This teaches us that first we need to be cleansed from our guilt; then that we are to be obedient servants of God, after He has made us fit to stand before Him; lastly, that by this obedience we shall obtain the peace of God, and thank Him for ever."[1]

[1] Ibid. p. 2, vi., vii.

Now, an important thing to remember is—to quote the same writer further—that "the sacrifices of the Law were only shadows of a better oblation yet to come. They had no value in themselves and by themselves, but drew all their strength from it, just as the sky at early dawn has its light from the yet unrisen sun. That better oblation, the only one that ever has been, ever can be, offered to take away sin, is the crucifixion of our Lord Jesus Christ (Heb. x. 12)."[1]

Now, the belief of the Christian Church has always been, as indeed the analogy of faith would suggest, that as the Jews were enabled to offer *a foretaste* of the great Sacrifice, so there must be some Christian *continuance* of it, otherwise we Christians would be worse off than Jews. If our Eucharist is only a memorial ceremony—strangely inappropriate it would seem in that case—if it is only bread and wine, if there is no Real Presence of the Divine Victim and no real showing forth before God of His death, then we are in a land of shadows indeed, and we have not reached the "good things to come," and the covenant between God and man, instead of being drawn close by the Atonement, would appear to a great extent to have been broken off.

We *have* such a means provided, my dear friend, as we very well know, in the sacrifice of the Altar, and this is (1) foretold in prophecy; (2) taught in the New Testament; (3) witnessed to by the Service-books and the great writers of the Early Church; (4) sanctioned by the formularies of the Church of England, and proclaimed by her great divines.

To touch on these points—without going deeply into them, as that involves much which, as I have said,

[1] Ibid. p. 2, viii., ix.

we shall have to treat of in speaking of the priesthood—will be my duty now. And, again, I must repeat that the *real* question before us is not so much whether the doctrine be true or not—though incidentally I hope to show that it is true—but whether or not the Church of England, in her appeal to Holy Scripture, in her appeal to the early Church, in the statements of her formularies, and by the witness of her divines, teaches the doctrine. If she does, as I think I can show she unquestionably does, then those who teach it—sacerdotalists or not—are her loyal children.

(1) As to prophecy, Isaiah foretells that there shall be a Church of the Gentiles, and that from the Gentiles should be taken Priests and Levites. The whole idea is the appointment of an order of ministers consecrated and set apart to offer a real sacrifice.[1]

The most remarkable prophecy of all, however, is that which immediately precedes and ushers in the New Dispensation. If this prophecy refers—as the great teachers of the Church have believed that it does—to the Eucharistic Sacrifice, it is at least intelligible. If its reference to it is denied, then at least *this* must be said—it will have to be carefully *explained away*. These are the words of the prophet: "For from the rising of the sun even unto the going down of the same My Name shall be great among the Gentiles; and in every place incense shall be offered unto My Name, and a pure offering: for My Name shall be great among the heathen, saith the Lord of hosts."[2]

Now, here, "the sacrifice which should be offered is designated by the special name of *meal offering*." It was not to be accepted from the Jews, but from the Gentiles. "It was a special sacrifice, offered by itself

[1] Isa. lxvi. 21.   [2] Mal. i. 11.

as an unbloody sacrifice, or together with the bloody sacrifice. . . . In the daily sacrifice it was offered morning and evening with the lamb; as *this* was typical of the precious blood-shedding of the *Lamb without spot* upon the Cross, so was the *meal offering* which accompanied it of the Holy Eucharist."

The early Church—to which the Church of England makes her appeal—saw the force of the contrast. They saw that the bloody sacrifices, which came to an end, foretold the one "full, perfect, and sufficient sacrifice, oblation, and satisfaction" which was made on the Cross; and so the *meal offering*, to be offered with incense, foretold the sacrifice of the Altar.

St. Justin Martyr was converted probably within thirty years of the death of St. John. He would be likely to know. What does he say on this verse? This: "God has, therefore, beforehand declared, that all who through this name offer those sacrifices, which Jesus, Who is the Christ, commanded to be offered, *that is to say, in the Eucharist of the Bread and of the Cup*, which are offered in every part of the world by us Christians, are well pleasing to Him."

St. Irenæus in the same century says, "He took that which is part of the creation, viz. bread, and gave thanks, saying, '*This is My Body.*' And the cup likewise, which is of the creation which appertains unto us, He professed to be His own Blood, *and taught men the new oblation of the New Testament.*"

Eusebius says, "The truth bears witness to the prophetic Word. . . . We sacrifice also the memory of that great Sacrifice, *performing it according to the Mysteries which have been transmitted by Him.*"

In the Liturgy of St. Mark it is quoted as finding its fulfilment "in the reasonable and unbloody sacrifice, which all nations offer to thee, O Lord, from the rising of the sun to the setting thereof." [1]

It can only be, I contend, by juggling with words, and emptying them of their meaning—in the way in which Protestant controversialists sometimes do—it can only be by ignoring the testimony of the early Church, that such a "sure Word of prophecy" can—according to the principles of the Church of England—be made to refer to anything but the Eucharistic Sacrifice.

(2) And as prophecy foretold, so the New Testament aught.

Our Lord Himself, in the Sermon on the Mount, alludes to "the Altar," to which, if the gift is to be brought, first of all care is to be taken to be "in charity." His reference can scarcely be *merely* to the Old Law—*that* was passing away; *He* was introducing a New Kingdom. If He refers to the *reality of heart* needed for the old worship, He cannot mean that it is *only* for that. If in the new worship there was to be *no altar*, it is difficult to imagine that He would not there and then have emphasized so great a difference.

The writer of the Epistle to the Hebrews tells us that "we have an altar, whereof *they have no right to eat* which serve the tabernacle." Opponents of Catholic doctrine interpret this solely of the act of sacrifice on

---

[1] Cf. Dr. Pusey on the Minor Prophets, *in loc.*; cf. also Thorndike (one of the Royal Commissioners at the Savoy Conference), who says, "In like manner it may be granted that the words of the Prophet Malachi ... is a prophecy of the institution of this Sacrament."—Chambers's "Thorndike on the Eucharist," p. 66. Grabe also says: "With Irenæus, Justin, Tertullian, Cyprian, Chrysostom, and a vast number of Fathers ... have interpreted this plan of the Sacrifice of the Body and Blood of Christ in the Eucharist."—"In Irenæus," lib. iv. p. 323.

Calvary. The expression "*no right to eat*" gains a meaning, otherwise wanting, if we view such a statement in the light of the Eucharistic oblation. Christ *is*, Scripture tells us—not *was*—"the Propitiation for our sins;" it tells us that Christians are "a royal priesthood;" it tells us that "Christ *is* "—not *was*—"a Priest for ever after the order of Melchizedek." "Therefore," it is justly said, "in some mysterious way His sacrifice is going on, though His pains and death are over."[1] Light is thrown upon this at once if we believe in the Eucharistic oblation. In it there is Priest and Altar and Sacrifice.

(3) The same truth is witnessed to by the early Communion Services (or Liturgies, as they are called) of the early Church. The testimony of these, I repeat, is important, for *the appeal* of the Church of England is to the early Church. What do they say?

Well, from out of their vast mass of evidence the following quotations will suffice:—

(*a*) From the Liturgy of St. Mark, which is nearly coeval with that of St. James, *i.e.* of earlier date than A.D. 200 : " Rendering thanks to Thee with Himself " (*i.e.* one Lord and God, and Saviour Jesus Christ), " we offer to Thee this reasonable and unbloody sacrifice, which all nations offer unto Thee, O Lord, from the rising of the sun until the going down of the same." And then come the words of Consecration : " For the Lord Himself, and our God and universal King Jesus Christ, in the night wherein," etc.

(*b*) From the Liturgy of St. James, certainly earlier than A.D. 200, which speaks as follows after the Consecration: " We, therefore also, sinners, remembering His life-giving Passion, His salutary cross, His Death, and

---

[1] Littledale, *ut supra*, p. 3, xii.

Resurrection from the dead on the third day, His Ascension into Heaven, and sitting on the Right Hand of Thee, His God and Father, and His glorious and terrible coming again, when He shall come with glory to judge the quick and the dead, and to render unto every man according to his works, *offer to Thee, O Lord, this tremendous and unbloody sacrifice,*" etc.

(c) From the Liturgy of St. Chrysostom: "In behalf of all and for all, we offer Thee Thine own of Thine own. . . . Moreover, we offer unto Thee this reasonable and unbloody sacrifice."

In this connection it is well to recall the fact that in the Institution of the Holy Sacrament *terms of sacrifice* are employed.

(1) The word translated "do"—the Greek ποιεῖτε—might be translated "sacrifice" or "offer." In Exod. xxix. 36-39 there occurs four times in our translation the word "offer." This is *the same word* which our Lord used in the Institution of the Sacrament, which is there translated "do." So it is in Lev. vi. 22, and ix. 7. *The same word*, again, is translated "sacrifice" in Exod. x. 25. Again, the same word is used constantly of the Passover (Numb. ix. 2; Deut. xvi. 1, 4; 2 Kings xxiii. 21; 2 Chron. xxv. 1, 2), and is translated "keep." The translation might have been, " Do the Passover," or, " Sacrifice the Passover." The words " Do this " may be, therefore, rightly translated, " Offer this," or, " Sacrifice this."

(2) St. Luke and St. Paul use the word translated "remembrance" (ἀνάμνησις), which is also *a term of sacrifice*. It corresponds to another word, μνημόσυνον. The one is an active form, the other a passive form. The one might be translated, perhaps, "commemoration," the other "memorial." By offering the "memorial" (*i.e.*

the μνημόσυνον) the commemoration (*i.e.* the ἀνάμνησις) was made.

(3) The term διαθήκη, *i.e.* "covenant" or "testament," is connected with this word in a religious sense in the Bible. A "covenant" (διαθήκη) was concluded by a visible instrument, which thus became a μνημόσυνον, or "memorial," *i.e.* a thing which could be pleaded or offered up to God, that He might "remember" the "covenant" and show mercy; and this was always an awe-inspiring thing. The "bow in the cloud" was the sign of the covenant with Noah, and so became a μνημόσυνον, or "memorial," before God. In the Mosaic "Covenant" the priest made an ἀνάμνησις—a "commemoration"—by the Blood of the Sacrifice, and this then became a μνημόσυνον, or "reminder," or "memorial," before God.

Now, in Christianity there is a "New Covenant," a "New Testament." The Blood of Christ is the instrument through which the "covenant" is made good. It is that Holy Thing on which God ὄψεται τοῦ μνησθῆναι, "will look to be reminded," and to give the benefits of the Christian Covenant.[1]

In the Institution of the Holy Eucharist we have the three terms, "Covenant" (διαθήκη), "Blood," "Memorial," together, *and* the sacrificial word "do," or "offer."

And then the whole runs thus: "The same night that He was betrayed, He took bread, and when He had given thanks (εὐχαριστήσας, made His Eucharist), He brake it, and said, This is My Body which is broken (κλώμενον) for you. Make this oblation (or 'offer this,' or 'sacrifice this,' or 'do this,') for that Memorial which peculiarly and alone can be Mine (εἰς τὴν ἐμὴν ἀνάμνησιν, *not* εἰς ἐμοῦ ἀνάμνησιν). After the same manner also (He

[1] Cf. "The Holy Eucharist," Lord Forbes, pp. 17, 18.

took) the cup, when He had supped, saying, This Cup is the New Testament in My Blood (the New Covenant made good through the instrument of My Blood). Make this oblation (or 'offer this,' or 'sacrifice this,' or 'do this') as oft as ye drink it for that Memorial which peculiarly and alone can be Mine (εἰς τὴν ἐμὴν ἀνάμνησιν)."

These solemn words, it has been truly said, "have an obvious reference to the Memorials of the Old Law, or Covenant, and our Blessed Lord seems to say, 'As God concluded a covenant with Moses through sacrifice . . . so God concludes a New Covenant through My sacrifice: My Body, My Blood, slain in sacrifice—this is the Holy Instrument of that Covenant, and it is that which is to be offered to God, for that Memorial which alone can be properly Mine.'"[1]

Read in this way, there is a deep and consistent meaning in all. The Old and New Covenants interpret each other, and are knit together. Holy Scripture has light thrown upon it, and is clear where all is cloudy by other interpretations. St. Paul has a real meaning when he adds that thus "ye do show or proclaim the Lord's death till He come;" and the Ancient Communion Services or Liturgies of the Church are seen to be in exact conformity with Holy Scripture.

(4) Here, then, is the Faith of Scripture as the Church has interpreted it and of the Ancient Church as to what St. Augustine calls "the Sacrifice of our Ransom." Has the Church of England denied and abandoned this? Is anything so terribly true as the saddening statement that "she teaches with absolute precision that the Lord's Supper is not a sacrifice"?

If such a statement were true, it would be sad

---

[1] Cf. "Theological Defence," Bishop of Brechin, pp. 75-80.

indeed. The worst that enemies have said of the Church—our Mother—would then be realized. She would have been unfaithful to her trust, unfaithful to her Lord, untrue to the Bible, untrue to the teaching of the Ancient Church. Our hearts might well sink within us were there any colouring for so dreadful a charge.

There is *no* truth in such a charge. We know, dear friend, that, amid all her sorrows, our part of the Catholic Church has been true in her witness to the Eucharistic Sacrifice.

Let us grant that many efforts were made by the new-fangled teachings of foreign heresies in the sixteenth century to silence her witness to this truth. A convulsion like that of "the Reformation," partly bad and partly good, could not well be passed through without its mark for evil and for good being left behind.

Let us grant that, as "the Churches of Jerusalem, Alexandria, and Antioch, and . . . Rome"[1] have erred, so also the Church of England, we may humbly believe, has not been *absolutely* immaculate, or always done the best thing in the world. This is a statement consistent, it seems to me, with truth and modesty.

Let us further remember, as I have already said, that the desire to restore—and the *right* desire to restore—*communion* to its proper place, may have induced the Church of England not to bring forward the idea of the sacrifice as prominently as Scripture and the early Church would seem to suggest.

Let us grant that it is possible to believe that some of the alterations in our Communion Office made it apparently less scriptural, and are to be deplored.

[1] Article XIX.

Grant all this to the utmost, and still the Church clearly, I submit, teaches "the truth as it is in Jesus," on this solemn subject; still she teaches "the Eucharistic Sacrifice;" still she teaches us to make "the great Oblation;" still she *shows before God* the death of Christ "till He come;" still she is true to the Catholic Faith in this matter; still the above statement of opponents is as contrary to fact as it well can be.

Now (1) remember the steady appeal of our Church to Holy Scripture, and remember what we have seen to be the voice of prophecy, and of the New Testament; (2) remember her appeal to the Ancient Church, and recall what we have said from the Fathers and the Liturgies, and recollect that—it is scarcely an exaggeration to say—a volume might be filled with similar testimony.

But then comes the question, Having made the appeal, has she been true to it? If "she teaches with absolute precision that the Lord's Supper is not a sacrifice," then she has, indeed, I acknowledge, been false to that appeal; but she teaches—as I now proceed shortly to show—nothing of the kind.

(*a*) In considering briefly the direct teaching of our formularies, naturally and rightly we *first* go to the Catechism.

The teaching of the Catholic Church is—that *one* great object of the Sacrament is to continually present before the Father the offering of the Precious Body and Blood of Christ, *really* present in a mysterious and *sacramental* manner "under the form of Bread and Wine;" and to plead thus the merits of His atoning sacrifice offered—in blood and sorrow—once for all upon the Cross, and so to apply effectually and with ever-renewed power the saving and life-giving virtues of that sacrifice,

—this is the meaning, I repeat, of the sacrifice of the Altar.

Well, what does the Catechism say? What does the Church of England teach her children?

"*Q.* Why was the Sacrament of the Lord's Supper ordained?

"*A.* For the continual remembrance of the sacrifice of the death of Christ."

I have already drawn your attention to the meaning of the word "remembrance" in the Institution. Here the meaning is, of course, the same.

The Church of England, then, teaches her children, *before* she goes on to dwell upon *Communion,* that the first object is "the commemoration," "the memorial;" in other words, "the sacrifice."

Nothing but a twisting of words, in a Jesuitical fashion, into non-natural meanings, can get over this. So far our Church teaches that the Lord's Supper *is* a sacrifice.

The Church is *exact* in this, for you first plead the Sacrifice before you feed on the Victim. That was the way with all sacrifices. You first, therefore, are taught of the Sacrifice before you are taught of Communion. The Church of England, whatever her faults, is exact and careful in her theology in teaching the young. She teaches in her Catechism the Sacrifice of the Altar.

(*b*) But, it is sometimes said, her Article on the subject—Article XXXI.—is entirely against this.

(1) If it *appeared* to be so, I repeat, "*Lex Orandi, Lex Credendi,*" we should have to interpret the Article by the Prayer-book. But—

(2) It is *not* opposed to the truth of the Eucharistic Sacrifice. The first part of the Article dwells—and dwells rightly—on the entire and absolute sufficiency

of the one great Offering on the Cross. The Article warns against *any* notion that *anything* except the offering of Christ can atone for sin. So far good. Then come the words which are supposed to *deny* the Eucharistic Sacrifice.

A form of error had apparently crept in at the time, of a very serious kind, viz. a popular notion that *something more* could be done, *besides and beyond* the Sacrifice of the Cross, in order to merit "remission of pain and guilt." This the Article rightly withstood. It was an error destructive of the meaning of the Eucharistic Sacrifice. "The Sacrifices of Masses, in the which it was commonly said that the priest did offer Christ for the quick and dead"—these were denounced. This was right. "It was commonly said"—a *popular notion* had grown up, apparently—"that the priest offered Christ *afresh*, that the Cross was insufficient," and so on. The results were serious. Masses viewed in this way became abuses for raising money, and encouraging irreverence and superstition.

Popular errors of this kind are dangerous. Compare the *then* state of things with more modern faults. Respectable people with fair income have in modern times hired cosy pews; they have kept out the poor; they have lived worldly lives, and got into the way of thinking that a quiet Sunday evening "in the roomy pew," where they could hear the form of heresy most satisfactory to them—which they called "the gospel"— preached, would do instead of Eucharistic Worship and a good life.

If Reformers *now* were framing an Article for such people, they might fairly say, "The sacrifice of Evening Service, in the which it is commonly supposed that making yourself comfortable in a cosy pew which is all your own, and listening to a "gospel sermon," will do as well as worshipping God in *the* service He appointed, and doing your duty in life, is a blasphemous fable and dangerous deceit." This would not mean that it is wrong to go to Evensong properly, or to listen to sermons in a right spirit, when desirous humbly to learn and practise the Catholic Faith.

The Article never condemns "the Sacrifice of the Mass." It only condemns a popular view of "Masses" which hinders the true view of the Eucharistic Sacrifice.

Christ, the Church teaches, is the One Victim. There can be no *fresh* sacrifice of Him. The Sacrifice of the Altar points back to—*is one with*—the Sacrifice of the Cross.

The Article guards the Eucharistic Sacrifice from perversion.

(*c*) Then we turn to the Service for the Eucharist, the Communion Service, the Liturgy, the Mass—by whichever name you call it.

(1) There is the first Oblation. The elements of bread and wine, and the alms of the faithful, are offered in "the Church Militant Prayer" to "the Divine Majesty." In this offering, the alms are set apart for sacred uses, for God's work; the elements are set apart from all common purposes, to be an acknowledgment of God's sovereignty over all created things, and the outward and visible signs of "the Holy Mysteries."

(2) There is the Exhortation, in which, after much teaching as to the Real Presence, and as to the necessity of right dispositions for receiving the benefit of that Presence, and the danger—as the Presence is Real—of receiving without these dispositions; *then* we are advised to call to mind that these "Holy Mysteries" are *both* "pledges of His love" in giving Himself for us, *and also*

the means of a "continual remembrance"—*i.e.*, as we have seen, a continual commemoration or memorial of His Death. Here we have the Eucharistic Sacrifice again.

(3) Then, in this connection, we come to the Consecration. This great Act is a solemn prayer first of all, for the priest is but a *minister*, and it is *not in his own power* that the thing is done. The priest is here appointed to act as an instrument—set apart by his ordination to fulfil the conditions in accordance with which the great promise is claimed—to speak, in fact, the appointed words.

What does he do? He appeals to the Almighty Father; he "reminds" Him—if I may say so—that His Son was given to "suffer death upon the Cross for our redemption;" he makes an "act of faith" in the "one oblation of Christ once offered" on Calvary, as a "full, perfect, and sufficient sacrifice, oblation, and satisfaction for the sins of the whole world;" he "reminds" the Father that His Son did, in order to perpetuate and apply the effects of that one Oblation, "institute, and in His Holy Gospel *command us to continue*, a perpetual memory" (*i.e.*, as we have seen, *a continual commemorative offering*) "of that His precious Death, until His coming again." Then, having thus "reminded" the Father of the atoning power of the Blessed Passion of His dear Son, and of the means instituted for the commemoration before Him, he goes on *to make the Memorial.* He first prays for the grace of a right reception, *and then* he does the very same acts and uses the very same words which the great High Priest did and used at the Institution of the Mysteries, and then he proceeds to use the sacrificial words,—after the Consecration which secures the Real Presence—"Do this" (or, "offer this," or, "sacrifice this") "in remembrance," or as a memorial, "of Me," making thereby, and as he says this, the offering appointed to be made.

In every celebration, then, of the Mysteries, the priest uses the same words and acts, making the Memorial, before God, of the great Offering.

Here, in the Act of Consecration, we have the Eucharistic Sacrifice.

(4) Then there is the Prayer of Oblation. In this the Father is besought to "accept the one sacrifice of praise and thanksgiving" (in other words, "this our Eucharistic Sacrifice"). Here we use the very terms of the Ancient Liturgies. Here also the Church prays that, as we have been pleading and applying the merits of the Cross, "we and all" His "whole Church"—the living and the dead, the whole Body of Christ—may "obtain remission of our sins, and all other benefits of His Passion." After this act of oblation, in which we bear *all* before God in union with the great Sacrifice, we offer "ourselves, our souls and bodies, to be a reasonable, holy, and lively (or living) sacrifice" unto God. Then, as this latter part of the prayer is specially suited to *communicants*—though not necessarily to those who communicate *at this moment*, for there may be those there who are in communion with Christ, but, for devout reasons, not *at that moment* communicating—we pray that God will accept "*this* our sacrifice," etc., for all, even those not yet old enough to be admitted *to Communion*, who may yet be present to join in the offering.

Here, again, my dear friend, is the Eucharistic Sacrifice. It seems to me that, examining even so much of our formularies, nothing can be further from the truth than to assert that the Church of England "teaches with absolute precision that the Lord's Supper is not a sacrifice"! The Church of England, with Holy

Scripture, with the Ancient Church to which she appeals, with the whole of the rest of the Catholic Church, " teaches with absolute precision " the great and precious truth of the Sacrifice of the Altar.

It might, perhaps, be advisable to show from the great divines of the English Church that such a reading of the Prayer-book is in conformity with their minds. This, as you know, would not be difficult. The difficulty is, with such an overwhelming mass of evidence, to keep within reasonable limits. I content myself, therefore, with reminding you of one or two examples.

Here is a statement from Archbishop Bramhall's views—and no man, you will remember, was stronger against anything merely *Romish*. " All the essentials of this sacrifice are contained in our celebration of the Holy Eucharist. . . . It was therefore truly said by the learned Bishop of Ely, " Take away your Transubstantiation, and we shall have no difference about the sacrifice." [1]

Here, again, is Thorndike: " The Apostle declareth that the same one individual sacrifice which Christ carried into the Holy of Holies, through the veil, *to present it* to God, is that which all Christians participate of, in the Eucharist always. . . . If the prayer of the Church be accepted of God in consideration of the sacrifice of the Cross appearing always before the Throne of God within the veil, to intercede for us, is it not all reason that the Church, when it celebrateth the remembrance thereof upon earth, should offer and present it to God ? " [2]

Again, " The elements so consecrate are truly the

---

[1] " Ordination Defended," etc., Bramhall's Works, v. 217.
[2] Thorndike, vol. i., part 2, p. 477.

sacrifice of Christ upon the Cross, inasmuch as the Body and Blood of Christ crucified are contained in them, *not as in a bare sign which a man may take up at his pleasure*, but as in the means by which God hath promised His Spirit; but not properly the sacrifice of Christ upon the Cross, because that is a thing which consists in action and motion and succession, and therefore, once done, can never be done again. . . . It is, therefore, enough that the Eucharist is the sacrifice of Christ upon the Cross, as the sacrifice of Christ upon the Cross is represented, renewed, revived, and restored by it, and as every representation is said to be the same thing with that which it representeth; taking representing here, *not for barely signifying*, but for tendering and exhibiting thereby that which it signifieth."

Think of Bishop Wilson's words: "May it please thee, O God, Who hast called us to this ministry, to make us worthy *to offer* unto Thee *this sacrifice* for our own sins, and for the sins of Thy people."[1]

But I would weary you if I went on. The testimony of English divines is overwhelming.

We may not forget, my dear friend, that this is no question of debating about words, but one of serious importance. I cannot express what I mean better than by quoting the weighty words of our dear friend Dr. Liddon, in speaking of the grave consequence of making light of Eucharistic truth.

"As our Lord's Divinity," he says, "is the truth which illuminates and sustains the world-redeeming virtue of His Death, so in like manner it explains and justifies the power of the Christian Sacraments as actual channels of supernatural grace. To those who deny

[1] "Sacra Privata," p. 104, edit. 1854.

that Jesus Christ is God, the Sacraments are naturally nothing more than 'badges or tokens' of social co-operation. The one Sacrament is only a 'sign of profession and mark of difference whereby Christian men are discerned from others that be not christened.' The other is at best only a 'sign of the love that Christians ought to have one towards another.' Thus Sacraments are viewed as altogether human acts; God gives nothing in them; He has no special relation to them. They are regarded as purely external ceremonies, which may possibly suggest certain moral ideas by recalling the memory of a Teacher Who died many centuries ago. They help to save His Name from dying out among men. Thus they discharge the functions of a public monument, or of a ribbon or medal implying membership in an association, or of an anniversary festival instituted to celebrate the name of some departed historical worthy. It cannot be said that in point of effective moral power they rise to the level of a good statue or portrait, since a merely outward ceremonial cannot recall character, and support moral sympathy as effectively as an accurate rendering of the human countenance in stone or colour on the lines of an engraving. Rites, with a function so purely historical, are not likely to survive any serious changes in human feelings and associations. Men gradually determine to commemorate the object of their regard in some other way, which may perhaps be more in harmony with their personal tastes; they do not admit that this particular form of commemoration, although enjoined by the Author of Christianity, binds their consciences with the force of any moral obligation; they end by deciding that it is just as well to neglect such commemorations altogether.

"If the Socinian and Zwinglian estimate of the Sacraments had been that of the Church of Christ, the Sacraments would long ago have been abandoned as useless ceremonies. But the Church has always seen in them, not mere outward signs addressed to the taste or to the imagination, nor even signs (as Calvinism asserts) which are tokens of grace received independently of them, but signs which, through the power of the promise and words of Christ, *effect what they signify.* They are 'effectual signs of grace and God's good will towards us, by the which He doth work invisibly in us.' Thus in Baptism the Christian child is 'made a member of Christ, a child of God, and an inheritor of the kingdom of heaven;' and 'the Body and Blood of Christ are verily and indeed taken and received by the faithful in the Lord's Supper.'

"That depreciation of the Sacraments has led, with general consistency, to the depreciation of our Lord's Eternal Person, is a simple matter of history. True, there have been and are believers in our Lord's Divinity who deny the realities of Sacramental Grace. But experience appears to show that their position is only a transitional one. For history illustrates this law of fatal declension, even in cases where Sacramental belief, although imperfect, has been far nearer to the Truth than is the naturalism of Zwingli. Many of the most considerable Socinian congregations in England were founded by the Presbyterians who fell away from the Church in the seventeenth century. The pulpit and the chair of Calvin are now filled by men who have, alas! much more in common with the Racovian Catechism than with the positive elements of the theology of the Institutes. The restless mind of man cannot but at last push its principle to the real limit of its application, even although centuries should intervene between the premiss and the conclusion. Imagine that the Sacraments are only picturesque Memorials of an absent Christ, and the mind is in a fair way to conclude that the Christ who is thus commemorated as absent by a barren ceremony is Himself only and purely human."[1]

It is, my dear friend, the solemn sense of the peril, thus eloquently described, which besets those who take a low view of the Sacraments, which makes it, so it seems to me, incumbent upon us all to do everything in our power to arrest so dangerous a decline.

As I close this part of my subject, I am reminded by the teaching of the Church to-day that the Church and all her teachings rest upon "the Foundation of the Apostles and Prophets, Jesus Christ Himself being the Head Corner-stone." May God give us all grace more and more so to hold the truth in love and faith, in loyalty and self-watchfulness, that we may be "living stones" in His temple, and may be so joined together in unity of spirit by their doctrines that we may be acceptable to Him at the last!

I am, my dear Dean, yours affectionately,
W. J. KNOX LITTLE.

THE COLLEGE, WORCESTER,
Feast of S. Simon and S. Jude,
October 28, 1893.

---

[1] Liddon, Bampton Lectures, 1866: "The Divinity of Our Lord," Lect. viii. p. 719.

PART IV.

THE APOSTOLIC MINISTRY.

My dear Dean,

We have now reached the last part of the question before us. In examining what was meant by " sacerdotalism " as it has been denounced by opponents, we have seen that Confession and Absolution, Fasting Communion and Eucharistic Worship,—that these devout practices, if taught, are believed to indicate in the teachers the " sacerdotalism " which is objected to. I have endeavoured to show that they are urged, or encouraged, or permitted, as the case may be, by the Church of England, and that so far forth " sacerdotalism " is her teaching, and those who teach it are, to say the least of it, not disloyal to her.

We have noticed also that to hold the doctrine of the Real Presence—which in no way implies Transubstantiation—and the doctrine of the Eucharistic Sacrifice —which in no way *interferes with*, but quite the contrary, the Sacrifice of Calvary,—I say, that to hold or teach these things also—so we are given to understand— implies this " sacerdotalism." I have endeavoured, accordingly, to show that these are the doctrines of the English Church, and consequently that in this matter also she teaches " sacerdotalism," and that therefore those who are " sacerdotalists " are the very reverse of being disloyal to her.

And now we reach that part of the question which is indeed the most important of all, namely, the question of the Apostolic Ministry. If there be a Christian Sacrifice, there must be a Christian Priesthood. If there be real gifts of grace, to obtain which it is—ordinarily speaking—*necessary* to make use of the ministrations of the appointed ministry, then that ministry must be *divine*. Those who hold the Catholic view contend that that ministry *is* divine; that it has its several functions and regulated orders; that it receives its official power from God the Father through Jesus Christ in direct succession from the Apostles; and that no ministry ordered and appointed in any other way than the ministry of the Church is a ministry according to the mind of Christ, or has authority to administer valid sacraments. Now, if this is "sacerdotalism," what I maintain is that in this particular also "sacerdotalism" is the teaching of the Church of England, and to be faithful to her—whether she be right or whether she be wrong—we ought in this respect also to be "sacerdotalists."

Before I go further, however, it is necessary, as far as possible, to remove certain misconceptions. The discussion about the Sacred Ministry has, it seems to me, been greatly darkened by fighting about *words*, and by the most extraordinary confusions of thought. Thus we hear strong statements, and even fierce declamations about there being "no sacrificial priesthood"! Again, we hear indignant denials of there being any "vicarious ministry," or of "presbyters" being able to perform "acts of sacrifice *as substitutes* for the people;" or of the "claims of priestcraft" robbing people of "the inestimable privileges of freedom which Christ purchased for them with His own Blood;" or of the Church of England interposing "no sacrificial tribe between God and man."[1] When we read statements of this kind, it is difficult to discover where we are. You do not want to fight with bogies; and devout persons who say things of this sort seem first of all to erect a scarecrow, or—if I may say so without offence—a kind of ecclesiastical "Aunt Sally," and then to throw at it and beat it as if *it* represented the teaching of those who maintain the Catholic character of the English Church. You and I, my dear friend, are quite prepared to join in the throwing if there is any special use in wasting our weapons upon gigantic ninepins. Who on earth—or anyhow who in the English Church—holds such absurd doctrines? Certainly not the instructed Catholic laity and clergy in our part of the Catholic Church. We may, then, clear the way in this part of the discussion by making four preliminary statements.

(1) The priesthood in the Catholic Church is *not vicarious*. The true doctrine of sacerdotalism does not deny, on the contrary it illuminates, the truth of personal and direct communion between the soul and God. *All* may pray; *all* may intercede. The difference in the power of prayers does *not* depend upon difference in official position, but upon the varying degrees of holiness of character and of love towards God.[2] A Christian priest does not act *in place of* the people, but he *does* act *as a priest* all the same, and his sacred office is not to be emptied of its meaning by riding off on the word "presbyter." While thinking of this, it is worth while noticing that probably, when fault was found with the "massing priests" of the Middle Ages, it was not meant that there was anything wrong in a

---

[1] *Contemporary Review*, July, 1892, 1893.

[2] Cf. Gore, "The Church and the Ministry," chap. ii., where the same view is upheld and stated *in extenso*.

priest being a priest, much less in the fact that he said his mass, but rather in the encouragement of the notion (*a*) that "masses" might be said one after another like magical incantations, with so much money value, and as something *separate from and independent of* the Sacrifice of Calvary;—notions of this sort, Article XXXI. condemned, and justly, as "blasphemous fables and dangerous deceits;"—and (*b*) the encouragement of the notion that the priest *so* acted *instead of the people, that they were relieved of all action and responsibility*. This—if it was held, and in so far as it was held—was undoubtedly wrong. *The Christian priesthood is not vicarious.* It is not, that is to say, *such* as to relieve souls of *their* responsibility. I quite grant that to drift into belief of a *vicarious* priesthood is a not uncommon failing in fallen man, arising from sloth and the dislike of taking trouble. It has been very justly said, " It is not only possible to believe in the vicarious priesthood of sacrifice, *but also in a vicarious priesthoood of preaching, which releases the laity from the obligation to make efforts of spiritual apprehension on their own account.*" You and I, my dear friend, must remember instances in our early days in which to hear dear pastor So-and-so "preach the gospel"—*i.e.* utter an accepted shibboleth with a fair amount of unction, and a little spice of denunciation of Roman Catholics and of affectionate feeling towards Jews thrown in—was treated as the whole duty of man, or, at any rate, the sum and substance of religious and Christian worship. A priest acting in his office in relation to the Body of the Church, can be no more a *substitute* for the proper and responsible action of individual souls, than the colonel of a regiment can be a *substitute* for the action of the regi-

[1] Gore, *ut supra* p 85.

ment he leads, and to the command of which he is appointed, *not by the regiment*, but by an authority above them both. I do hope, in discussions on "sacerdotalism," we shall hear no more declamations and denunciations in regard to *vicarious* priesthood, which are quite beside the mark.

(2) Again, true sacerdotalism does *not* teach a priesthood *independent of* the everlasting Priesthood of Christ. The Christian priesthood is an expression and application of *that* everlasting Priesthood. It is the manner in which, the means by which, the Lord has willed that *His* priestly functions should have their continuance among men.

(3) And then, again, true sacerdotalism does *not* mean a priesthood *independent of* the Church, as if it were a *caste* or *tribe* quite outside the Body. *In the Church*, as the Body, receiving life from her Divine Head, and never, of course, separated from that Head—as He is the Head and she is the Body,—*in the Church*, I say, indwelt by the Holy Ghost, reside those supernatural powers which are called into play in various ways, and for their own specific purposes. Some of these supernatural powers for special ends are exercised for the whole Body, and in union with the whole Body, by the priesthood properly set apart and ordained by Apostolic hands for such exercise of such powers. That priesthood, by such ordination, receives from the great Head of the Church special commission and special grace to act in this *representative*, not *vicarious* character.

(4) And then, lastly, true sacerdotalism does certainly *not* imply an arrogant spirit of insolent exclusiveness. The appointment to exercise solemn functions—coming from God, and not from any mere congregation of men—*ought* to be productive of only a deeper sense of

responsibility, and—from some realization of the vast chasm between the greatness of the *office* and the nothingness of the *man*—of a deeper humility of soul and a temper corresponding to the sense of being "servant of all." An arrogant and overbearing temper or attitude of mind,—as though one holding a priestly office were *thereby* better than others, or had a right, so to speak, to "give himself airs,"—*this* is a base and false sacerdotalism indeed.

For these forms of sacerdotalism, you will agree with me, my dear Dean, *wherever* they are found—and I fear they may be found even among ministers of bodies which have separated from the Church, even also among those *in* the Church who are not backward in their denunciations of true sacerdotalism,—for these forms of sacerdotalism, I say, the Catholic Church, and the Church of England as a part of the Catholic Church, can have nothing but condemnation.

There is, however, a true sacerdotalism, and to disparage or to find fault with *it*, is, it seems to me, to find fault with or disparage the teaching of Christ, of His Apostles, of Holy Scripture, of the whole Catholic Church, *and*—for that is the real question before us—of the Church of England.

And now to a certain extent we have, I hope, cleared the ground. Our opponents have been apt to confuse the argument, by mixing up their attack upon what is the true teaching of Christianity and the Church, with their attack upon corruptions and falsehoods which *we* condemn as strongly as they. There is, however, I fear, still a serious difference between us; and what I maintain is this—I repeat it again—that the Catholic doctrine of the Apostolic Ministry is true, so it seems to me, to Scripture and the early Church, *and*—above all for the purposes of our discussion, which is *the* point—to the teaching of the Church of England, and that the doctrine of the ministry held by our opponents is *not* true to any one of these authorities.

What we hold and assert as true "sacerdotalism" is this—I can best state it in the form of the following propositions.

(1) Christianity is not merely the statement of an *ideal*, nor is it a *philosophy* only; nor is it a system of morality only; nor is it a posture of sentiment or feeling caused by oneself; it is, in order to effect these—so far forth as they are true and needful—a revelation of *Truths* of a supernatural character which must be embraced not as mere opinions, but must be received *by faith*.

(2) It makes clear to man his *end*, and teaches him the means by which he may attain that end, and may be changed by God's power—though not without his own will—into a new state of spiritual life; *i.e.*—

(3) Christianity implies, in fact, a revelation of supernatural *truth* and a gift of supernatural *grace*.

(4) Further, it teaches that in order to bring *truth* and *grace*, a corporate Body has been established in this world by Christ and continued in it. The Catholic Church is a visible Society. It is not a mere religious club or department of State for purposes of religion; or *congeries* of good people who happen to hold the same opinions, and to be moved, more or less, by the same class of motives; and who, for sake of order and decency, make regulations about their services and their ministry, though *what* these regulations are does not very much matter.

(5) Consequently, it is *not* an *invisible* Body, consisting of *really* good people who are known to be such by God alone. On this point I think I have written

before, viz. on the consoling fact that while there are what I call "crypto-Catholics," who, through no fault of their own probably, are not getting the full benefits of the Body, while yet they are receiving blessings from God, still the Catholic Church—the *executive* of the Divine kingdom is *not* a select company of *good* people devoid of any Divine organization whatever.

(6) That the Church, then, is—as an *executive*, so to speak—a *visible* Body; that it is *the* appointed witness in this world to God's *truth*, and *the* appointed channel in this world of God's *grace*.

(7) Therefore, that if spiritual gifts are to be given to any individual soul, those gifts, according to God's ordinary laws, cannot be fully received without association with others, in the way in which God has regulated that association—*i.e.*, as we say, without being in communion with the *Church*.

(8) And then, that in order to the ministration of *grace* and the witness to *truth*, this Church has a ministry. This ministry can only be exercised—as the work of the ministry is God's work—by an appointment from *God Himself*.

(9) That God Himself has appointed a way for handing on the supernatural graces necessary for the exercise of the ministry. That He, through Christ—the eternal Word of God, Who "was made man"—gave commission and authority to Apostles with power to transmit the necessary supernatural gifts. That the Apostles *received*, and so, as God willed, had power *to give;* i.e. that in the Church, in order to an effective ministration for the whole Body, there is, by the Divine will, a necessity of the *grace of Orders* given by a proper and apostolically valid Ordination.[1]

---

[1] Cf. St. John xx. 21-23.

(10) Then, further, as ministers need an *outward* call and a regulated manner of appointment to their office, that the right of giving this call and making this appointment belongs only to one order of the ministry, viz. the bishops; that is, that in order to have a valid ministry according to the mind of Christ, you *must* have *Episcopal Ordination*.

(11) And then, lastly, seeing that there is no new commission, no new revelation issuing from God from time to time; so, in accordance with the usual method of Divine government in nature as in grace, the *grace of Orders must be handed on*. The succession in the earlier dispensation was by *natural* generation; the succession in the new dispensation, *i.e.* in the Christian Church, is by *spiritual* generation.[1] God sends His Son, Who becomes Incarnate "and a Priest for ever." As *He* is sent, so *He* sends others; and others send others, and so on. This seems to me to be scriptural; this is in accord with God's regular ways of working; this is common sense; this is the doctrine of *Apostolical Succession*.

Now, my dear friend, these propositions seem to me to express our Faith as regards the Sacred Ministry. They may, I repeat, be defended from Scripture; they certainly represent the belief of the rest of the Catholic Church at this moment. They represent, as I think may be shown, the Faith of the Ancient Church from the first, and—which I again remind you is *the* point in question—the teaching of the Church of England.

For all I have said, in fact, amounts to this: that the Church is a *divine* Society, and the arrangement of its officers is a *divine* arrangement. It means that

---

[1] This is *why* the Church calls the bishop "Reverend Father" and "Father in God." Otherwise such titles would be meaningless.

without bishops—who have received the grace of Orders by regular succession from the Apostles—you can have no priests, and that without bishops and priests you can have no certainty of true sacraments. This, of course, is important, for sacraments—where they may be had, and at least where men are not hindered from using them by ignorance, or prejudice, or necessity—are, by Divine revelation, a necessary *means* of union with Christ—in other words, a necessary means of salvation.

The contention is that it has pleased God to appoint *means*, by the use of which the human race may attain to the end of their being; that these means are, therefore, not invented by men, are not a gradual growth arising from their needs and from their experience, but that they are appointed by Christ; and that among these *means* is to be found the threefold ministry of bishops, priests, and deacons, without which the Church cannot be. This is the belief of all Catholics. This, I maintain, is the teaching of the Church of England.[1]

Now there is another view put forward by those who denounce the Catholic view of the Apostolic Succession and of the Sacred Ministry, both outside and inside the Anglican Church. Those who are *outside* we cannot blame. Those who *dissent* from the teaching of the Church, and therefore become "Dissenters"—however full of sorrow we may be about them because of the loss, as we believe, they are under—are, so we must acknowledge, at least consistent. It is more painful, however, when the *divine* character and the solemn functions of the Sacred Ministry are denied or minimized by those who have undertaken its responsibilities and been ordained to its duties themselves. It

---

[1] Cf. Haddan, "Apostolical Succession in the Church of England," chap. iii.

becomes still more painful when—practically holding the doctrines of Dissenters, although remaining in the position of Churchmen—they denounce as "sacerdotalists" those who in good faith hold, and act upon, the teachings of the Church as to the Sacred Ministry.

Now, my dear friend, I have, I think, stated with sufficient explicitness the sort òf "sacerdotalism" which is condemned by all good Catholics. I think I have also made it plain that they believe in Apostolical Succession, and that any other system of the Sacred Ministry seems to them to be at once contrary to common sense, to Divine Revelation, and to the teaching of the Church of England. I think, also, I have made it plain that—as it seems to me—they believe in a *real* priesthood, a *real* sacrifice, a *real* altar, and that they will have nothing to do with the habit of juggling with words, and playing with expressions, and calling men "presbyters" when they mean they are "priests;" and that in this they teach *true* sacerdotalism and repudiate *false* sacerdotalism, and also repudiate a non-natural and, as it seems to them, a dishonest interpretation of terms. In plain English, we *do* hold that the English Church—in common with the rest of the Catholic Church, of which she is the part sent by God to this land—teaches that a true Church must have the ministry of bishops, priests, and deacons, *not* as a matter of convenience, but as a matter of Divine appointment. I hope this is quite clear. I hope there can be no mistake about it. To throw overboard the doctrine of Apostolical Succession and of a *real* priesthood, altar, and sacrifice, is, according to the belief of Catholic Churchman, to be untrue to the mind and teaching of the Lord Jesus Christ, and—because, again, that is *the* point in our discussion—to be out of accord with the teaching of the Church of England.

Well, to go back to what I have said, there appear to be those—even, alas! *in* the Church of England—who deny, as it seems to me, *her* teaching on the two important questions, which really run into one, and which are now before us. I take these questions, then, in order; and the first is—

THE APOSTOLICAL SUCCESSION AND THE EPISCOPATE.

It has been asserted, and lately with special emphasis, as you will remember, my dear Dean, that we may love and cherish Episcopacy with all our hearts, that we may "believe it to be the best form of Church government," but that we are not to say "it is the only form." We are told that we may "care for Episcopacy," that we may go so far even as to say that we "do not believe that any Church can be vigorous and powerful so as to fulfil her mission in the world as she ought to do except under Episcopal government;" but we are told in the same breath that "the Church of England has nowhere said that Episcopacy is necessary to the existence of a Church," and we are challenged, any one of us, to "bring forward a passage from any author of the Church of England in which he has said so much as that." I believe that this "challenge" has been since modified into a challenge to any of us "to bring forward any passage from the *authorized formularies* of the Church of England" in which Episcopacy is spoken of as necessary to the existence of a Church.

Now, my dear Dean, what does this amount to? It amounts surely, to this: (1) That Episcopacy is not necessary to the existence of a Church; (2) it is, therefore, a human, not a divine institution; (3) it is in the opinions of some people—*but that is a matter of opinion*—the best form of Church government, but not the only form. This, surely, is plain. If this be true, I do certainly confess that "sacerdotalism," as taught in the Bible, and by the Ancient Church, and by the whole Catholic Church at present, cannot be defended by English Churchmen; and, therefore, what is more, that, if this is true, the English Church has not a leg to stand upon; she has played fast and loose with language; she has trifled with men in the most solemn moments of their lives; and, from my point of view, no bishop or priest who respects himself, or has any respect for the morality of language, would serve in her ministry for another day. But, my dear friend, this is *not* true; our part of the Catholic Church is *not* so faithless, so immoral, and so false.

We may do well, then, to examine the above propositions, first of all, in the light of practical common sense. If Episcopacy is not *necessary;* if it is only a *human* institution, and not *divine; if* this is so,—can the opinion that it is the *best* form of Church government be justified? I do not think it can. Remember, we are now on the plane of natural, commonplace, human things. We have given up the idea of Divine appointment; we are only to reason on the question on the hypothesis that the thing is altogether a matter of human convenience.

Well, (1), those who say these things are greatly led to say them from a kindly motive. "Reunion" is a word to conjure with; and they amiably believe that men who dissent from the teachings of the Church of England may be reunited with her if Episcopacy be represented as a mere matter of taste or opinion, and not as a necessity. Thus, Dissenters are invited—after being told that Episcopacy is the *best* form, but not a *necessary* form, of Church government—to what is called "submit to Episcopal Ordination." One eminent minister of a body which dissents from the Church of England, on realizing this position, is reported to have said that he did not think that the presence of a bishop at his ordination *would do any harm!* Do men seriously believe that, in so grave a matter as Divine Faith and Divine Grace, anything is to be gained by persuading conscientious people who differ from you on many points, to "submit" to what turns out to be, in their minds, a harmless but senseless performance which—considering the gravity of the occasion—would appear rather of the nature of a solemn farce? For my part, I must say, my dear friend, that if I were a Dissenter, nothing would induce me to join a Church which would be playing so fast and loose with truth and honesty as the Church of England would, according to this theory. I do not think that such statements can be justified by an amiable desire for what looks very like a hollow "Reunion."

For (2) *is* Episcopacy the very best form of Church government, if we are to treat it as a merely human question? For my part, I think the affirmative answer to this question is not, at first sight, evidently the right one. There have been plenty of bad bishops in the Catholic Church; plenty of pretty bad, certainly worldly, and often very inefficient bishops in the English Church, before now. These things ought to be borne with, and they have been borne with, *if* the Episcopate is a necessary and divine institution, only darkened, like other things in the Church on earth, by the sins of men. But, if it is only a *human* institution, and it is a mere matter of opinion whether it is *best* or not, then why should it be borne with? It is not *necessarily best*. Very well; then, under certain circumstances, it may be far from best. A bishop is—so it seems to me—a divine necessity, *or else* he is an expensive luxury, *or*, under some circumstances, an expensive hindrance, *or* at best a relic of the past of doubtful utility. You cannot get out of that dilemma. It is worth while submitting to anything, enduring anything, going to any amount of expense for anything, *if* it be according to the mind of the Lord Jesus Christ. But if—as the teaching we are examining indicates—it is a human arrangement, a matter of opinion, and open to argument, it is quite another question. Try the Episcopate, then, on this hypothesis, in three particulars, and say whether it is necessarily the *best* form of Church government.

(*a*) In modern times a great deal of the work of the diocese must depend upon finance. Is it certain that financial matters can be managed better by a bishop, appointed as our bishops are, than by a committee, say, of businesslike laymen? You must have known, as I have, instances in which we clergy of the second order have been warned to keep in mind our own natural unbusinesslike ways, while always remembering the—apparently innate—intelligence of the laity. If Episcopacy is a mere matter of opinion and taste, we may well imagine that, in this kind of thing, "the intelligent laity" in committee might possibly be more useful than some bishops.

(*b*) Or, again, take the question of Confirmation. According to the theory we are considering, this can be nothing more than a more or less impressive ceremony. We have suffered sometimes, we priests—have we not? —when we have brought young people to Confirmation from what I must call the extraordinary "fads" of some bishops. Either there was some special time when alone Confirmation could be held; *or* a peculiar arrangement as to places, and the answering of the question by which baptismal vows are renewed, has had to be attended to; *or* variations of feelings in a particular bishop as to age for Confirmation have had to be submitted to; *or* only a certain number could be confirmed at once, therefore some have had to be put off, to the probable damage of their spiritual life; *or* young people have had to be taken to great distances, with much inconvenience and sometimes expense, and running the dangerous risk of turning a day of serious spiritual import into a day of dangerous pleasuring; *or*, after weeks of hard work and careful preparation, when candidates have been deeply impressed and really in earnest about spiritual things, sometimes an unfortunate parish priest has had the pain of feeling that half his work has been—in so far as it could be—undone by the coldness, or perfunctoriness, or evident want of experience as to young people's trials and difficulties, of the bishop. I speak of cases that I have known in the past. I have to be very thankful, dear friend—as I have no doubt *you* have—for a very different state of things under some bishops of whom I have had experience; but the point is this: there *are* difficulties, and very grave difficulties, about our Confirmations. If our bishops be not a divine necessity, if they are only—in the opinion of some persons—the *best* executors of the Church's mind, I think many of us may fairly—on merely *human* principles—differ from that opinion in regard to this. It is no great stretch of imagination to realize a Confirmation in a little country parish, or in a parish in the town, conducted quite as much to edification by "presbyters" or pious laymen—if, indeed, it is worth while conducting it at all—as by a bishop, since his presence, so we learn, is not really *necessary*.

(c) And now take the case of *Ordination*. You must remember Ordinations which, in their coldness, dreariness, and perfunctory character, were enough to chill any young soul, however burning the zeal might have been which impelled to a life-surrender to the priesthood. Things in this particular, indeed, have, thank God, in later years greatly improved, though for this we have certainly not to thank that party in the Church which denounces "sacerdotalism." Still, Ordinations were in the past very far from perfect, and I suppose there are places in which they are by no means altogether satisfactory now. Now, if the episcopate is not *necessary*, it is quite possible to imagine how Ordinations might be managed by ordinary "presbyters," or laymen, in a kindly and loving and spiritual manner— if, indeed, Ordinations be needed at all—and with quite as much spiritual help as the ordinands, in some cases, receive now.

If, then, Episcopacy be not divine and *necessary*, if it be only defended as a matter of *human* regulation, and is to be discussed on a merely *human* platform, it is very far from being evident that it *is* the *best* form of Church government. But further; on this supposition, the position of the Church of England seems to me to be quite indefensible. It is true that to get over the difficulty about Episcopacy is not to get over all the difficulties between ourselves and those good persons who dissent from the teaching of the Church. It is true that even after some English bishops or priests have tried to empty the teaching of their Church with regard to the Sacred Ministry of all its meaning, with the charitable desire of clearing the way for a patched-up peace with Dissenters which they call "Reunion," they are still met with difficulties from honest Dissenters who deny various details of the Faith, and have the straightforwardness to say so. It is true that abandonment of *principle* can never lead to a solid and valuable "Reunion." Still it is also true that the existence of Episcopacy is *one* serious bar which stops the way for Dissenters who do not believe in it. Well, then, my dear friend, it seems to me that a Church like the Church of England, if she considers Episcopacy as not *necessary*, but only one permissible form of Church government out of many, is acting in a most immoral way. If it be not necessary, it is a hindrance. If it be a hindrance, it should be swept away. Episcopacy is valuable in the eyes of any serious believer only because of its divine authority. We have no right, I maintain, on Christian principles to preserve an antique form of Church government—which has sometimes worked well, and sometimes badly—as a matter of taste or opinion; seeing that—if it is only *that* and not a divine ordinance—we are, by preserving it, adding unjustifiably yet another difficulty in the way of "Reunion."

I may, perhaps, strengthen my contention—which indeed seems to me to be obviously true—by reminding you of the words of our dear friend Liddon on the matter. He says—

"If bishops are not of divine obligation, is it right to uphold a cause and symbol of division with which essential Christianity could dispense? The Protestant historian, Ranke, has drawn attention to the barrier which is raised by the Episcopate between the English Church and the Lutheran and Reformed communities on the Continent. The maintenance of such a barrier is more than intelligible, if we believe that upon a true Episcopal Succession depends the validity of the Eucharist—our chief means of communion with our Lord. But when we consider the present pressure of infidelity upon all reformed Christendom, is such an obstacle to unity even defensible, if in our hearts we deem the Episcopate to be only an archæological treasure, or only, as the phrase goes, a very interesting form of Church government?"[1]

There can be but one answer, I maintain, to such a question. Bishops are a *divine necessity*, or their maintenance is *a sin* against the spirit of Christian brotherhood, *a sin*, therefore, against Christ.

Then there is another thing to be noticed in this connection. It is actually proposed that in order to effect this—as, I think, conscientious Dissenters would agree with me in thinking—*hollow* "Reunion," that the present existing ministers of "other denominations" should be admitted to minister in the Church, although not episcopally ordained, but that all future ministers should be ordained by a bishop. This is, to my mind, an astonishing proposal. If men without Episcopal ordination can administer valid sacraments *now*, why, in the name of common sense, can men so appointed not administer valid sacraments in the future? If you can do without Episcopal ordination *now*, you can do without it for all time. In one word, if Episcopacy be not *essential*, as being *divine* and according to the mind of Christ, then, (1) it is by no means evidently the *best* form of Church order; and (2) it is a hindrance and a stumbling-block, and ought not to be retained. Our whole position, on this hypothesis, is untenable, and if

[1] Liddon, sermon, "A Father in Christ," p. 13.

untenable, it is unchristian. Bishops are *necessary* to the constitution of the Christian Church, *or* they are a distinct *hindrance* in the way of Christian fellowship, and they ought to be abolished.

But the fact is, Episcopacy, carrying with it Apostolic powers for the continuance of the Church, according to the mind of the Church's Founder, is—according to our convictions—*necessary;* and if to believe this is "sacerdotalism," then "sacerdotalism" is, as I think may be shown, in accordance with Scripture, with the teaching of the Catholic Church, *and*—which again I say is *the* point in our discussion—the teaching of the Church of England.

I. Now we may deal for a moment with the general lines of the argument from Scripture.

The Church of England, as we know, distinctly asserts that the existence of the Three Orders from the first is evident from Scripture, if Scripture be studied with care, and its teachings illuminated by the other records of the early Church. The well-known words are as follows: "It is evident unto all men, diligently reading the Holy Scripture and ancient authors, that from the Apostles' time there have been these orders of ministers in Christ's Church; Bishops, Priests, and Deacons."

Now as to the testimony of "Holy Scripture," not to dwell upon the question of "ancient authors." We have to remember in this, as in other things, surely, that the New Testament is not a precise handbook or directory as to Church government, any more than as to other things. It is a collection of biographies and letters, and what might be called Episcopal charges, and so on. It is written by men who believed in, and lived in, a visible Society—the visible Church of Christ. That Society was a *teaching* Society, and a home of supernatural grace, and an organized Body with its own special ministers. The writings of the New Testament, as they are meant to put on record the life and acts of our Lord, or to correct mistakes, or to enforce truths, would naturally only touch on the ministry by passing allusions, and so on. The strength of the argument, then, lies in this: that you find certain *facts* alluded to, or taken for granted, in the New Testament, and that these facts, when they are rendered into precise ecclesiastical language, imply nothing else than the Three Orders and the Apostolical Succession. In other words, take for granted the Three Orders and the Apostolical Succession, and you *make sense* of the statements and allusions to the subject in the New Testament, when no other theory will make sense of them; or—again to use mathematical language—the doctrine of the *necessity* of the Three Orders and the Apostolical Succession *satisfies* the conditions of the problem as put before us in the New Testament as nothing else can *satisfy* them. We can imagine a person in future years, when, say, the present kingdom of England has developed, or changed, or gone, desiring to know what was the constitution of that kingdom in earlier times. We can imagine such a one unable to get hold of any regular treatise on the constitution, and yet coming to the conclusion, from various allusions which he discovered here and there in writers speaking of other subjects, that there had been a Monarchy more or less limited at different times; that there had been a Parliament, consisting of two Houses, with varying degrees of influence at different times, and regular Convocations as the representative Bodies of the Church; and although—on the supposition—he could find no formal treatise, still he would attain to certainty that those who talked of the kingdom either as a pure Autocracy like modern Russia, or a Republic like the United States, were wrong. Or, again, we are in the habit of gathering out and inferring the customs and laws of classical nations from the allusions which we find in classical writers, and we are really all the more certain that our knowledge of them is trustworthy, just because the writers in question are not writing *for the purpose* of proving their existence, but writing in a natural way and *taking their existence for granted.* Now, if we act on such principles in relation to our present subject in reading the New Testament, we find there the Three Orders, and we find that their power is conveyed to them from Apostles, and evidently meant to be handed on. It ought to be remembered that this is not a question of *words,* but of *things.* Too often, I imagine, difficulties have arisen because *this* has been forgotten. We do not, of course, find in the New Testament "bishops," "priests," and "deacons" always spoken of together in that regular manner and with these very names, in which and with which the thing would nowadays be done; but we *do* find the three *offices* under whatever *names.* (1) We have the Apostles holding plenary power; (2) then we have another order, sometimes called bishops (ἐπίσκοποι), sometimes called priests or presbyters (πρεσβύτεροι); (3) and then we have deacons (διάκονοι).[1]

At first the Apostles correspond to what we should now call bishops, and the bishops or presbyters correspond to what we should now call priests. Then we find that the presbyters and deacons could not of themselves continue their own order, and when the Apostles

---

[1] *e.g.,* cf. Phil. i. 1, where Church-people—"the saints" and *three* orders come in; or 1 Tim. iii. 1, 12, and iv. 6, 11, where *three* orders appear, though the *names* not *settled* as now.

could not undertake the work of Ordination in any particular place, special officers were sent by them, with special power to do the work. It was by "means of" the laying-on of his hands that the grace of Orders was committed to Timothy; the "presbytery" were associated *with* St. Paul, but the Apostle was the Ordainer.[1] The allusion may have been to Timothy's original ordination to the priesthood, and the ordination alluded to in 2 Timothy may possibly or even probably have been to the Episcopate.[2] This sense of the two passages is, of course, not their *necessary* sense, but it is a probable one. In the same way, if we believe that Epaphroditus, the " Apostle " of the Philippians, who receives a special message, and who is called St. Paul's " true yokefellow," —I say, if we believe him to be *the Bishop* in our sense of that Church, with its priests and deacons, this interpretation gives the fullest and most natural meaning to the words used.[3] In the same way, if we consider Archippus, specially referred to in the Epistle to Philemon, and specially warned to take heed to his ministry in the Epistle to the Colossians,—I say, if we consider him *the Bishop* of Colosse, a passage otherwise rather inexplicable becomes clear.[4]

Again, Timothy and Titus are marked out from all other "presbyters" as having *special function and power;* viz. the power of administering discipline—and this over presbyters and deacons, as well as over others —and the power of filling up the ranks of presbyters and deacons, when necessary, by Ordination. If *all* presbyters had these powers, there would be no sense whatever in St. Paul's directions to Timothy and Titus. And here I may quote the words of an able writer: "If

---

[1] 1 Tim. iv. 14.
[2] 2 Tim. i. 6.
[3] Phil. ii. 25; iv. 18.
[4] Philem. 2; Col. iv. 17.

the laying-on of hands in 1 Tim. v. 22 means, or includes (as it almost certainly does), Confirmation," then the Apostolic power of confirming, as well as other Apostolic powers, was given to them. "In other words, as the Churches grew too large for the supervision in each charge of one Apostle, and as the Apostles themselves felt the time of their own departure to draw near, . . . each Apostle appointed others, within portions of his own especial charge—as notably St. Paul appointed St. Timothy and St. Titus—not to be presbyters only, but above presbyters; and, in brief, to take the Apostle's place in all his permanent offices."[1]

Then, again, we find that they who have to discharge their office have a special gift of grace ($\chi\acute{a}\rho\iota\sigma\mu a$) for its discharge, and that this is given to them by the laying-on of hands. This gift of grace God alone, of course, can give; there can, therefore, be no confidence of receiving it, unless it is sought for in quarters where God has placed the authority to convey it. If we think what this means, it means nothing else but *Apostolical Succession*. We find, of course naturally, as the Church developed and became more fully organized, all sorts of arrangements as to dioceses and metropolitical sees, and so on; and the later history of the Church throws light on the allusions in the New Testament. Those allusions, as I have said, cannot give us exact information on all points; for instance, the different *functions* allotted to the different orders of ministers are not clearly drawn out in the New Testament as we find that they were afterwards. None the less, we *do* find in it that from the first there *is* a ministry with different grades of function and power, and in that ministry, it is *only* the Apostles, or "Apostolic men," "who have the power to

---

[1] Haddan, "Apostolical Succession," etc., pp. 88, 89.

communicate the gift of the Holy Ghost by the laying-on of hands." We *do* find, as we have seen, "the ministry of 'bishops' (or presbyters) and 'deacons' appearing there, as an almost essentially subordinate ministry, and we have clear evidence that the *Apostolic* office admitted of being extended and localized, as in the case of St. James and (more or less) of St. Timothy and St. Titus."[1] And we do find, as we have seen, that a gift of grace (χάρισμα) given by the laying-on of Apostolic hands is necessary for the discharge of ministerial function. And we do find that "there is no provision whatever in the New Testament either for the proper and adequate administration of discipline, or for any continuance at all of the ministry, save as by the hands of the Apostles, or of bishops as successors of the Apostles."[2] We do find also that in the case of every Church alluded to, where the matter is touched upon at all, that it seems in the highest degree probable, to say the least, that *that* Church is "placed under single government, distinct from and above that of its presbyters."[3] And what, my dear friend, I ask you, does all this amount to? It amounts, surely, to this: that whatever changes in detail there may have been afterwards, or whatever developments of duties, or whatever variation of arrangements in different parts of the Church, great *principles* which are *essential* to the divine organization of the Church are evident from the first—viz. the principle of Three Orders of ministers; the principle that only the highest Order could hand on the grace of Orders and recruit the ranks of the ministry; the principle, in fact, of *Apostolical Succession*, as according to the mind of Christ from the first.

---

[1] Gore, "The Church and the Ministry," p. 270.
[2] Haddan, *ut supra*, p. 93.   [3] Ibid.

II. As to the witness of Church history, of the sub-Apostolic and later ages, this is too large a question, you will feel, for me to enter upon now. It seems to me that men must strain the ʹmeaning of words and distort the statements of history to an astonishing degree, in order to doubt what the mind and action of the Catholic Church—whether they think her right or wrong—in all these ages has been in this matter. Those who wish to study the question, when they have not the opportunity of going into researches for themselves, will find it, as you know, treated in a temperate and scholar-like and very thorough manner by Mr.·Gore, in his book on "The Church and the Ministry."[1] It is, however, notorious as she has—as we have seen—stated the fact,[2] that the Church of England interprets the history of the Church from the first, as witnessing to the three-fold ministry. And this brings me to the *real* point of our discussion under this head.

III. What is the teaching of the Church of England as to the *necessity* of Episcopacy? What is her teaching as to *Apostolical Succession?* We have seen already, I think, that if our Church does not consider Episcopacy *necessary*, her conduct in relation to many who dissent from her form of Church government is unchristian and indefensible. But I think it may be shown that she *does* consider Episcopacy *necessary*, whether she is right or wrong in doing so, and that she *does* hold and teach the doctrine of *Apostolical Succession.*

Men *cannot*, of course, deny that the teaching of the Church of England is, that there have been from the first the Ministry of the Three Orders. What they do, however, is this: they ride off on the phrase "Historic

[1] Gore, "The Church and the Ministry," chaps. iii. and vi.
[2] Preface to the Ordinal.

Episcopate," and seem to maintain that whilst *historically* there has been an Episcopate, and that the Church of England acknowledges the *historical fact*, still some other form of Church government, if not *quite* so good, is good enough, and that the Church of England, while acknowledging an *historical fact*, does not admit a *divine necessity*.

Further, it has been asserted that as to the doctrine of the Apostolical Succession, it is not held by the Church of England at all, and as a proof of this we are reminded that the *phrase* is not used in her formularies, and it is even asserted—strange to say—that it is *an invention of the Oxford Movement!* This latter assertion is really astonishing in any thoughtful person. Whether they hold the doctrine or not, they ought to know that it has been held by the whole Catholic Church for many centuries, and that the ministerial system of our own part of the Church now, as always, long centuries before the Reformation of the sixteenth century, is based upon the assumption that that doctrine is true.

However, my dear friend, I can best deal with this extraordinary assertion by quoting the words of one of the greatest, if not *the* greatest living historian—a man who entirely understands what he is talking about, as well as being himself also an English Bishop. After dealing with the attacks of Roman controversialists,— with which we have nothing to do now, as the Roman Church entirely agrees with the Anglican Church as to the *truth* of the doctrine, though some of her controversialists have, when they have been in straits to find some stick to beat us with, impugned the genuineness of *our* succession,—I say, after dealing with attacks of this sort, which are so entirely baseless that they are not difficult to rebut,—he goes on to touch upon the startling statement of Puritans within and outside the Church of England, who deny "altogether the need of Apostolic Succession, and summarily reject the claim of the Episcopate, to primitive authority or historic descent." According to these, he says justly, " there is no such thing as Apostolic Succession, and the whole fabric based upon the assumption is a false pretence to authority, not only baseless in itself, but used as an instrument of exclusion of faithful Christians from the privileges to which they are entitled as believers, and as a ground of persecution against those who reject the form of government to which it belongs. Then," so he says, "comes in the assertion of another school—that the men who carried on the work of Reformation and Church government during the first age of the Reformation did not believe it themselves." Then he notices the further teaching of another school—that "the doctrine of the historic Episcopate" (used in its strict sense, that is, as including the doctrine of the Apostolic Succession) "is a comparatively modern invention in relation to the Church of England, and in fact a figment, so far as we are concerned, of what is called the Tractarian Revival." Then this able writer continues as follows: "The arguments of the Puritans against Episcopacy altogether, are, of course, quite beyond a possibility of handling now; and they turn on quite a different sort of evidence. But the statements as to the historic use of the term 'Apostolic Succession' in the Church of England, and the modern idea of its real acceptance, may be dismissed briefly. Up to the period of the Reformation, *there was no other idea of Episcopacy except that of transmission of Apostolic Commission;* that the ministry of the Episcopal government could be introduced without such a link, was never contemplated, until Bugenhagen reconstituted a nominal Episcopate in Denmark, and this was an example not likely to be taken in England nor was it so accepted. There is, then, no occasion to test the writings of the Elizabethan divines in search of traces of a belief in their own official existence. Archbishop Parker's own work on the history of the Church of England suffices to prove *the importance which he attached to succession.* A catena of authorities, from the days of Hooker onwards, is framed without much trouble. The use of the *exact term,* 'Apostolic Succession,' is a matter that involves a little more research, *but it is forthcoming.* The work of Mason on the English Episcopate, the language of Bishop Forbes of Aberdeen in the seventeenth century, of Bishop Beveridge on the Articles, of Law and Wesley, and of the American Prayer-book of 1805, not to speak of books that were written between 1805 and 1833, are enough to prove that *there is no element of innovation or invention in question;* but whether or not the two words are in common use, the writings of Mason, Jeremy Taylor, Bramhall, and Lindsay, on the material point, are sufficient to prove that *the doctrine was definitely held.* It is not to be denied that, like many other great truths which controversy has done its worst to smother, the great meaning and force, both of word and thing, needed, and still needs, to be more fully realized." And then, when noticing the terrible troubles through which our Church passed at the Reformation, and the dark view taken by some of the characters of various persons mixed up with the Reformation movement, he adds this: "Surely there must be something of *Divine organization* and Divine guidance in an institution and history which has persistently continued under such an array of disadvantages, and has done so much good in the world, as its enemies cannot deny."[1]

These weighty words, my dear friend, will suffice, I think, to meet any such astonishing statements, as that the Church of England does not hold the doctrine of *Apostolic Succession*, and that the doctrine was an invention of the Oxford Movement. Both these assertions, as this great writer shows us, are untrue to fact.

But let us look for a moment more closely into the statements of the Church of England. Of course, no one can deny that in her ministry she accepts the Three Orders, and declares they have been in the Church from the beginning. But the contention of opponents is, I repeat, that this is only an ecclesiastical or human arrangement; that, looking at the date of its origin, we think it is Apostolic; that it is not essential, but only expedient; and that, in fact, we only keep it because there it is. I have already maintained that, if this be all, to continue this ministry under modern circumstances is morally, and on Christian principles, indefensible.

We maintain, I repeat, on the other hand, that the Threefold Ministry is a divine institution, and therefore *essential* to the constitution of a Church according to the mind of Christ; and that this is the teaching of the English Church.

(1) As to the Articles, the least determined statements on the subject would be likely to be found there. Well, turn to Article XXIII.; we there learn that "it is not lawful for any man to take upon him the office of public preaching, or ministering the sacraments in

---

[1] Charge delivered at his Second Visitation, 1893, by William Stubbs, D.D., Bishop of Oxford, pp. 49, 50, 51. [The italics throughout are mine.—W. J. K. L.]

the congregation, before he be lawfully called, and sent to execute the same." We know from the statements in the Ordinal what "lawful" and "lawfully" mean here, viz. according to God's law. In Article XXXVI., ordination by bishops, including mission, according to the English Ordinal, is declared to be an act of those that *have* such authority, so that those who are so ordained *are* "rightly, orderly, and lawfully consecrated and ordered." In these Articles, except by an inevitable inference, the Church of England is not engaged in passing judgment upon others, but she is laying down an *essential* law for herself. As to the first of these Articles, I may quote the words of an able theologian—

"We have distinct evidence, at the end of the second century, that the hierarchical constitution prevailed universally, without any known exception throughout the whole of Christendom. . . . It is impossible to account for this hierarchical uniformity without presupposing an original, divine institution. If we consider the difficulty of transmission of intelligence, the rarity of the occasions of communication, the deep-rooted, ethical peculiarities of the varying tribes which were converted to Christianity, we can in no way account for it, save on the supposition of the Threefold Ministry being a part of the original constitution of the Christian Church.

"No new form could thus have established itself universally without exciting some opposition; of that opposition there is no trace in any of the earlier records. In the fifth century, indeed, we find the existence of opposition—in the case of Aerius and Vigilantius—but this opposition actually tests the universality of the organization. It was left to the religious exigencies of the foreign reformers to frame, first, a theory of the non-necessity of bishops, and then to erect the platform of their polity without reference to them. By some, indeed, the new constitution was justified only on the plea of absolute necessity. Calvin regretted this imagined necessity.

"The gravity of the matter consists in this. That while we are not in any way to limit the mercy of God, and therefore can understand that, in exceptional circumstances, exceptional conditions of things may be allowed; yet, in the course of the guidance of the Church, it is a truth universally accepted by all who have any pretensions to be sound theologians, that the validity of certain rites depends upon Episcopal ordination, *i.e.* upon the Apostolic Succession; and, as a result of the character of Holy Orders, none but one so appointed can bind or loose in the name of Christ, or consecrate His Body. As a matter of fact, in the Bodies who have not Apostolic Mission, the belief in both these functions has disappeared, and that disappearance is not the least terrible result of the schisms of the sixteenth century." [1]

(2) And next, we may notice the great strength of testimony which comes to our contention from the various *allusions* in prayers and collects. For these allusions are, so to speak, unpremeditated evidence; they are words which the Church could never rightly put into the lips of her children, unless she had believed in the *Divine* appointment of the Sacred Ministry in its threefold order, and in the doctrine of the Apostolic Succession. Thus she prays for the "bishops and pastors of Thy flock," as being the sole ordainers; and bishops and pastors *there* are one class of persons, not two, as our Lord is called "Shepherd and Bishop" in 1 Pet.

---

[1] The Bishop of Brechin on the Thirty-nine Articles, *in loc.*

ii. 25. Again she prays to God saying, "Who by Thy Divine Providence hast appointed divers orders in Thy Church." It may be said, of course, as to *this* prayer, that it only recognizes an historical fact as being providential, like any other historical fact; but it is surely more in accordance with the whole tenor of the Church's teaching, and less a straining of language, to recognize that it means that when the Apostles appointed these "divers orders," it was *by Divine direction* that they did so. In another collect, the Church directly compares the clergy of the present time with the Apostle St. Peter. In another collect, she compares the bishops with all the Apostles, to whom God first "gave many excellent gifts," and then charged them to feed His flock. What I contend is this, that as *lex orandi* is *lex credendi*—the law of prayer is the law of belief—the Church would never have made allusions of this kind in her collects if she had not held the doctrine which we are discussing.

(3) And now we turn to the great statement in the preface to the Ordinal: "It is evident unto all men diligently reading the Scriptures and ancient authors, that from the Apostles' time there have been these orders of ministers in Christ's Church; bishops, priests, and deacons."

It has been truly said that this is not stated as a bare fact, but as a fact which *implies a law*, so that none "shall be accounted a lawful bishop, priest, or deacon in the Church of England" who has not had "Episcopal consecration or ordination."[1]

But, further, direction is given that the sermon preached at the ordination both of deacons and priests is to declare, among other things, "how *necessary*" both

---

[1] Haddan, *ut supra*, p. 142.

"orders are in the Church of Christ." It is to be remembered that, according to the Church of England, neither of these orders can be given except by a bishop properly consecrated.

Surely no one can say after that, that the Church of England does not consider that Episcopacy is *necessary*. And here I cannot do better than quote the words of a weighty writer, to whom frequent reference has been already made, on this subject.

"We have," he says, "further, in the Ordinal itself, the change of the words 'by His Divine Providence' (in the Ember Day prayer) into 'by His Holy Spirit'—the ascription of the sending of ministers to our Lord Himself after His ascension; the description of their office in the same place as 'appointed for the salvation of mankind;' and above all the solemn words of the ordination itself. And if we turn from the Ordinal to the comment upon it, derivable from the other services, besides the entire framework of these services, and the rubrics respecting the ministers of them,—the plain words of the well-known form of Absolution in the Visitation Office show unmistakably, what indeed ample evidence demonstrates, to have been not only the allowed, but the pronounced and decided meaning of those who remoulded our service-books at the Reformation. Orders, then, in the view of the Church of England, are (historically) an Apostolical ordinance; but one both in itself *necessary*, and in its origin, a direct appointment of Christ Himself by His Holy Spirit with no less an end than the salvation of men's souls, and with no less a power than that of administering sacraments and conveying instrumentally God's gift of forgiveness of sins. And those orders, of course, are asserted to be so, and none other, that are set forth in the Ordinal itself, viz. bishops, priests, and deacons, with their several powers as there distinguished and declared."[1]

It is important to remember, when speaking of the belief of the Church of England as to the *necessity* of Episcopacy, that in the preface above alluded to, she affirms that she cannot account any one to be a lawful bishop, priest, or deacon, and cannot suffer them to execute any of the functions appropriate to those offices, unless they are consecrated, or ordained according to her own rite, or have "*had formerly Episcopal consecration or ordination.*" These words are strong, but action is more eloquent even than words. If the Church of England *receives*, as she has done,—and in the above words states, that she *can* receive—a Roman or a Greek priest who may join her Communion without re-ordination, while she *cannot* admit a minister from any Dissenting body unless he—I will not say "submits to," but—"has the privilege of." receiving the grace of Orders at the hands of the bishop,—I say, when she says this and does this, is it possible for her more strongly to assert the *necessity*, according to her teaching, of Episcopacy to the constitution of the Church in accordance with the mind of Christ?

If, in view of this, men deny that she asserts that necessity, it seems to me to be useless to attempt to argue with them. Words to them must have a totally different meaning from that which they have to you or me. It may well be said, as it has been said, that the powers which the Church of England declares to be committed to those who are consecrated or ordained, are "powers certainly in their own nature such as none but Almighty God can give, and which, therefore, only the authority of Almighty God can ever excuse, much

[1] Haddan, *ut supra*, p. 143.

less sanction, men in claiming to bestow. Beyond all power of gloss," the same writer justly goes on, " our services are rank and fearful blasphemy, *or* they rest upon the doctrine here laid down,"[1] viz. the doctrine of the *necessity* of Episcopacy and of *Apostolic Succession*.

I might, as you know, my dear friend, bring abundant testimony from the documents of the time of the Reformation to show the intention of our reformers in the same direction. In spite of a very natural, and in some respects a very justifiable sympathy with foreign reformers, our divines of the Reformation period would never allow themselves to be drawn away from the true doctrine of the Apostolic Ministry. The strongest things that can be produced in an opposite direction were the stray opinions of stray divines; but *the Church* stood firm. If any irregularities did occur in stormy and difficult times, it would not be an astonishing thing. The striking thing is, that whilst desiring to be comprehensive and sympathetic towards various bodies of Dissenters, the Church has felt this matter of Orders to be so *essential* to her existence as a part of the Catholic Church, that she has never wavered. The justification for her firmness in this matter, as I have already maintained, is, that *it is essential;* were it not so, I repeat again, her faithful adherence to it, under all the circumstances of the case, would be a thing deserving of grave condemnation.

You will quite understand me, my dear Dean, when I remind you that I am not at present engaged in an *attack* upon other religious bodies, but in a *defence* of our own position. Of course, to defend the Catholic position of the Church of England is—by implication—to differ from and condemn systems endorsed by religious

[1] Haddan, *ut supra*.

bodies which are separated from her. But it is a very different thing to condemn a system, and to condemn individuals who are under that system. It is possible to make large allowances for Dissenters and others, who deny what we believe to be Divine truth. The Church herself, in the past, has been greatly to blame for their secession. They are often *where* they are, we may well believe, through no fault of their own. Sometimes they have been brought up in a system, and it has been difficult to shake off old habits and a long training; sometimes they have an entirely wrong view of what we *mean*, and think that we are putting something "legal" and "carnal" in the place of spiritual religion. We know that God's grace often "overflows" the sacraments, and that where people have acted with sincerity and an honest heart, even in irregular systems, God has worked with them and given them blessings. In most cases, indeed, "we only part where they deny." In inviting them to consider more carefully their position, and hoping that they may realize that the Church's way is the way which has the *imprimatur* of her Divine Founder, we are mostly not asking them to deny truths which they have learnt, but to advance into fuller truth. We cannot, then, be justly called "narrow" because we refuse, in the interest of a hollow comprehension, to deny the principles of the Church; and others cannot be justly represented as "large-minded" and "generous" if they are prepared to surrender that which they have no right to surrender, and to act under the plea of "charity," in defiance of the Church's teaching, and of her long-established tradition as to the real character of the Sacred Ministry. It would be grossly unfair to us to represent us as treating Dissenters as "social lepers," because we are obliged, by the very terms of our engagements to the Church, our Mother, to say that in all honesty we do not believe them to possess a valid ministry. For myself, some Dissenters are among my very dear friends. I recognize, and rejoice in, their goodness. I know that I have much to learn from them. I am sure that God's grace is evidenced in their lives and characters. But that, I submit, is no reason why I should go, not only contrary to what I believe to be the witness of Scripture and of history, but also—which is my point here—contrary to the teachings of the Church to which I am bound as an ordained priest. You do not fail in *charity* because you are faithful to *principle*. Believing that Dissenting Bodies are *under loss* by their abandonment of the Apostolic Ministry, one is bound to say so—although certainly without bitterness, or pride, or scorn. "He that is not against us is on our part," said our Lord Himself; but the same Lord also said, "He that is not with Me is against Me." We surely have to exercise *charity*, but we learn also the necessity for *decision* and faithfulness to principle. Longing as we do that all who "name the Name of Christ," and are trying to serve Him, although in ways that seem to be irregular, and are "departing from iniquity," should act in the closest conformity to His will, there is nothing "narrow" or "uncharitable" in putting forward the Church's system and the Church's teaching as being His own revealed way. Stating this clearly, we cannot but hope that many may be drawn more and more to realize that they have the highest blessings by treading in "the old paths."

"What is commonly understood," said a masterly writer on this subject, already quoted, "to be meant by the doctrine of the Apostolic Succession, was a commonplace among Christian ideas, and was bound up with the whole fabric of the life of the Catholic Church."

And again, "It will appear at once as a consequence" of this, "that the various Presbyterian and Congregationalist organizations, however venerable on many and different grounds, have, in dispensing with the Episcopal successions, violated a fundamental law of the Church's life. It cannot be maintained that the acts of Ordination, by which presbyters of the sixteenth or subsequent centuries originated the ministries of some of their societies, were covered by their commission, or belonged to the office of presbyter, which they had duly received. Beyond all question, they '*took to themselves*' these powers of Ordination, and consequently had them not. It is not proved—nay, it is not perhaps even probable—that any presbyter had, in any age, the power to ordain; but it is absolutely certain that for a large number of centuries it had been understood, beyond all question, that only bishops could ordain, and that presbyters had not Episcopal powers; and that no exceptional dignity, belonging to any presbyter-abbot, had ever enabled him to transcend the limits of his office.

"It follows, then—not that God's grace has not worked, and worked largely, through many an irregular ministry, where it was exercised or used in good faith —but that a ministry not episcopally received is invalid, that is to say, falls outside the conditions of covenanted security, and cannot justify its existence in terms of the covenant.

"This conclusion, once accepted, has, of course, an immediate bearing on the obligations of individuals who may find themselves members of Presbyterian or Congregationalist bodies; but it has also another and more general bearing on the relation of large communities of Christians to the properly constituted Church. 'How can you suppose,' they indignantly ask, 'that we can accept conclusions which would falsify the prolonged experience we have had in our Churches of the systematic action of the grace of God?' The answer to such pleading is surely this: We do not ask you to deny any spiritual experience of the past or the present. The blame for separation lies, on any fair showing quite sufficiently with the Church to make it intelligible that God should have let the action of His grace extend itself widely and freely beyond its covenanted channels. We ask you, then, to be false to no part of experience, but, rather to be more completely true to experience in all its aspects."[1]

This seems to me to be true and just. It would seem, surely, then, to be disastrous and wrong for Churchmen to allow themselves to speak—in the interest of a desired "Reunion"—as if Episcopacy and Apostolic Succession were matters of comparatively little moment. To do so is scarcely likely to attract Dissenting Bodies. Why should they rejoin a Church which keeps up an unnecessary condition for "Reunion," and *appears* to teach a doctrine which turns out not to be of *Divine* origin? To do so, also, alas! plays into the hands of Rome. *Few*, on the one hand, would be likely to join us in consequence; *some*, on the other hand, might be tempted to join a Church which speaks determinedly of the *necessity* of Apostolical Order, if they are led to imagine that our part of the Catholic Church does not.

But, as we have seen, *she does*. If, then, to believe

[1] Gore, "The Church and the Ministry," pp. 339, 345, 346. See also generally Boyd, "On Episcopacy."

in the *necessity* of Episcopacy, and the truth of the *Apostolic Succession*, as a condition of a Church's life according to the mind of the Divine Founder of Christianity, be "sacerdotalism," then "sacerdotalism" *is* the teaching of the Church of England, and those who uphold it are, to say the least of it, not disloyal to their Mother Church.

II.

The Priesthood.

I have dwelt, my dear friend, on the necessity of the Episcopate, and the truth of Apostolic Succession, not only because there is a tendency to abandon these truths of Catholic Christendom and of, therefore, the English Church, out of a desire to promote "Reunion" with our brethren who dissent from the faith of the Church, but for another reason. The denial or abandonment of this truth—always held in the Church—would be ineffective as well as wrong, however amiable or kindly be the motives of those who encourage such a thing. This we have seen. But, further, this truth is in fact a part of the doctrine of the Priesthood, which is an integral and necessary department of the Christian revelation.

The doctrine of the Priesthood in the Church of England is assailed as that evil "sacerdotalism" which is so loudly condemned. It has even been denied that the Church knows anything of "priest, altar, or sacrifice;" that the sacerdotal idea is foreign to the Church of England, and so on. If this were true, then, indeed, we could have no more to do with the English Church, for she would have parted company—that is our contention—with the teaching of Catholic Christendom, and, indeed, with the gospel of Christ.

This, however, is *not* true, as I shall try to show.

I. Well, first let us glance at the opposing theories. According to this view, the Sacred Ministry, as we know it, is more or less a matter of convenience. The Episcopate is a venerable institution, supposed—in the minds of Churchmen who hold these views—to be the *best* form of government, but no way necessary, and in the minds of those who dissent from the Church to be neither necessary nor the best.

The Priesthood, or Second Order, is supposed to be also a more or less convenient ministerial arrangement. The *name* "priest" is considered a misfortune, as it leads men to think they *have* priests when they have not; and, in truth, the ministry means that there are three sets of persons, bishops, presbyters, and deacons, appointed for sake of order and convenience, holding no *Divine* office at all, and exercising different powers, not because they alone can exercise them by gifts of grace, but because it is convenient to have different officials to perform different functions, as—in civil matters—you might appoint policemen or magistrates to discharge various duties with a view to maintaining the public peace. According to *this* view, ministers are really laymen, called for convenience (or inconvenience!) "bishops, priests, and deacons," and appointed to perform ministerial duties which could be done just as well by any one else, except in so far as it is wise in life to have a regulated division of labour.

Further, according to this view, the Second Order *really* ought to be called *presbyters;* the word *priest* is misleading. In so far as *this* order is concerned, in so far as it has come down from early days, each member of it is to be considered a successor, so to speak, of the Jewish *elder*, not of the Jewish *priest*.

Well, as to *this*, the comparison is certainly an *imperfect* one, for the Jewish elder was not a minister of religion at all; he was an ecclesiastical magistrate. He assisted the ruler of the synagogue in looking after the affairs of the synagogue, and in supplying readers, and in maintaining discipline. Any person in the congregation might expound or teach just as well as he.

To keep the parallel: those who hold this low view of the Priesthood have to *add on* a ministry of religion to the original view of eldership.

Now, it is interesting to remember this, because those who deny the *sacerdotal* teaching of the Church make, as one of their great objections to it, what they consider a point in argument, viz. that it cannot be true because it *adds on* certain duties and functions, which do not lie in the original term *presbyter*. In fact, then, *both* theories *add on* to the offices supposed to be represented by the original term.

A notion that there is no Priesthood proper in the Christian Church, but that our word *priest* really means *elder* and nothing more, springs from the idea of parallelism with the Jewish *synagogue*. It has really taken form and impressed itself on men's minds only within the last few centuries, and gained much of its force from the learned Dutch Presbyterian Vitringa, who wrote about 1759. As to any English divines falling in with this notion, *he* quotes Lightfoot and Thorndike, because they *speak* of the *synagogue*. But when the term "synagogue" is used, it is used to express *the entire Jewish system;* and Thorndike, who alludes to the resemblance between a Christian minister and a Jewish elder, dwells upon the still closer resemblance between the Christian minister and the Jewish priest! Nothing can be imagined as a better illustration of the weakness of the case of those who would saddle the English Church and English divines with this mistaken notion than the fact that Thorndike, of all men, should be quoted by Vitringa in favour of his Presbyterian theory, considering that no divine of the English Church can be more full and strong and uncompromising in his teaching on the doctrine of the Sacrifice of the Altar than Thorndike.[1]

Lightfoot also, the other divine that is quoted, uses —as Vitringa himself acknowledges—the term "synagogue" in its *widest* sense, and speaks at the same time of "sacrifices, priests (*sacerdotes*), deacons, or Levites," as points of correspondence between the Jewish and the Christian system. This view as to the second order of the ministry is certainly not the view of the divines of the English Church.

This, then, is the opposing theory of the Christian ministry. Ministers may be *called* bishops, or presbyters, or priests, or deacons, or whatever you please, but their difference of grade or order only arises from religious convenience. If you are to have a bishop, it is because you think it advisable to have a general "overseer." But another arrangement would do as well, or nearly as well. If you are to have a priest— whom you had much better call "presbyter," for fear of mistakes—you mean that his office and his name have been suggested by those of an officer of the Jewish synagogue. Christianity is a revelation of an ideal of life and of redemption by the death of Christ. It is practically a philosophy. It implies philanthropy and social duties. Its sacraments are badges of fellowship; they can be done without—each soul can carry on its

[1] Cf. Carter, "The Doctrine of the Priesthood," p. 3, and Thorndike, "On the Eucharist," *passim*.

own religion with God without the intervention of others. There is one High Priest, indeed; but His "One Sacrifice once offered" is "finished," in such a sense that we have no more to do with it except to *believe* that He offered it for us. He does not present it for us in heaven, and whilst we remember it, we cannot of course, therefore, present before God that Sacrifice on earth. We call our Lord High Priest: the high priest of the Jewish system symbolized Him, but the other priests of that system symbolized nothing; there is nothing corresponding to them, in any measure, in the Christian system. We have no priests, no sacrifices, no altar. When we speak of sacrifice, we mean it *only* in the sense of praising God, or thanking Him with the "fruit of our lips;" and to speak of a Christian Priesthood now, except in so far as that term may be used in an ideal or metaphorical sense of all Christian people, is entirely misleading and erroneous; and consequently all that in any way encourages the notion of the existence of a priesthood on earth, such as the teaching of Confession and Absolution, or the advisability of prayer and fasting in preparation for Communion, or the presence of worshippers at the Communion Service joining "the Church's prayer-meeting" at a moment when they themselves are not communicating, or the teaching of the Lord's Real Presence instead of His Real Absence in the Sacrament, or of the truth of the Commemorative Sacrifice as a memorial before God of the One Sacrifice once offered in blood and suffering on the Cross,—all these teachings which encourage the notion of a Priesthood are unscriptural and erroneous, and imply that evil "sacerdotalism," which is to be withstood by all faithful Christians!

Well, my dear Dean, you and I believe that *all*

these things—which are thus denounced by opponents—when properly understood, are true; and that this view which opposes them all is erroneous and a mistake, and represents at least a very insufficient Christianity, according to the witness of Scripture and antiquity; but *the* point, again I say, is this—What is the teaching of the English Church? Supposing for a moment that all the above view was perfectly right and sound;—in that case, I maintain, the English Church would be wrong, for the above view is not *her* view. *If* we come to the conclusion that she is wrong, not true to Scripture or to the Catholic Faith, it might be our duty at least to cease to exercise our ministry in her; but whether she is right or whether she is wrong, *we cannot be disloyal to her by teaching what she teaches.*

II. The "Presbyter view" is *not* then, I maintain, the view of the English Church. Her teaching is that there are three orders of ministers by Divine appointment; that as to the Priesthood, it is not a thing separate from, much less opposed to, or interfering with, the Priesthood of Christ, but is *that very Priesthood* exercised according to His will through human instruments. It is the great Office of the Christian Church; for a bishop is, after all, a priest with the added powers given by God, to give the Holy Ghost by the laying-on of hands, as the Apostles did, and to continue the Sacred Ministry by *handing on* the priestly Office which none but a bishop can do.

(1) Now, this is *not* opposed to proper *independence*. The idea that it is, lies at the root of a good deal of the opposition to this truth. There are two aspects of religion for a Christian. There is, of course, personal responsibility, and direct communion of the soul with God. But it is also true that we are members of a *Body*. Our

greatest sin is to act as if we were independent of *God*, and a kindred sin is to act as if we were independent of *one another*. By being *members of the Body of Christ*, we have union with the Great Head. Our new life in Christ is a *gift communicated to us*, and the ministerial succession and the Priesthood of the Church are valuable, among other things, because they impress this fact upon us. Christ's gifts and graces are given to us from without; of course, when we reach the age of responsibility, we are bound to appropriate them *within* by faith. Our souls are saved through the strength of a living faith *within*, but by the instrumentality of grace given to us from *without*. As covenanted channels of grace, the sacraments have ever been used in the Catholic Church: it is possible to quote St. Ignatius, Justin Martyr, Irenæus, Tertullian, in proof of this, to say nothing of the strong teachings of Holy Scripture; but I have said enough on this head in speaking of the Real Presence, and need not weary you with quotations now. Such a belief in the sacraments implied that Christianity did not merely teach personal independence, and the administrators of those sacraments were ever believed to be men set apart for the purpose of dealing, by power from on high, with such Divine things. A Priesthood, receiving gifts of grace handed on by succession from Christ and His Apostles, does not *interfere* with the communion of the soul with God; but its appointment has been needful in conformity with the economy of the Incarnation, for bringing man into, and continuing him in, that state which makes such *personal* communion most fully possible. If sacraments are, as they are, covenanted channels by which God's grace from above is given to the soul, that it may be in a position to have close communion with God, then the men who administer such sacraments require a special calling from on high. "There is not in the world," says Bishop Taylor, "a greater presumption than that any should think to convey a gift of God, unless by God he be appointed to do it."[1] The doctrine of the Priesthood, then, does not at all interfere with proper Christian *independence*, but it is doubtless a reminder that there may be *improper* independence, which would make a man forget the Christian's place as a member of the Body of Christ.

In this connection I may remind you, my dear Dean, of what you have, I think, dwelt upon yourself, and what seems to me to be quite obvious, that the principle of "sacerdotalism" is the *principle* of Divine government in life. Turn it out of religion, and you introduce the idea of an inconsistency in the Divine dealings with man. I have dwelt upon this before, I need not enlarge upon it now; suffice it to remind you, that the great leaders of thought, great scientific discoverers, nay, our natural parents, our very food, our medical men, do not *interfere* between us and God, do not destroy our proper independence, but are *means*, according to God's appointment, by which in various ways we receive His gifts.

I may, perhaps, in passing, allude to another point. The fact that the Catholic Church accepts lay Baptism does not contradict this rule as to the Priesthood, nor lessen the weight of the saying of Bishop Taylor's quoted above. "I will have mercy, and not sacrifice," *i.e.* "I will have sacrifice, but not without mercy," is God's way in dealing with His people. God has His general *methods* of dealing with His people; but He is,

---

[1] Taylor's works, "Ductor Dubitant," xiv. p. 26. Quoted also by Gore, "The Church and the Ministry," p. 82.

of course, not hampered by those *methods*. The Catholic Church puts before us His revealed way; but she is large and wise and generous, like her Divine Founder. Holy Baptism is of the extremest importance if it may be had; the proper minister for it *is* the ordained priest; but, being so important as the way of entrance into the Christian family, the Church has been guided to permit the administration of it, in extreme cases, by other baptized Christians, if done in good faith, and with the form and matter appointed by our Lord. The administration is then *irregular*, but not *invalid*. To make *systematic use* of what is an *exceptional permission* in cases of extreme necessity would, of course, be wrong. But this by the way.

(2) Then, again, the doctrine of the Priesthood as taught by the Church is objected to on another kindred ground, viz. that it is said that *all* Christians possess a priesthood, and that the Catholic doctrine of the *ministerial* priesthood interferes with this truth.

Far from *interfering* with it, my dear Dean, the one is the complement of, and illustrates the other. In this connection men usually quote 1 Pet. ii. 9, in order to deny the Catholic doctrine. That passage is important. In it the Apostle is applying a statement of the Old Testament to show that a "royal priesthood" is inherited by all Christ's people; this calls our attention to the fact that in *both* covenants there is unity of purpose, and therefore that it is probable that *both* priesthoods would appear in a Christian Church, as they were in the Jewish Church; it gives a high probability to the existence of a *ministerial* priesthood in the Christian as well as in the Jewish Church, as the priesthood of the people in one is reproduced in the other.

For redeemed man is saved through the death and atonement of Christ, *and* being thereby in a state of salvation, he is able willingly to offer his transfigured nature and his renewed powers to God. This power and this duty of offering one's self, one's soul, one's body, one's gifts to God, constitutes the *individual* priesthood of the Christian. But just as there is this power and duty in the individual, so—*God's people being a corporate Body*—there is a *ministerial* priesthood for the whole Body. Further, it is by means of Sacraments — Baptism and Confirmation — which are administered by the *ministerial* priesthood, that the individual soul is consecrated to God's service, and "ordained," so to speak, to a share, in his proper measure, of the Priesthood of Christ. Men need not suppose—and it is this supposition which so often closes their eyes to this particular truth of the gospel—that the act of the *ministerial* priesthood can *take the place of* individual effort and faith on the part of those who must exercise their *individual* priestly function in their own souls towards God. The two must go together. "Repent, and be baptized every one of you in the Name of Jesus Christ for the remission of sins, and ye shall receive the gift of the Holy Ghost," is an instance—as has been truly said [1]—of this combination of the inward condition and the ministerial act. Thus it is that we have the "Amen" at the end of the Consecration Prayer, in reference to which St. Paul objects to the use of an unknown tongue, lest, if used, an unlearned man would not know when to say his "Amen" at the Eucharist at the close of the Consecration Prayer: [2] thus it is that the "Sacrifice" in the Prayer of Oblation is spoken of as "*our* sacrifice of praise and thanksgiving"

[1] R. Carter, "Doctrine of Priesthood." [2] 1 Cor. xiv. 16.

(*our* Eucharistic Sacrifice), and "*our* bounden duty and service." The Priesthood, according to the teaching of the Church, is, as I have said, *ministerial* and *representative*, not *vicarious*. But it is a *real* Priesthood; it does not contradict; it falls in with; it illustrates; it is a necessary consequence of, the priesthood of the people.

(3) All sorts of arguments—if arguments they can be called—are brought from *etymology*, from names, and their original derivation. This is an instance of the way in which—so it seems to me—men will allow themselves to dwell on *words* instead of *things*. We are told that there is no such thing as priesthood in the Catholic Church, or in the Church of England, because the word "priest" is derived originally from "presbyter" (πρεσβύτερος), which means "elder," or older person. A great deal of stress is laid upon the fact that Christian priests are not called in the Bible by the title ἱερεύς, which was the term used for sacrificing priests. It is really astonishing that such arguments should be seriously advanced; it is an example of the shifts to which men are driven who oppose the doctrines of the Church. For, if it comes to that, the word ἱερεύς itself means simply "one who deals with holy things," and I believe that the proper word corresponding to ἱερεύς in the Hebrew is not used where it would naturally be expected. But all this is absurd. Words themselves are not things with *necessary* meanings. When "they come into contact with new ideas" they "become representatives" of these ideas. It is a matter of usage, and according to usage they are as good representatives of the new ideas as they were of the old. "What notion," it has been truly said, "of a sacrament" would be likely to be gained by finding that originally it had meant

the oath of a Roman soldier? What notion of Holy Baptism would be gained that originally it only meant washing? Words change their meaning or enlarge their meaning, and in the difficult relation in which the Catholic Church stood in the earliest age to the Jewish Church, it was quite natural that another term for the priesthood should be appropriated, instead of the old Jewish term, to avoid confusion; not because it was not to represent a real priesthood, but because it was to represent a larger and more real priesthood, dealing no longer with types and shadows, but with substantial realities.

The same sort of change or enlargement had, in their degree, passed over former words of the same kind. There is no doubt that the idea of a real priesthood, involving sacrifice, is an idea well known and universal. There is no doubt that this idea was well known throughout Eastern and Western Christendom. Well, the word "priester" in Germany, "prêtre" in France, "presbytero" in Spain, "priest" in England, were unquestionably all used—this no one can contradict—to express *that* idea, as meaning precisely the same thing as "sacerdote" in Italy, and ἱερεύς in the East, and "sagart"—derived from "sacerdos"—in Ireland, and "offeiriadd," offerer, in Wales.[1] It has been the way of the Christian Church to take up words and rebaptize them, so to speak; and it is, I submit, perfectly absurd to argue against the priesthood on the ground that some Christian nations and some parts of the Catholic Church have used, to express "priest," a word derived from "presbuteros," whilst others, to express the *same idea*, have used words more directly related to the old sacerdotal expressions.

[1] Cf. Carter, "The Doctrine of the Priesthood," *ut supra*.

(4) I need not trouble you by ranging over the various arguments which are advanced from Holy Scripture as against the Catholic doctrine. They chiefly turn upon something more or less like what we have considered, viz. the old Jewish name of "priests" not being given in the New Testament to the ministers of the new dispensation. I may as well call your attention to three considerations which have been very properly advanced in answer to such arguments—[1]

(*a*) It was clearly not the will of God that there should be a sudden break between the old dispensation and the new. "At first they continued daily with one accord in the temple." They clung to the Holy City and its past, to the old worship, till they were *forced* to relinquish it, and they observed the Levitical Sabbath. While they were still receiving some ministration from the hands of the Jewish priests, there would have been serious confusion had the same *name* been used for the new ministry as for the old.

(*b*) Besides that, as we have seen, the old ideas as to the Levitical law clung about the old terms, and it was necessary for Christians to learn the *larger* meaning of the Christian priesthood. It has been quite truly said, therefore, "that the disuse of the term may therefore be regarded as a merciful provision to facilitate the progress of the Jewish mind to the spiritual realities of the new kingdom. It certainly could not have been meant to teach them that there were no *such* realities; but if this argument is to prevail, it must prevail for the abolition of the Christian duty of observing "the Lord's Day." Our opponents will scarcely say that we are

[1] Ibid., where this is argued *in extenso*, from which the following considerations are, in part, condensed.

wrong in maintaining the "Christian Sabbath," and interpreting the Fourth Commandment, *mutatis mutandis*, to apply to a real observance of the Lord's Day. Protestants can scarcely object to the term "Sabbath;" the term "Sabbath," however, is nowhere used in the New Testament in regard to Christianity; indeed, very strong language is used by St. Paul about the observance of Sabbath Days as well as Holy Days;[1] and a merely superficial study of some passages of the Epistle to the Hebrews would lead one at first sight to suppose that all Sabbath observance was abolished, of every kind, and that the *only* rest contemplated by Christianity is the rest of the soul in God.[2] And yet, side by side with this, the Apostles and the whole Church were keeping the Lord's Day as the Christian Sabbath; and we can trace up to the very earliest antiquity the observance of Passiontide and Easter, and Wednesdays and Fridays. The *principle* involved in both terms, "priest" (ἱερεύς) and "Sabbath," was maintained and consecrated by the Christian Church, while the *terms* themselves were disused. There is no strong language in the New Testament against the word "priest" (ἱερεύς), as there is against "Sabbath" and "Holy Days;" but the fact is that it was necessary from circumstances to use new terms and fresh arrangements while the great *principle* was maintained; and those who argue from Scripture that the Christian Priesthood is abolished, and is replaced by a mere Eldership or Presbyterate because the old *word* for "priest" was not used of the Christian ministry in the New Testament, ought to argue much more strongly against any *divinely* appointed day of rest, and should maintain that the observance of the Lord's Day is of very questionable propriety, considering the way in which the

---

[1] Cf. Col. ii. 16, 17.   [2] Heb. iv. 4-11.

New Testament treats the "Sabbath," and at best can only be defended as a matter of human convenience and having nothing whatever to do with Divine Revelation.

This can scarcely be done with consistency by those who show Puritan proclivities, and therefore a devotion to the word "Sabbath." On this point I may quote pregnant words: "This remarkable similarity in the use of these two terms forms a very strong presumption that the same *principle* has operated in both cases. While there was danger to be apprehended from Jewish ideas becoming attached to the new system, from mere confusion or from the appearance of antagonism, the Jewish *terms* were suspended, though the *ideas* of 'Priesthood' and 'Sabbath' passed into the Christian system. When this danger no longer existed, and the separation of the two systems was complete, the *terms* themselves were again freely used. . . . Such a change of names . . . where the inner life of an institution was developed under a new aspect, occurred in other cases, marking, as it would seem, a general law. Thus the Passover survives in Passiontide and Easter; Pentecost in Whitsuntide; the Feast of Tabernacles in Advent and Christmas."[1] No imperfect forms of Christianity, it seems to me, my dear friend, mark the consistency of God's dealings, and the expansion of Judaism into Christianity, so clearly as is done by the Catholic Church.

(c) The whole Mosaic system in its detail is represented by St. Paul, in his Epistle to the Galatians, as a kind of interlude between God's original revelation in patriarchal times, and His fulfilment of that revelation in the Christian dispensation. Thus, while certain features of the Mosaic system were allowed to die away in the Christian Church, certain rites of *patriarchal*

[1] Carter, *ut supra*.

times which had held their ground, but in a secondary place, under the Law, were brought into striking prominence in the Christian Church. Baptism was a very *early* custom; but it was *secondary* in Judaism; and it was raised to be a sacrament in the new kingdom. Laying-on of hands was a solemn custom in *patriarchal* times; it has no great prominence, to say the least of it, in Judaism; and *it* becomes the outward sign of two sacraments in the Christian Church, and is stated in Holy Scripture to be one of the "first principles" or "foundations" of the "doctrine of Christ."[1] So the term "elder" came from the times of the *patriarchs*, as a solemn and honoured term, to express that mysterious, *priestly* power that lay in the head of the family; and this term was chosen as the name for *that* minister of the Christian Church who "begets sons unto God," and has the power "to feed them with the bread of immortality." The new dispensation, then, looks back especially to the patriarchs. And when we remember this, we see that the Church selected *not* an unpriestly, but *the most priestly* name possible. The gospel is the carrying out of the promises made to the Fathers. We expect from this the patriarchal development of the Priesthood. St. Paul himself says that the Priesthood was not abolished, but "changed." The "change" seems to have been this: *the new Order came, not from the Mosaic covenant, but from Christ Himself*, and, like *His* Priesthood, *this* great Priesthood of the Catholic Church, which is only an expression and application of His own, has been formed "after the order of Melchizedek." The Priesthood of the Old Law was not the source from which *it* sprang; it was its type and shadow. Think in this connection of the

[1] Heb. vi. 1, 2.

words of Eusebius: "Our Saviour Jesus Christ does, even to this present time, celebrate sacrifice among men by His ministers after the manner of Melchizedek; for as he, being a priest of the Gentiles, nowhere appears to have used material sacrifices, but blessed Abraham in Bread and Wine, in the same manner our Saviour and Lord, and *afterwards all priests that derive from Him*, performing in all nations their spiritual functions by Bread and Wine, do express the mysteries of His Body and Saving Blood."[1]

If, then, we had no real Priesthood, we should be altogether out of joint, so to speak, with the teaching of Scripture in these particulars. And further, the existence of the Priesthood *falls in with* the economy of the Incarnation. It has pleased God that invisible things should be presented to us under the form of what is seen, and that *through* such form they not only show themselves, but *act*. It pleases God thus to approach His creatures. In the Old Covenant all this was done in part, and was expressed in symbol. In the New Covenant God is "with us" in Christ made man, and that Incarnation is *extended* with all its powers and blessings to all who will to use it, in loving faith, by the means of a ministerial priesthood, ministering sacraments which are outward and *effectual* signs—that is, signs *effecting* what they signify—of inward grace. The "presbyter view" of the ministry is "out of joint" with the whole economy of the Incarnation; the "sacerdotal view"—and, I submit, it alone—is consistent with the great principles of that mighty mystery.

(5) Then one may perhaps notice the strong point that is made against Christian teaching as to the Priesthood, by what seem to me to be misunderstandings and

[1] Lib. v., "De Dem. Evan.," c. 3.

misinterpretations of the Epistle to the Hebrews. I think that you were present lately on an important occasion, and heard, as I did, these objections, put in what I must call a very masterly and telling way. It was then denied that our Lord represents in heaven the sacrifice that He offered on earth. This assertion was supported, if I remember rightly, by the statement that the attitude of a sacrificing priest is not to be *sitting* for ever on the right hand of God; further, it was asserted that in the Jewish ritual no sacrifice was ever carried into the holiest of all, and that our Blessed Lord, therefore, could not be presenting Himself as a Sacrifice in the true Most Holy Place; that, therefore— that was the argument—as our Lord did not do it in heaven, the Christian priest could not be doing it on earth. It was argued that the sacrifice of our Lord was so entirely finished that its value and influence spread throughout all ages, and it needs no representation.[1]

Certainly, if all this be true, the Catholic Church is a vast breakdown. We have no business to go on saying in the Creed that "I believe in the Holy Catholic Church;" we ought to say, "I repudiate the Holy Catholic Church," for a great part of her teachings about Christ and His sacrifice is wrong. We ought, I submit, to make our Act of Faith instead under some such form as this: "I believe in a variety of Protestant interpretations of verses of Holy Scripture, even though those interpretations are contradictory to the teaching of the Church, and not infrequently contradictory to one another." But this argument, my dear friend, although it was well put, and stated with excellent temper, in a succinct and masterly way, is, I think, full of fallacy, and chiefly valuable as a short and

[1] By Archdeacon Perowne, at the Church Congress at Birmingham.

handy statement of erroneous interpretation of Scripture and of heretical teaching as to the Priestly office of Christ.

The Epistle to the Hebrews argued against the Jewish notion that their ceremonial law was sufficient for their justification. They had forgotten that its character was *typical*, and that it could not therefore be *lasting*. Against this, the Epistle argues that the blood of slaughtered animals cannot take away sins; that if *new* sacrifices have to be offered perpetually, it shows that they are not effective; and that if their priests were *all* that they had to act for them, the fact that they had to offer for themselves as well as for the others, and that they passed away and died, showed *their* ineffectiveness. The Jews, in fact, had got into the way of trusting to their priests and sacrifices without any idea of their relationship to the covenant in Christ. Against this the writer of the Epistle argues. In opposition to this, he places the faultless sinlessness of Christ; the offering up of His own Blood; the impossibility of His dying any more; and the fact of His having entered into the heaven itself, and having taken His seat at the right hand of His Father, proving that His offering was eternal and inexhaustible in its effects, and prevailed with God.

The Epistle, therefore, teaches that there is one only true High Priest Who can meet the wants of mankind; that to Him there can be no successor, in such sense that He hands on His Priesthood to that successor and dies, and goes away and gives up the office Himself; that there is one only Sacrifice for the cleansing of the soul; that it can never be *repeated*, and that there are no defects in it which have to be *supplied*. The argument in the Epistle in the plainest manner teaches that there cannot be a priesthood which offers sacrifices *separate from and irrespective of the Sacrifice of the Cross*, and that there never can be a *fresh* offering in blood and slaughter and sorrow of the one true Lamb of God.

But the question, which is the real question in point now—as to *the ordained means* for applying the virtues of the Sacrifice of the Cross, and *pleading* its efficacy; and as to the appointment of an order of priests, who, in the power of the one High Priest, are the appointed agents for applying those means — and for such pleading—does not come into the scope of the argument at all. The Catholic doctrine teaches, in accordance with the argument in this Epistle, that the sacrifice has been *once offered*, that there is *one great High Priest;* but it goes on to remind us that that sacrifice can be *pleaded*, that its perfected merits are *applied* to individuals, and that a ministerial priesthood has been appointed by Him on earth to *plead* that one sacrifice and to *apply* those merits. As to the remark that the *session* of our Blessed Lord, the Eternal High Priest, on the right hand of the Father, proves that He does not present or show for us His meritorious Death and Passion before the Father—it is one of the most inexplicable statements I have ever heard. The idea seems to be that His *sitting* at the right hand of the Father is inconsistent with the attitude of a priest, and that He could not show His meritorious death in Heaven because there was no altar in the Holiest Place of all, in the Jewish temple. To argue in this way seems to be seizing upon one detail meant to emphasize *one* particular fact, and to make it do duty for everything else; and upon it I have to say—

(*a*) Our Lord *sitting* as the Eternal High Priest

does not tell against the appointment by Him of an earthly priesthood, any more than God Almighty *sitting* upon the throne of heaven can tell against the existence of earthly sovereigns, ruling by His providential guidance over earthly kingdoms.

(*b*) Then as to the *attitude* of the Great High Priest; *this* figure is meant, of course, to emphasize His triumph and the *completeness* of His sacrifice, but certainly is *not* meant to teach that He does not show Himself, with the merits of His Passion, before God for us, for this very epistle asserts the contrary.[1] Now, to show Himself there—He, being both Priest and Victim—in the power of His great sacrifice, *is* to plead His Passion for us. He is Himself, indeed, Priest and Victim and Altar. Besides, we have read, I suppose, of "a Priest upon His throne;" we have read, also, in Scripture, I think, of "the Lamb as it had been slain," standing upon the altar; and we read in this very Epistle, "For Christ is not entered into the holy places made with hands, which are the figures of the true; but into heaven itself, *now to appear* in the presence of God for us."[2] The Catholic doctrine is, that just *as* our Blessed Lord so " appears " for us there, *so* by His priests, acting with His people on earth, He "appears" for us. The great Day of Atonement has at length arrived; it does not lose its power, as the old Day of Atonement did. It is able to give to *all* acts of sacrifice "a continually availing power, and to all priests and worshippers an enduring acceptableness." There is no more constant repetition of a mere shadow; there is perpetual memorial of the Substance.

It has, however, further been said, as you know, that the Catholic doctrine of the Priesthood and the Eucharistic

[1] Heb. ix. 24.   [2] Ibid.

Sacrifice is inconsistent especially with two expressions in this Epistle to the Hebrews: (1) "By one offering He hath perfected for ever them that are sanctified;" and (2) "Now where remission of these is, there is no more sacrifice for sins." But, in the first place, the Catholic doctrine teaches that, in the sense here meant, there *is* but one offering. The objectors close their eyes to the fact that the Eucharistic Sacrifice is *not a new sacrifice*, separated from the offering on the Cross, but the *same one Sacrifice* shown forth before God. They lose sight of the fact that the Catholic doctrine teaches that "there *is* no more sacrifice for sins," in the sense of some further victim being put to death, but that *there is the memorial of that one Sacrifice*. If they mean that everything has been already done which is required to reconcile God and man, *in such a sense* that the Church and the children of God are to do nothing at all, then "it follows that sin is pardoned before it is committed;" and as for faith, and prayer, and penitence, and the reading of the Bible, and Church services, and Sacraments—well, of course, these and all other means of reconciliation are works of supererogation, and ought to be given up.

Teachings of this kind seem to me to lead, if they are to be followed out, to utter Antinomianism; and, indeed, these erroneous and defective statements of the gospel have often led men into an easy-going and unreal religionism—a religion of phrases and of cant; the halfway house, to those who *think*, towards Unbelief. Sacraments are nothing, *or* they are great realities. They are not *substitutes for* Christ; they are ordained means of *union with* Him. Those who administer them can do so, dare to do so, only by a Divine ordination to a sacred office, in which they act in the power of His

Priesthood. He is the one High Priest for ever; they are His divinely appointed subordinates; they are agents, in accordance with the ordinary law of His working, which He uses to express His supernatural power. Anyhow, nothing can be more absurdly beside the mark than the notion that the Epistle to the Hebrews tells against a department of gospel truth, which in fact it illustrates. Indeed, while the main drift of the epistle is, as we have seen, concerned with that great truth on which the Eucharistic Sacrifice and the Christian Priesthood depend, there is, at least, quite possibly in one passage an allusion to the Christians' approach to the Holy Mysteries, and certainly to the Sacrament of Holy Baptism.[1]

III. I need not dwell upon the testimonies of antiquity and of the early Church as to the fact of the Priesthood. I have said enough on that head in discussing the question of the Real Presence and the Eucharistic Sacrifice, and it need not be repeated now. If what the whole Church has taught as to the Sacrifice be true, then there must be an Altar, and there must be a Priesthood. Indeed, it should never be forgotten that, if for nothing else than because the Church of England appeals to antiquity, those only can be loyal to her who hold the doctrine of the Priesthood and of the Sacrifice, for the Liturgies and the Fathers are *full* of both.

But now, as to the various statements about some of the early Fathers using the expression "altar" in a metaphorical sense, they prove nothing against the Catholic doctrine, for they certainly never would have used the expression in illustration of certain truths if they had not been accustomed to a *real* altar, by

[1] Heb. x. 22.

which the expression was suggested. I don't suppose English people even would speak of marriage in such an expression as "she was singularly young and graceful when he led her to the altar," unless, besides the idea of mutual love and self-sacrifice between man and wife, they had been used to the fact of a *real* altar before which their marriage vows were made.

However, my dear friend, after all, although I have touched upon them, because their arguments, such as they are, are constantly brought up, I have to remind you again that the real question before us is, What—rightly or wrongly—is taught us by the English Church? Such arguments as those which I have noticed are legitimate enough in their place; but Churchmen are placed in this position—they "believe in the Holy Catholic Church;" they believe that the true representative of that Church, to them, is the Church of England. She is, then, the *interpreter* to them of Holy Scripture in all doctrinal matters. We do not, then, expect to find in Holy Scripture an exact directory. Important doctrines are taught there; nothing that is not contained there or, "may be proved thereby," is required as a matter of faith for salvation; but it is the Church, as a Divine Society, guided by God, which tells us, in all grave and important doctrinal discussions, what it is that Holy Scripture *means*. Our own part of the Catholic Church is especially free and above-board, so to speak. She does not *maximize*; she does not pile on details of doctrine, as being of necessity unto salvation. She rather *minimizes*. She states the *least*, rather than the *most*, that is possible. If she clings—as she does cling—to sacerdotal doctrines, we may be pretty sure that we had better not drift off into new-fangled Calvinistic theories; but that we shall be acting wisely, and in accordance with common sense, if we cling to her moderate and sensible teaching, and if we take care to interpret Holy Scripture according to her witness in important doctrinal matters.

Well, now, I maintain that the Church of England, *in the clearest manner*, teaches the doctrine of the Priesthood. I have ventured already to call your attention to those false forms of sacerdotalism which she does *not* teach, and I have ventured to remind you that true sacerdotalism, accordingly as we believe to be the mind of Christ, she *does* teach; and that *it* implies the following truths—the Apostolical Succession, the *necessity* of Episcopacy, the truth of the Eucharistic Sacrifice, the Real Presence of the Lord's Body and Blood under the form of Bread and Wine in the Sacrament, the Penitential system, including Confession and Absolution, and so on; and now it only remains for me to recall to you what has been already implied—that she is consequently *quite clear* in her teaching—as against a mere " presbyter " theory—*quite clear*, I say, as to the truth, witnessed to by the whole Catholic Church, that in Christianity, as our Lord has revealed it to His Apostles, there is a real Priesthood.

If we are to examine, then, the teaching of the Church of England on this important subject, about that we can have very little doubt. Language must be strained to snapping; non-natural senses must be put upon the plainest words; casuistry and special pleading must be employed to the utmost before the teachings—the plain teachings—of the Church of England can be made to square with the assertions of Puritanism, denying the reality of the priestly office.

(1) It is, indeed, almost a miracle that, in the midst of the storms of the Reformation, the Church of

England preserved this and other Catholic truths at all. There was a general upheaval. The Latin part of the Catholic Church, under the influence of the Papal See, put off the necessary reforms, until it was all too late to avert a catastrophe. Lutheranism, represented by the Confession of Augsburg, preserved with tenacity much Catholic *doctrine;* it taught the true doctrine of Regeneration in Holy Baptism, of Confession and Absolution, and of the Real Presence. But the stress of circumstances had led the followers of Luther to abandon the Episcopate. When the divinely appointed *means* for continuing the sacred ministry was gone, the truth of the gospel soon began to die; and modern Lutheranism is in sad contrast to the Confession of Augsburg, and a terrible warning that if the divinely ordered system of the Church is tampered with, Catholic doctrine cannot long survive.

Calvin, on the other hand, did *not* cling to Catholic doctrine any more than to the Church system. He was a dominant character, a great genius, and a thorough-going opponent of the Church and the Faith. To oppose his imperious will was to suffer for it, as all Geneva knew to its cost, and as Servetus showed by his sufferings at the stake. Calvin's desire was to preserve some semblance of Christianity, while abandoning the Priesthood and the Sacraments. He had to find something to do duty for the authority of the Church. It was found in this way: (1) In discarding the Priesthood and in teaching the novel doctrine that to believe in that office was to derogate from the everlasting Priesthood of Christ; (2) in teaching that the ministerial office only implied presbyters, pastors, teachers; (3) in inventing the heresy of final perseverance and indefectible grace. Calvin was a genius, and he was a heretic. His influence was immense. The mischief he did, strictly speaking, incalculable. The Helvetic Confession is the standing witness at once to his genius and his opposition to the Catholic Faith.

Calvinism has had, and even now has, extraordinary power. It discards Divine commissions. It is purely human. It has the power coming from a system which ignores and parts company with many supernatural truths, too exacting in their consequences to be pleasant to "the natural man," and yet does not altogether ignore or part company with that longing for *some* sort of religion which is one of the noblest and most lasting attributes of human nature.

Calvinism left its mark upon England, and the trail of its evil influence across the English Church. The foreign reformers of the Calvinistic school were unceasing in their efforts to corrupt the English Church. Under their influence truths were temporarily suppressed or watered down. Under their influence the natural and healthy course of our Reformation was seriously injured. The Second Prayer-book of Edward VI. is the low-water mark of the struggle in the English Church, and a gauge of the utmost influence upon us of Calvinism. Even *here*, however, the doctrine of the Priesthood was preserved. Even in her saddest moments our part of the Catholic Church clung to *this* truth.

(2) Turning to our authoritative formularies, they are strictly sacerdotal.

The priestly power *in its fulness* resides in the Episcopate. From the Episcopate, with the laying-on of hands and the giving of the commission, it is bestowed on the Second Order. There is this reserve. The Sacrament of Confirmation—a *full* consecration of the laity to the Royal Priesthood of all Christian people—and the

Sacrament of Order, or the power of conveying the grace for the continuance of the Sacred Ministry, remain with the bishop. The authority of the Priesthood proper, when so conveyed, is then—so far forth—*inherent in the Second Order.* The Third Order—the diaconate—receives a measure of what in a less exact sense may be called priestly power, viz. the power to baptize and teach, but *this depends for its exercise on the bishop's licence.* All this has been preserved in the English Church. And a clear evidence of her faithfulness to the *sacerdotal,* and not the *presbyterian,* view of the ministry is to be found in this, that in giving her sanction to the marriage of those who enter the Sacred Ministry, she does not in the Latin copy of her Article—which is of the same authority as the English copy—say De Conjugio *Presbyterorum,* but De Conjugio *Sacerdotica,* when referring to bishops and deacons as well as to the Second Order, recognizing thereby the priestly view of her ministry in its full extent. The special functions of the Second Order, however, of priests, that is, properly so called, are the power to administer Absolution to penitent sinners, to bless in the Name of the Lord, and to consecrate the Bread and Wine in the Holy Sacrament, so that, under their form, there may be, according to the Lord's promise, the Real Presence of His Body and Blood in the Divine mystery.

As to Absolution in its most general and most individual application, this we have dwelt upon in considering the question of Confession and Absolution; and this is carefully committed by the Church of England only to those who strictly and imperatively have received the commission of the Priesthood.

In the Holy Eucharist the same is the case. Here it is only one who has received the same commission who makes the offerings of the alms and the Bread and Wine as consecrated to do so by God, and as the representative of the people. In the consecration by which, through the power of the Holy Ghost, the "inward part or thing signified" is connected with "the outward and visible sign," it is still one who holds the commission of the priest who alone is empowered to act. In the Great Oblation, wherein is represented before God the Death and Passion of Christ, it is again the commissioned priest who alone can present the sacrifice. It is the priest, again, who feeds the faithful by administering to them the Body and Blood of the Lord. It is he who leads the people of God in the further offering of "ourselves, our souls and bodies." It is he who gives the final benediction. It is the Priest, then—by the power given him by Christ, through his Apostles, and transmitted to him in Ordination by the bishop—who is *the* appointed minister in this great act of the Christian religion. In this, in many details—not necessary to refer to again, as we have considered them before in discussing the Real Presence and the Eucharistic Sacrifice—the English Church is true to the custom and teachings and sacerdotal idea of the Catholic Church by using the ministration only of the priest.

This is as plain as daylight in the Prayer-book, and cannot be denied. Well, then, my dear friend, think of the light that is thrown upon all this by the solemn words in which the great commission is given, in the Ordination of Priests; and think, on the other hand, how *this* draws out the meaning of these words.

The bishop, you remember, says at the laying-on of hands, "Receive the Holy Ghost for the office and work of a priest in the Church of God, now committed unto thee by the imposition of our hands. Whose sins thou dost forgive, they are forgiven; and whose sins thou dost retain, they are retained. And be thou a faithful dispenser of the Word of God, and of His Holy Sacraments; in the Name of the Father, and of the Son, and of the Holy Ghost. Amen."

Now, on such words I should like to call your attention to several points which are, I think, worthy of notice.

(a) Here we have an echo of our Lord's own words.[1] If Apostolic Succession be believed, such words then are intelligible. Without *that* they are not so much unmeaning as daring and even profane. It is not a *prayer;* it is a *commission* given with a gift of the Holy Ghost, to authorize and enable for its exercise, by one who had *received* himself (from one who had the power to give), not only *this* gift, but the power to transmit it from Christ.

(b) Here are the several functions of the Priesthood—the power of Absolution, authority to teach, and power to administer sacraments. You remember Archbishop Bramhall's saying, "I answer again, that in our very essential form of priestly ordination, priestly power and authority is sufficiently expressed. We need not seek for a needle in a bottle of hay. The words of our Ordinal are clear enough."[2] One cannot but say with the archbishop, clear enough they certainly are!

(c) Then you may remember—what makes the matter clearer still—that whereas originally in the wording of the commission it ran simply, " Receive the Holy Ghost; whose sins ye remit," etc., in 1662 the present form was adopted, so that " for the office and work *of a priest,*" etc.,

---
[1] St. John xx. 21-23.
[2] Bramhall, " Defence of Ordinations," discourse v. 486.

might be inserted to make clear the mind of the Church on that point. And then the Savoy Conference made it clear, beyond reasonable doubt or question, in a more marked way. The Nonconformists were at the time opposed to Churchmen on this very question of the Priesthood. The Calvinistic view of "presbyter" was what they desired to see introduced. They asked the bishops to remove the word "priest" from the Prayer-book, and to introduce the more general word "minister" in every place instead. The bishops felt that to give up the Priesthood would be to depart from the will of our Lord as always understood by the Catholic Church. "It is not reasonable," they said, "that the word 'minister' should be only used in the Liturgy. For since some parts of the Liturgy may be performed by a deacon, *others by none under the order of a priest—viz. Absolution and Consecration*—it is fit that some such word as 'priest' should be used for these offices, and not 'minister,' which signifies at large every one that ministers in that holy office, of what order soever he be."[1]

The bishops went further. They not only declined to give up the term "priest;" they even replaced it in two important places, instead of "minister," where it was of doctrinal importance. The term "pastor," the characteristic and favourite term of the Nonconformists, was removed. "Bishops, Pastors, and Ministers," in the Litany, was changed into "Bishops, Priests, and Deacons." Here the question was raised and discussed, and was settled in a Catholic sense, with the full knowledge of all parties concerned as to what was involved.

Under such circumstances it is impossible, my dear friend, for any one with the smallest pretence to accuracy to assert that the Church of England in her teaching

[1] Cardwell, "Doc. Ann.," ch. vii. prop. ii.

is not sacerdotal. She may be right or she may be wrong, I repeat, but if to believe in a real Priesthood—an order of men ordained to absolve and consecrate and offer "the Sacrifice of our Ransom,"—if this be "sacerdotalism," then "sacerdotalism" is the teaching of our Church, and they who hold and teach it are the very reverse of disloyal to her.

(*d*) Drowning men will always catch at a straw, and those whose minds and convictions are leavened by Calvinism, and who would gladly, in the face of overwhelming evidence, deny the supernatural character of priestly acts, and the evidently sacerdotal teaching of the Church, fall back, in their difficulties, on the one consoling fact left for them, viz. the removal of the word "Altar," and the substitution of "Holy Table," in the Second Prayer-book of Edward VI. What consolation they can get from this cannot be grudged them. In that darkest moment of the Church's struggle, the Reformers certainly went to the extreme limit for purposes of conciliation. But they did so because they knew it was a question of *words*, not *things*. It may have been unfortunate that they gave even this slight chance to opponents of the Catholic character of the Church to cavil; still they knew well, that if a *priest* and a *sacrifice*, then of necessity an *altar*. To priesthood and sacrifice they were faithful, and so there was no sort of change of doctrine in what they did, as they knew well enough that "Altar" and "Holy Table" meant precisely the same thing, and both terms were used for the same thing by the Fathers. The term "Altar" prevails universally in the traditional and familiar language of all; and the *word* itself is preserved in the Coronation Service.

But, indeed, this foolish and, I think, somewhat

disingenuous effort to prove that the use of the term "Holy Table" instead of "Altar" in some way committed the Church to a denial of the doctrine of the Priesthood,—this effort, I say, ought to have been precluded by the words of St. Paul.[1] He contrasts the "altar" of sacrifice or "table," as he calls it, with the "Table" of the Lord. The comparison and contrast —where false worship and true worship are placed face to face—is entirely meaningless, but for the *one idea*— the idea of sacrifice, and therefore of the Priesthood —being common to all men, and therefore rightly *used* by Christians, though wrongly by heathen. The "altar" and "table" here are equally related to this idea. Then, again, men naturally and rightly speak in common language of "the altar." Not to do so would be affected and foolish. It is impossible to silence the witness of ordinary common sense to the truth of the Christian Priesthood and Sacrifice; and the good old English custom of "bowing to the altar"—only neglected or interrupted by the new-fangled ways of Puritanism—was a witness to the sense that *that* part of the sanctuary *could not but* specially remind all of the special Presence of God, by its close connection with the Priesthood and the sacrifice. But, indeed looking at our formularies as they stand—as we clergy of all three orders have bound ourselves to accept them —it is surely to play fast and loose with language in a very serious fashion to attempt to deny the doctrine of the Priesthood. And it is difficult to imagine anything more calculated to empty the young, who look to entering the ministry, of all warmth and zeal, than that they should find bishops who ordain them using the solemn words of the Church, and then denying

---

[1] 1 Cor. x. 16-21.

the doctrines they plainly teach. Whether or not, however, men be faithful or unfaithful, our Church speaks in no uncertain voice on this truth.

Tremendous as the crisis was, my dear friend, through which the Church of England passed in the convulsions of the sixteenth century, tremendous as the forces were which were at work to lead her wrong, in God's mercy she remained true to the Catholic Faith, true to the Apostolic Succession of her bishops, true to that Sacerdotalism which is involved in the Divine structure of the Catholic Church.

There are only three other matters, besides those which have been discussed, which are frequently instanced by opponents as proofs of the sacerdotalism they condemn. I need not weary you by dwelling on them at length, but I notice them ere I close.

(1) Some Churchmen are said to show their "sacerdotal" tendencies by decrying the Reformation.

Well, I dare say extreme and one-sided things have been said on the subject. But, then, it must be remembered that such things have been provoked by equally extreme things said by those of more Calvinistic or Puritan sympathies. Every reasonable and temperate person who comes to study history, and is not carried away by controversial passion, must look upon that period of our Church's history with very mixed feelings. It was a cruel time and a sad time in all directions. A great writer whom I have already quoted, speaking of it, says justly, I think, "The state of religious life was realized as a state of war, with all the moral evils of a quasi-martial law."[1] We may thank God for the way in which then He brought "light out of darkness," and for His mercy in preserving our Church in her

[1] Bishop of Oxford's Second Charge, 1893.

unbroken continuity true to the Catholic Faith and Apostolic organization; but to talk of it as if it were all "bright and blessed," as if it were a new revelation, as if a new and glorious Church were suddenly founded on the ruins of a wrecked and ruined one, is to indulge in baseless and foolish fancies, and to neglect historical truths. These things may serve to catch "popular" applause from those who have never learnt the truth, and where religion consists chiefly in Calvinistic prejudices or abuse of Rome. Churchmen, especially those who are called to the Sacred Ministry, ought surely to be ashamed of using extravagant language as to the Reformation when they must know its mixed character, if they take the trouble to study its history; when they ought to know that the Church of England has *always* from time to time been reforming herself, and when they cannot but be well aware of "the legal and constitutional," and doctrinal and spiritual, "continuity of the Church before and after the Reformation" of the sixteenth century.[1] There is nothing specially "sacerdotal," I submit, in trying to see history as it is, and refusing to canonize that very mixed movement—partly good, partly bad—called commonly "the Reformation."

(2) Sacerdotalism is charged to those who use the word "Mass" sometimes to describe the Eucharist.

Well, it is surely a matter of taste and opinion. The use of the word is, anyhow, as old as St. Ambrose, A.D. 385. It occurs in the First Prayer-book of Edward VI., and that Prayer-book is spoken of with the highest approval. It is not a "scriptural" term, and Roman Catholics use it,—these seem to be the objections to it. As to the first, *that*, I must submit, is ridiculous. "Lord's Supper" is not a "scriptural" term for the Eucharist, as

[1] Cf. Bishop of Oxford's Charge, *ut supra*.

Mr. Keble has shown. "Matins" and "Evensong" are not "scriptural" terms. We need not dwell on such an argument; it arises out of a total misconception of the use of Scripture. As to Roman Catholics using it, there is but *one* Blessed Sacrament instituted by our Lord. Roman Catholics don't have *one* and we *another*. I should have thought it would be rather a recommendation to a term that, as we have to differ in so much from our fellow-Christians of the Roman Communion, we can recognize points in which we do agree. Whatever the *derivation* of the word may have been, by the "Mass" is meant neither more nor less than the Eucharistic Sacrifice; and if any man in any part of the Catholic Church likes to call the Mystery,—Eucharist, or Holy Communion, or Holy Mysteries, or Blessed Sacrament, or Lord's Supper, or Mass, surely he may exercise his lawful liberty—as *all* these *terms*, with more or less appropriateness, apply to the same thing—without people going wild about a word, and denouncing the use of it as a proof of evil sacerdotalism!

(3) And then, lastly, this dreaded "sacerdotalism" is supposed to be indicated by Prayers for the Dead.

That is a devout practice, I am glad to say, which prevails among many who, by no stretch of imagination, could be called "sacerdotalists." Natural duty and natural affection prompt us to it. Our Lord almost certainly took part in it. Scripture points to it. The Church has always done it from the first. Only modern prejudice, and a kind of pagan temper which has leavened Puritanism, and a spirit of violent reaction against some abuses connected with "the Roman" (not the Catholic) "doctrine of Purgatory," have unhappily, in modern times, led even good people to unloving neglect of the dead. The Church of England has, alas! owing to her difficulty in dealing with some popular errors in the sixteenth century, allowed it too much to be obscured, but she has preserved her witness to its truth, by her appeal to antiquity, in which it always prevailed, and by her prayers for the dead, in at least the Prayer of Oblation in the Eucharist, if not in the "Church Militant Prayer." The present Dean of Lichfield has, as you know, my dear friend, cleared up the matter in his usual temperate and scholar-like way, and shown that the practice is in accordance with the Church's mind.[1] There can certainly be no evil sacerdotalism in anything so loving and devout as this; no evil sacerdotalism in "casting *all* your care"—that about your beloved dead as well as other care—upon God, as "He careth for you."

"Sacerdotalism," then, wrongly understood, means, I imagine, that men holding Apostolic orders are supposed to teach that they receive these in some *mechanical* fashion. This—if any teach it—is wrong. It means, I suppose, further, that some imagine that there is a *vicarious* Priesthood, and a sacrifice which, in some way, *takes the place of* the sacrifice of Calvary. This—if any hold it—is profoundly erroneous. It means, I suppose, that those who are ordained to the Priesthood form a caste or tribe which comes *between the soul and God*. This, again, is, of course, entirely false. It means, I suppose, that—in consequence of being priests —men "give themselves airs," assuming an arrogant or dictatorial temper, and so on. Nothing can be imagined more entirely unchristian, or more contrary to the teaching of the Catholic Church.

If any think or act in this way, *their* "sacerdotalism" you and I condemn most cordially. I am

[1] Cf. Luckock's "After Death."

bound to say, however, such teachers I have never had the ill fortune to meet in the English Church. If *this* is "sacerdotalism," let us repudiate and condemn it with all our hearts.

But a "sacerdotalism" which insists on the truth of the Apostolic Succession, on the *necessity* of Episcopacy to the constitution and working of the Church in accordance with the mind of the Founder, on the *reality* of the Priesthood, on the *reality* of the Presence in the Holy Sacrament, on the *reality* of the Eucharistic Sacrifice, on the wisdom of Confession where needed, and the *reality* of Absolution, on the liberty of the children of God to be present at "the Church's prayer-meeting" when not communicating, on the piety of *fasting* as well as *prayer* in preparation for Communion, on the necessity of believing in the gifts of the gospel being real and supernatural and needed by us all,—this is true "sacerdotalism." In *this* sense I— and I imagine *you* join with me in this—I am a "sacerdotalist" from head to heel; and I maintain that, *in this sense*, the English Church—so I have tried to show —as all the rest of the Catholic Church, teaches "sacerdotalism" to her children as an integral part of the gospel of Christ.

Then as to those "without," those who *dissent* from the teaching of the Church, we have, I repeat, no hard word to say. God forbid! We are misrepresented if it is said that we, in the Church of England—who cling to Catholic faith and practice—have anything narrow or unkind to say of them. I can't express better the feelings we have, and ought to have, about the good and holy ones among them, who, alas! are not able to accept the teachings of the Church, than in words which you will, I know, remember well—

"*They* are members of the *soul* of the Church, who, not being members of the visible Communion and Society, know not that, in not becoming members of it, they are rejecting the command of Christ, to Whom, by faith and love and in obedience, they cleave. And *they*, being members of the *body*, or visible Communion of the Church, are not members of the soul of the Church, who, amid outward profession of the faith, do, in heart or deeds, deny Him Whom in words they confess. The deliverance promised in that Day is to those who, being in the *body* of the Church, shall, by true faith in Christ and fervent love to Him, belong to the *soul* of the Church also, or who, although not in the *body* of the Church, shall not, through their own fault, have ceased to be in the *body*, and *shall* belong to its *soul*, in that, through faith and love, they cleave to Christ its Head."[1]

This is what we feel. Surely a decisive faith in the revealed way of the Church is not incompatible with large love towards those who are — more or less — "without."

Indeed, after all, the Church has one great end—to bring souls into union with God through Christ. Not those who can *state* doctrine exactly, but those who *live* it, even if they state it imperfectly, are the children of God. We *must* be loyal to truth, if we know it. In an age like this, when "Undenominationalism"—a pleasant word for indifferentism, and hollow religion—is face to face with Christianity, we are *bound*, in loyalty to our Master, in education, as in religious ministration, to stand firmly by the system and teaching of the Church which has come to us from Him, and to give no quarter to any, however apparently pious, variety of heresy so

[1] Pusey, "Minor Prophets," on Joel ii. 32.

likely to degenerate into hollow sham which professes to do duty for the Catholic Faith. But goodness is of God wherever we find it. " Love, joy, peace, long-suffering, gentleness, goodness, trustiness, meekness, self-restraint,"—these are fruits of the Spirit, these the Catholic Faith is meant to produce in the soul. If it does not produce them, so far forth fails. *If* they are produced, and *wherever* they are produced, they mark the *real* " sacerdotalist," and we hail such with joy.

And now, my dear friend, I have finished the task that lay before me. I end as I began, by reminding you that I do not love controversy. Honestly, I detest it. Never can controversy be right or wise unless it is forced upon us as a duty. I have thought that this was forced upon me. I have not wished to *attack* any one. My business has been to *defend*. I have tried to maintain that it is not fair to charge with any *evil* " sacerdotalism " those who, like myself, hold or use the doctrines and practices which have been impugned. These doctrines and practices I believe to be justified from Holy Scripture and the early Church; but my point has been to show that they are—to speak with restraint—in accordance with the teaching of the Church of England.

Dissenters I can understand. They dissent from the teaching of the Church, and, as they *dissent*, they act consistently and become *Dissenters*. I am sorry that they part company with the Church. I think they are under loss accordingly, under very grievous loss, but I *understand* them and *respect* them. I am sorry if any of them feel bitterly towards us. Towards them I, for one, can feel no bitterness.

" Low Churchmen " I cannot pretend to *understand*.

They are a constant enigma to me. To go no further, how bishops of the Church who strenuously deny the *Divine* succession of the Episcopate, and the reality of the sacerdotal office, *can* administer the laying-on of hands, using the awful words of our Ordinal, when continually they denounce Confession and Absolution, and would be quite angry with the men they ordain if *they* ventured to assert the fact of their priesthood, or to act upon the assumption that the words of Ordination are meant in good faith,—this I don't pretend to understand. How men can receive the grace of Orders, given with such awful words, and accept the Prayer-book with its thorough Catholic teaching, and then act not one bit as Catholic priests, but as if they were Protestant ministers,—this is a riddle that I cannot read. But it is not my business to judge them. We may well believe that, in some way we cannot understand, they explain things to themselves. We may well credit them with honesty and good faith, but we certainly have a right to expect that to us *they* will do the same. We cannot but regret their action, if we refrain from judging their motives. It tends to weaken our position as well towards our Dissenting brethren as towards our brethren in the Roman part of the Catholic Church. Still there it is; and it is none of our business to narrow the border of the English Church, but rather to pray and strive that any who have "shortened thoughts" as to the truth which they are to witness to, and as to the grace they are to dispense, may be led by Him Who alone can lead them to the fuller knowledge and practice, to the fuller realization of the blessedness of the Catholic Faith.

Their methods of controversy also, I acknowledge, are to me astonishing. They seem to treat Holy

Scripture as a sort of *directorium* to be referred to, so that each of them, according to his private interpretation, settles what is true in doctrine or practice quite irrespective of the teaching of the Church. This method is, it seems to me, a most fallacious one. But in the case of Dissenters there is nothing inconsistent in employing it. In Churchmen, it is quite another matter. If they *do*—as they say—"believe in the Holy Catholic Church," then *her* interpretations of Holy Scripture have settled the question in any doctrinal matters where her interpretation is given. For instance, I submit no one in the sacred ministry of the English Church is justified in interpreting the third chapter of St. John in any way whatever but as teaching Regeneration in Baptism, once they have accepted the Prayerbook *ex animo*, and have bound themselves, therefore, by its statements in the Baptismal Service. Many things, I maintain, are open questions; but doctrinal matters, settled by the Church's plain interpretation of Holy Scripture, or continuous witness of what has been taught in the "Apostles' doctrine," are *not* open questions.

Believe in the Holy Catholic Church; take her for your guide in doctrinal and practical decisions as to the mind of Holy Scripture; and you hold the Catholic Faith, and see the meaning and beauty of Catholic practices. Reverse the process. "Put the cart before the horse." Interpret Scripture by your own mind, quite irrespective of the Church's witness, and you may call yourself a Churchman or anything else, but it is, humanly speaking, a mere chance into which, out of many, heresies you land yourself, or *how* crippled and insufficient your belief may be. It seems to me that we differ essentially in our *methods* in this—that *they* believe in Scripture as a storehouse of doctrine which *they* are to ransack *for themselves*, and make what they please of, quite irrespective of the Church's teaching; while *we* believe in a Divine Society into whose hands God has put a Divine Book. *They* believe in unrestrained private judgment; *we* believe in the Holy Catholic Church.

However, many men have many minds; and Truth is a large thing, and has many aspects; and it is not your business or mine, my dear friend, to judge our brethren so long as we boldly witness to and cling to the truth, so long as we give no countenance to the idea that indifferentism is religion. We are convinced that "Low Churchmen" hold an insufficient faith, and are quite astoundingly untrue to much of the teaching of the Church. The way, however, to lead to better things is the way of love and faithfulness and prayer. It is sad, and it is injurious—it seems to me—to true religion when men *will* go out of their way to stir up strife. If they do, however, and if in doing so they misrepresent us, or malign the truth, then it may be a duty—though always a painful duty—to defend it; it may be a duty to remove as far as possible any danger of misunderstanding.

We do not desire to conceal anything. In so grave a matter we are bound, I think, to be quite above-board, and to make all plain. Men may not agree with us, but they ought not to be allowed to misunderstand us. We are *bound* to make our positions clear. I hope, in doing so, I have avoided any mere bitterness or denunciation. I pray that God in His mercy may bring us to the "unity of the Spirit," and to "peace through the truth;" that we may learn to bear and forbear, so that mists of prejudice and passion may clear away; that, remembering our different points of view, we may all make large allowances for one another; that, recalling to ourselves that the love of God in Christ is *the* great thing; that, knowing how "toilsome and incomplete" are all our efforts, we may—each one, without mere cant, without indifferentism, without pretending that it is not important to be exact and thorough as far as we may—hold the truth as far as we know it in love, and not forget that, when all is said—

> "God's greatness flows around our incompleteness,
> Round our restlessness His rest."

I am, my dear Dean, yours affectionately,
W. J. KNOX LITTLE.

THE COLLEGE, WORCESTER,
All Saints'-tide, 1893.